Henry Willard French

Oscar Peterson

Ranchman and Ranger

Henry Willard French

Oscar Peterson
Ranchman and Ranger

ISBN/EAN: 9783337149611

Printed in Europe, USA, Canada, Australia, Japan

Cover: Foto ©ninafisch / pixelio.de

More available books at **www.hansebooks.com**

Oscar Peterson Ranchman and Ranger

444/56

OSCAR PETERSON

RANCHMAN AND RANGER

BY
HENRY WILLARD FRENCH
Author of "Lance of Kanana."

BOSTON
D LOTHROP COMPANY
1893

Copyright 1893,
BY
D. LOTHROP COMPANY.

All rights reserved.

To the Boy I Love

2072229

CONTENTS.

Chapter		Page
I.	Coming Events Cast their Shadows	1
II.	Who Fired that Shot?	11
III.	News from the Mansion	22
IV.	Oscar's First Duty	33
V.	Bagatawa	44
VI.	Not for Gold	67
VII.	At the Ranch-house	82
VIII.	Brighter Prospects	97
IX.	With Shot-gun and Rifle	108
X.	Over the Prairie	131
XI.	Oscar Has a Personal Experience	153
XII.	Through the Wheat Fields of Dakota	173
XIII.	A Doubtful Host	192
XIV.	Dead or Alive	224
XV.	Deadwood	256
XVI.	The Indian Question	291
XVII.	The Last of the Trail	325
XVIII.	The Man Inside	343
XIX.	"I am Afraid to Die"	361
XX.	The Past and the Future	373

ILLUSTRATIONS.

Held Up!	Frontis.
The First Wolf	5
The Missing Heel	9
"Who Fired that Shot?"	13
A Fight for Life	16
"Wenononee, Shut the Door!"	23
Oscar's Two Friends	34
The Squaw's Cabin	37
A Conversation Without Words	47
The Black Against the White	53
Bagatawa	62
Black Dog and his Squaw	65
"Were You Shaking your Fist at Me?"	71
"Wenononee!"	78
Upon his Mission	81
Weno and Sancho	91
Weno Paused, to Gather Courage	93
The Indian Messenger	104
He Turned to Run	113
On the Lake	118
Every Head Was Lifted	121
Six Inches from the Mark	127
It Was an Indian	150

ILLUSTRATIONS.

A Withered Old Medicine-man Appeared	159
"That Will Do"	164
Panza Settles the Question	170
Oscar Looked Eagerly Forward	174
A Run to the Dalrymple Farm	186
"That's what I call Farming"	190
Old Settlers	194
The Prairie Post-Office	215
Dead or Alive	227
They Emerged from the Gulch	253
Meeting on the Deadwood Trail	260
"Only Waiting for a Show"	263
They Entered Deadwood	265
"The Boy Was Crying"	286
The Last of Deadwood Gulch	293
"Steering over the Trackless Plain"	303
"Looking up the Gorge"	305
He Was Pulling off his Boots	312
"He Won't Do It Again"	317
The Cowboys' Serenade	323
A Real Cow-town	327
"That's what We Shall Indulge In"	338
"I am Oscar Peterson"	366

OSCAR PETERSON:

RANCHMAN AND RANGER.

CHAPTER I.

COMING EVENTS CAST THEIR SHADOWS.

"Who'd have thought the snow could be so deep? When I left England the grass was green," said Oscar Peterson.

His father smiled as they tramped along together through the dense forests on the north shore of Manitoba Lake, where the snow still lay in drifts in the shaded hollows, and his face showed every sign of pride as he watched his only child — a strong, sturdy boy of sixteen. Oscar's mother died in that wild frontier country when he was a baby. For five years he had been cared for by an Indian nurse, then for ten years he had been at school in England, and now he had returned for a year before finishing his course.

"The banks of the Thames at Oxford, and these

forests are two very different places, Oscar," he replied. "The grass is growing green about the village, you know, and in a few days more wild flowers will be in bloom right where these snowdrifts are. Don't make up your mind to be disappointed with Manitoba till you have time to become a little better acquainted."

"Look here, father, I'm no tenderfoot," Oscar said, laughing as he spoke the name commonly applied to newcomers. "I'll be tougher, of course, when I get my sea-legs on; but don't you forget that I was born on the shores of Manitoba Lake, and that I'm just as much a part of this country as an Indian. The day after I got home I was out in the sheephouse, and I saw that old sign which you carved for me. Don't you remember it? It was 'Oscar Peterson: Ranchman and Ranger.' You nailed it up for me over the shed end of the little log cabin we lived in then. I tell you I was just proud of it; and while I stood looking at it, the whole time between seemed to vanish. The ten years in Oxford were like a dream. It was a bang-up dream, and I've learned lots that will help me all my life; but when you come right down to facts, it's hurrah for Manitoba every day of the week, and I'm Oscar Peterson, ranchman and ranger, and you see if I don't make a good one."

"I'm thinking you'd make a good one, Oscar, whatever you undertook," replied his father. "Try that, for instance."

The words were not spoken when Oscar's rifle was at his shoulder. It flashed, and a duck fell flopping in the snow.

"I told you so," Mr. Peterson observed, smiling. "I shall be rather surprised, but very glad, if you continue to like this life after the novelty is worn off. Study has a tendency to make a boy feel too fine for frontier slang and high-topped boots, but it doesn't hurt him for them in any other respect; and I tell you the wise development of a new country is the grandest thing a fellow can do for the world, and for those who come after him."

"I'd have come back before if you'd let me," Oscar replied, shaking the snow from the duck and tying it.

"Indeed I did not want you to," said his father. "Every hour at Oxford will help you at ranching and ranging, if you care to turn it that way. I should not have asked you to come back even for a year, only that I needed you so much. The fact is, I took up a mining claim in the States, and put a man in charge who was very well recommended to me. I have heard that the mine has turned out something wonderful, but I suspect that the agent is a fraud. I must go down and see to it. I may be gone only a month, or it may be all summer, and while I am away you must take charge of the property here. Experience is the best teacher, so you had better run everything just as you like. It will be the quickest way to learn to run them right. I wrote to the agent that I should leave here this month; but I did not say anything to you about it before, for I didn't want you to have a chance to get too much advice out of me."

A low whistle was Oscar's only response, as he slung the duck over his shoulder. "The property" had been wonderfully transformed since he left it, ten years before. Instead of the pioneer's log cabin, he found his father living in a substantial stone house, on the brow of a butte overlooking the lake. Instead of the clearing that surrounded the cabin, he found one of the finest stock farms in the province. Instead of a few huts and wigwams on the lake shore, there was a practical little village, with its store, its church, and its doctor. Instead of vague prospects of ore in the wild lands at the north, there were several successfully operated mines. Instead of buffalo and Indians over the broad prairie to the south and west, there were great fields of wheat near the village, and farther away herds of cattle belonging to his father were pastured. They had come up the lake in their yacht to select a site for a saw mill, to open another industry. All of this was included when his father said, "While I am away you must take charge of the property here." No wonder Oscar's only response was a low whistle.

The whistle was cut short by a series of yelps, and short, sharp barks, followed by the piercing shriek of a horse.

THE FIRST WOLF.

"Wolves!" muttered Mr. Peterson. "And hungry ones. They've got a horse. I wonder who brought him up here at this season? Come on!"

Hurrying forward, with their rifles ready, they entered a gorge where the snow lay deeper, and soon approached a rude log wigwam. Beyond the tepee a horse lay on the ground, just breathing his last, with four large wolves already beginning their feast.

"Indians?" Oscar asked, as they paused for a moment behind the tepee.

"Not now," replied his father. "Indians may have built it, but the snow lies over the smoke hole. They have not been there for a long time. That is no Indian pony, either. I think it belongs to Black-dog, a half-breed, who works at the mines, and I wonder how it came up here?"

"Can't we get a shot at the wolves, father?" Oscar asked, cautiously peeking about the wigwam.

His father hesitated a moment. His face showed that he was troubled; but quickly recovering himself he said, "Why, yes, if you want to; and of course you do. I forgot that you had not had shooting all your life. If we can do it without disturbing them, let's climb to the top of the tepee. Come carefully. Keep well on this side. There! Have you a good place?"

"Jolly," Oscar replied in a whisper, as he balanced himself and leveled his gun. "Which shall I take?"

"Take the fellow at the throat with one barrel, then swing over to the one next him, on the shoulder. I'll wait, and if you kill them both I'll take another."

Oscar fired as his father directed, and each wolf with a savage yelp rolled over into the snow. One of the remaining fellows evidently knew what the report of a rifle meant, for, like a flash, he bounded away into the forest. The other stopped to look up at the top of the tepee and show his teeth, with an ugly growl. The next instant he, too, was stretched out upon the snow.

"Now let's be quick about the skins, Oscar," his father said, slipping down from the tepee, "for it's getting late, and it will take us till long after dark to beat back against the wind, unless it changes."

Oscar followed him, and they were not long in having the three skins tied in a bundle, with the skull left upon one of them, to use the brains in dressing them.

"Seems to me the skins are the heaviest parts of animals," Oscar said, as they put a pole through the cord to carry the bundle between them. His father did not reply at once. He was examining the horse. "It is Black-dog's, as sure as fate," he was saying to himself. "Four white feet, the top of his right ear cut off, and a hump on his hip. I don't believe Black-dog himself ever left him here."

They started at a rapid pace for the lake, but a little later Mr. Peterson laid down the pole, and going to one side bent forward to examine a track in the snow. As Oscar came up he said: "That boot was made in the States, but it has one of Wawanka's slug-holds on the heel. Somebody from the States must have been at the village not very long ago, for the slug is sharp,

THE MISSING HEEL.

and that boot would not last to do much tramping through these forests."

"Here's a track without any hold, father," Oscar said; and his father, examining it, replied: "It has no heel, either. See! every other one is that way. The slug on one boot must have dug into a log and torn the heel off. I told you those boots would not last long here."

Oscar's eyes were busy in an instant, and following the trail back a little way, he called to his father that he had found it, and with his hunting knife pried the lost heel from the log where the slug had caught. He examined it for a moment, and was about to throw it away when his father said: "Put it in your pocket, Oscar. These tracks may have been made by some one who has been stealing horses."

They picked up the skins and went on, but Oscar noticed that the troubled look did not leave his father's face; that he did not speak again, and that he kept a very close watch in every direction as they advanced. The incidents did not seem to him to amount to anything at the time, but before long he was glad to recall even the most trifling of them as something of very grave importance.

CHAPTER II.

WHO FIRED THAT SHOT?

THE skins and duck were safely disposed in the yacht. The sail and jib were set. The rifles were carefully placed in the stern. Oscar stood with his foot on the rail, with a boat-hook in his hand, holding her to the rock upon which his father was still standing, when his eye caught a mass of tawny fur half-way up the trunk of a pine-tree that had been broken at the roots, but was still standing, leaning against its fellows. "O, father! what a shot," he cried. "Look at that bear climbing a tree."

"That is not a bear, Oscar, it is a"— Mr. Peterson paused abruptly, and Oscar felt a gust of cold wind strike his face, and saw his father look quickly toward the sky. "How those clouds are piling up!" he exclaimed. "It means a blizzard if it means anything, and we don't get home without a struggle."

"Oh! but, father, can't I have just one pop? I'll come back to-morrow for the skin," Oscar pleaded;

but another gust of icy-cold wind struck his face at that instant, taking his breath away, and making the yacht reel till he almost lost his hold. "Guess you're right, father," he gasped, tugging on the boat-hook. "Better jump aboard, quick!"

Mr. Peterson sprang on to the yacht, but stood for a moment looking anxiously back into the forest. Oscar let her go, and was bending forward adjusting the boat-hook when the sharp report of a rifle rang upon the air.

As Oscar sprang to his feet and, catching his rifle, threw it to his shoulder, Mr. Peterson sank upon the bottom of the yacht and leaned back against the stern seat. One quick glance told him that his father was wounded, but not killed.

"Who fired that shot?" he ejaculated, and stood with his finger on the trigger, and his eyes fixed upon a point in the forest where a thin white cloud of smoke was curling away among the trees.

"It was a mistake. A friendly Indian. The ball glanced," his father said, in short, gasping sentences. "It is not serious. Get out of this cove. Be quick!"

"It was not a mistake, father, and it was not an Indian," Oscar replied, without moving. "Just let me see the tip of his shoulder."

"Coward!" he shouted; "come out from behind those trees."

"If you wait for him to load he will fire again if

he is in earnest. You make a good mark standing there," Mr. Peterson said, in a weak voice; but Oscar was conscious of a strange feeling which he had never realized before, and which no one can explain or understand who has not felt it. It was more than vengeance and far more than revenge. It would have

"WHO FIRED THAT SHOT?"

held him there, with his rifle at his shoulder, against all advice or authority, against all reason and in the face of any possible danger, in the one hope of sighting that rifle upon the one who had fired the shot at his father.

Unnoticed, however, the yacht had been silently gliding down the cove under the effect of the breeze and the circling current. The forerunner of the blizzard that had been slashing and swaying the giant pines dropped suddenly. Oscar felt the icy flaw as it struck his face. The same instant he caught the flash of a rifle to the right of where he was looking. Before he could turn sufficiently to fire, before he heard the report even, the yacht had careened till her rail lay on the water, and Oscar was thrown heavily backward against the sail.

Quickly recovering himself, Oscar found that his father had caught the tiller in his hand, barely saving them from capsizing, while a bullet had cut the sail beside him, and buried itself in the bundle of skins on the seat.

"That lurch was all that saved you," his father said, as Oscar grasped the tiller and let out the sail just in time to avoid the bristling rocks at the entrance to the cove. The next moment the yacht swept out on to the lake beyond the ledge, and out of sight of any one in the forest, upon the sheltered bay. But the wind, in irregular, fierce and fitful gusts, came tearing down the lake till Oscar could hardly hold her, with all his strength.

"Are you much hurt, father?" he asked, turning anxiously to his father, but forced to look back again even before he was answered.

"Not much, I hope," said Mr. Peterson. "The ball struck my side, a little above my hip. I am glad you are here. Don't mind me now. You can't do much more than watch the yacht. I'll get up forward, out of the way."

For a moment the wind, though still fierce, had been steady, and setting the course so that there should be clear sailing room ahead, Oscar made the ropes and tiller fast, and helped his father. Mr. Peterson faintly warned him not to, but he had hardly strength to speak, much less to get forward by himself. He tried to make light of it, that Oscar should not know, but the moment he reached the spot he sank, unconscious, by the mast. As he felt himself fainting he roused enough to whisper: "Too much sail, Oscar. Be quick!"

Indeed he had to be very quick. Another fierce flaw had struck the yacht. He drew his hunting knife and cut the tiller free, then sprang to the sail. There was no time to unwind the ropes. He cut them, too, as quickly as the sharp blade could sever them. The great sail bulged, and for an instant Oscar thought they must surely go over, but he caught the tiller and dragged it round with all his strength. The sudden motion relieved the strain for an instant, and the sail came rattling down. There was no time to stop and think what next to do, however. The sudden gust was not followed by a lull, but by another and another, each fiercer and colder than the last, till the wind howled and roared along the lake, the water flew like rain from the tops of the rising waves, and the ropes twanged like bowstrings. Only the jib was out, but the strain upon that was terrible. He tried to bring the yacht about a little to relieve it, but the moment the wind caught the broadside

A FIGHT FOR LIFE.

it lifted it clear out of the water till the lee rail dipped. Back again went the tiller just as the rudder itself was being lifted out of the water, and before the jib could break away, like a flash Oscar unwound the rope and twisted it about his own arm. It was the only way that he could manage it.

If that jib or jib line broke, the wind would roll them over as it pleased. One moment he must let it loose to save it, the next he must drag upon it for his very life. The wind blew harder and harder, and the waves rose higher and higher, till suddenly a torrent of icy rain broke from the dense clouds, then changed to sleet, then to snow, and then to rain again, while the fierce wind froze it where it fell.

Winding the rope around his leg to hold it, Oscar tore off his overcoat and leather jacket, and, springing forward, threw them over his father. He bent down for an instant, to be sure that he was breathing, and back again to his post. They were tossed and whirled from wave to wave in the blinding rain and sleet. Ice formed on the ropes and rail, and icicles hung from the sail that lay in a mass where it had fallen.

He had lost his hat in the cove, and icicles hung from his thick brown hair as he sat in his shirt sleeves, drenched to the skin, holding the tiller under his knee, and tugging upon the rope that was twisted round his arm.

"There's no use trying to run ashore this side of home," he muttered. "It would only mean staying there all night, and we might as well go to the bottom. No! I'll keep her up if she'll stand it, and I'll keep her nose toward home."

"We're going at a frightful rate. We must be almost there," he said a little later, to cheer himself;

for his hands were so numb that he had to watch them to see that the rope was held fast and not slipping through his fingers; and it began to be evident that he could not hold out much longer.

The yacht reeled and trembled as it leaped forward in its desperate struggle. It seemed to Oscar that he had been there for hours when, at last, through the rain and sleet he discerned the faint outline of the village, far in the distance, and a little to his right. He shuddered as he saw how hard it was for his stiffened muscles to bend and change the course, and a dull, cold tremor crept over him with the conviction that he could not do it. Home was too far away. With every lurch he thought the yacht was going under, and it began to seem as though he did not care much if she did.

What! He started with a shiver. Did not care? He cast one quick glance toward the white, still face beside the mast. Did not care? "The wind is still rising. It is not that I am giving out," he gasped. And as he ground his teeth he muttered, "Oscar Peterson, don't you dare give out! Do you hear me?" and he gave the rope another twist about his arm.

What was that? Was some one calling? He listened intently. It sounded again. Above the shrieking of the wind he heard the shrill cry which an Indian can send so far. His eyes were almost blinded by the storm, but after searching for a moment he discovered a canoe approaching with a single Indian. It seemed as though the little thing must swamp. Every wave that rushed toward it was ready to engulf it, but keeping the bow in the eye of the wind the Indian paddled it swiftly and steadily nearer and nearer. At last it was not more than twenty feet away, but as he rose above it on a wave he saw to his horror that it was filling with water, and was almost beyond the Indian's control; while worse yet, at the rate and course of the yacht, he was going to pass it, out of reach, and leave it behind.

Gathering all his strength he made one tremendous effort. He braced his feet upon the rail, leaned back upon the tiller and, as far out as his arm would reach, left the jib line slack. But his feet were numb with cold. His legs were cramped and half-frozen. The position was a dangerous one at the best, and when the yacht reeled and lunged, in answering the helm, his foot slipped, and before he could make one motion to save himself, the tightening jib line dragged him over and he slid into the water.

Even then he only half-realized that it was he himself who was overboard, and that he must do something or drown. The water was warmer than the wind, and his first thought was that he was more comfortable there. But something began pulling fiercely upon his arm. He thought of the jib line he had twisted there. It roused him, and he clutched it in both hands. In reality he not only saved himself, but saved the yacht by doing so.

As his head came out of water he gulped a breath before it was dragged un ler again. When he came up again he was close beside the yacht, and some one was pulling on the rope. Then some one was pulling on his arm. The Indian was leaning over him. He heard a voice say, "Young master, hold fast. Heap big storm, but all come right," and a moment later he was dragging himself into the yacht, while the Indian quickly unwound the rope, caught the tiller, and skillfully brought the yacht back into her course.

"Young master go see father," said the Indian. "Me heap good sail canoe. Heap time sail wid father."

For an instant Oscar stood clutching the mast and staring at the little figure so quietly and skillfully managing the helm. It was not a veteran brave or even a young buck who had dared to face that fearful storm in a frail canoe to lend him aid. It was a little Indian girl. He was too bewildered, however, to fully comprehend it all, and chiefly realizing that one who understood the work had relieved him, and that he was free at last to care for his father, he knelt beside the prostrate form and at once became oblivious to everything else, even to the danger which still was so great.

He did not realize whether much or little time had

passed, when he was roused by a sudden thump that started the seams, stove a hole in the bottom of the yacht, and drove out the mast. Then all was still.

The mast and rigging fell across him so that he could not move, for a moment, and while he was freeing himself he heard the Indian say, "No mean do dat. Heap try get shore quick." When he lifted his head and looked about him the Indian girl had disappeared, but the yacht lay fast between two rocks well up the shore.

Other voices sounded, and in a moment the yacht was surrounded by a throng of rough-handed, coarse-tongued, tender-hearted frontier settlers, all ready to do their best for the master whom they all loved.

In the gathering dusk they made a rude litter of the seats of the yacht. They laid their coats upon it to make it as comfortable as possible, and, placing the unconscious form of Mr. Peterson there, they lifted it upon their shoulders as tenderly as rough men could, and started, in the darkness which had suddenly closed in, through the village street and up the butte to the stone mansion of the master.

At every step of the way the little procession increased. Women came out with lanterns to lead the way. Children, sobbing and trembling, timidly followed on behind. The doctor was there and the minister. Indians and half-breeds were there. Every one who could be was there.

CHAPTER III.

NEWS FROM THE MANSION.

"Shut the door, Wenononee! Shut the door!" cried old Wetamoc, an Indian squaw, throwing her arm over a bundle of dried sweet grass lying on a chair beside her, while she drew her blanket about a pile of bright-colored shavings from which she was weaving baskets, as her granddaughter entered the log cabin and with her a savage gust of wind, rain and sleet. It pulled the door away from Wenononee the moment she lifted the latch, and made a grand rush through the cabin and into the fireplace, tossing the ashes in every direction.

The Indian girl caught it quickly, and bracing her moccasined feet on the earth floor and her shoulder against the heavy oak door, she pushed with all her strength before she could force it back. Gust after gust swept against it, and the door shivered and creaked on its iron hinges before it settled into its place and the broad wooden latch fell into the slot to hold it there.

For a moment Weno did not move, but stood with her cheek resting on her extended arm, the rain dripping from her long black hair and loose dress, and gathering in little pools upon the floor about her feet. Solemnly and slowly, in true Indian instinct, her bright

"WENONONEE, SHUT THE DOOR!"

black eyes wandered from one object to another about the room, as though they were something new to her, and not at all as though she had been born within a stone's throw, and had lived in that log cabin almost all her life.

It was no tepee, but a very sumptuous wigwam for an Indian in the province of Manitoba. It was a substantial cabin, with the logs hewn smooth on the inside, and the chinks well filled with clay. There was real glass in the windows, a solid stone chimney, a broad fireplace and a little room overhead which Weno called her own.

Wenononee lived here with her mother and grandmother. Her father and grandfather were killed before she was born. The village had grown up about the cabin, and it now stood in the very center of the settlement, between the village street and the lake; though only sixteen years before it was a solitary pioneer's cabin, in the midst of a great wilderness, surrounded by wandering tribes and wild animals. Mr. Peterson was the pioneer, and it was here where his son was born, here where his young wife died. It was here where Weno's mother came to nurse the little pale face baby, and at the shed end of this same cabin the little sign once hung: "Oscar Peterson: Ranchman and Ranger."

During the half-breed insurrection, Weno's father and grandfather renounced their tribe to defend this pioneer cabin. With Mr. Peterson they held it till General Lord Wolseley put an end to the insurrection. But they were branded as traitors by their people, and an Indian never forgets. Shortly after the war they were both killed while out hunting. No one ever knew why or by whom, yet no one doubted that it was their reward for having defended the pale face pioneer. Mr. Peterson gave the log cabin to the two squaws for their home, and had never ceased to provide for them in every way. It was only a verbal gift lest, if the property were legally theirs, they might foolishly dispose of it, to their own sorrow, as so many Indians have done before and since. No one who knew Mr. Peterson, however, ever doubted that his word was as good as his deed, and that the log cabin and the little farm extending to the lake belonged to the Indian squaws just as truly as though a dozen deeds were recorded in their favor.

It was not a long journey for Wenononee's eyes to wander about the room. Here and there a bright-colored print was fastened to the wall. Bunches of dried grass and narrow strips of dyed wood hung from the rafters. A lump of smoked venison was swinging on its string with a bunch of dried golden-rod on one side, and onions on the other. Indian shawls and blankets, beads and belts, leggings and moccasins hung on the wall or lay in a pile in the corner; for Wenononee's people were no half-breeds. They were true Indians, of the tribe of Hiawatha, and they were very proud of it. Not a word of English was ever heard in the cabin, and in the peculiar characteristic, so common among border Indians, the squaws would not even admit that they so much as understood a word of it. Weno, however, had attended the English school in the village to please "The Master," as, high and low, far and near, they all called Mr. Peterson; but she was still an Indian. Then there were skins upon the earth floor and skins upon the wall. There were two pairs of antlers, of which Weno was quietly very proud — as the result of her own hunting — bows and arrows, an old gun and no end of litter; otherwise it would not have been an Indian's wigwam.

Against the wall at one end of the room there were two box beds, one above the other. In one of them Weno's mother was lying, slowly dying of that combination of lung troubles which is destined, in time, to settle the Indian question in America without the aid of cruel and unjust legislation.

Beyond the beds and near the fire, Wetamoe, the old grandmother, sat upon a skin on the floor, using a chair to hold her grasses. Then came the fireplace, with its embers and ashes lying about in confusion, where the wind had left them.

When her eyes reached this point Wenononee turned slowly from the door, crossed the room, and began replacing the fallen sticks and poking back the glowing coals, while she sang a quaint Indian song. Aided by the brighter light and inspired by the song, the old squaw's fingers flew among the colored shavings and sweet grasses till one could see the basket growing under her touch.

Weno paused in the song for a moment and, with a shudder, muttered, "It is awful on the lake." The old squaw gave a peculiar grunt, but did not look up from her basket.

"The master was out in it, and the young master, in the bird canoe," Wenononee said a little later, as she still crouched before the fire, looking steadily into the glowing coals.

Again the old squaw responded with a grunt. It was different from the other, however, and one who understands the Indian understands his grunts as well as spoken words.

"They might have been drowned," Wenononee added; and the old squaw paused in her work to lift her hand and make a circle in the air, saying, as plain as words, that all things are in the hands of the Great Spirit.

Wenononee shook her head slowly, as though she were not quite sure of that philosophy, and, after a pause, continued: "The master has been badly hurt, and the young master fell into the water and would have drowned, they say, if it had not been for an Indian." But the stoical old squaw only responded with another grunt and another circle in the air.

Weno sat for some time in silence, trying to solve, in Indian fashion, the great orthodox problem of foreordination and free agency, while she wrung the water out of her hair, letting it fall into the ashes.

"Like these drops of water are we all," she whispered. "We were not, we are, we shall not be. We come, we hurry, we go. Who knows and can say more?"

With a sigh she turned and threw herself upon the skin beside her grandmother, with her face resting in her hands, her elbows on the skin. She lay there in silence for a while, watching the old squaw's fingers — long, and gaunt, and ghostly, in the flickering firelight — deftly and swiftly twisting the shavings and braiding the grasses.

"Was it so very much that my father and grandfather did for the master that he has always been so good to us?" she asked, at last.

The old squaw's hands dropped upon her knee, and for a moment she sat staring over Weno's head into the fire beyond. The sudden question had recalled those terrible days before the child was born, and in the howling of the storm as it lashed the rain and sleet against the windows, and in the deep thunder of the waves she heard again the war-whoop of her tribe, the clatter of their horses' hoofs, the splash of their thousand paddles, the twang of their bowstrings and the whirr of their arrows. Her old eyes shone and flashed in the firelight. Her face lost its wrinkles and a deep frown gathered upon her forehead.

With instinctive admiration Wenononee lay watching the old squaw. She knew the story of Wetamoc's marriage, well; how the brave who led her to his wigwam was then one of the great chiefs of the tribe, and how they all said that of all the women he could not have chosen a better wife. And Wenononce was enough of a true Indian still to recognize and appreciate the qualities which had made Wetamoc worthy. She loved the wild, roving life of her people; she could not help it; and the warm weather rarely found Weno sleeping under the roof of the log cabin. She could shoot an arrow straighter than any Indian boy of her age who came to the village. She could ride the wildest pony in Manitoba, or paddle a canoe as skillfully as any brave. She knew where game was found and how to trap it; and with the old rifle which the master had given to her father she could shoot in a way that put to shame many of the settlers who were much better equipped. She possessed all of the Indian instincts of loyalty, too, and when the vision had passed away, and with a grunt Wetamoc returned to her work, though Weno did not think it wise to repeat the same question, she asked another in the same line.

"If we were ever in trouble the master has given us aid?" she said.

Wetamoc assented with a grunt.

"If the master or the young master were to be in trouble again wouldn't it be our duty to " —

Weno paused abruptly, lifted her head, listened

intently for an instant, then sprang to her feet and hurried out of the cabin, pulling the door after her before the tempest had time to discover that it was open.

The moment the door was closed her hands fell idly by her side. She stood still in the darkness, silently watching the glimmer of the lanterns which some of the settlers were carrying in advance of the men who bore the litter, as the solemn procession moved up the village street toward the stone mansion on the hill.

As it came nearer Wenononee shrank back into the open shed at the entrance to which Oscar's sign once hung.

It was a curious throng that slowly and solemnly tramped past the log cabin, weird and strange in the flickering light of the lanterns that left many black shadows and slowly moving mysteries unsolved. There were German peasants in their rough, dark clothes and small flap caps, Frenchmen and half-breeds in jaunty buckskin jackets and bright-colored scarfs, Indians in their blankets, shod with moccasins, gliding noiselessly on, like ghosts, and Scotch farmers and rough English miners making as much noise with their feet as a horse. In the center the litter was borne upon men's shoulders, and notwithstanding the storm and night, the rough men who bore it walked with uncovered heads. Behind the litter walked the doctor and the minister, and between them — they were supporting him, each holding an arm — was Oscar Peterson. When they had passed, Wenononee came from her hiding-place and followed with those who were walking in the rear.

It was broad daylight when Weno returned to the cabin. The storm had blown itself away and given up its struggle to bring the winter back again. The bright sun was streaming through the east window as though there never had been and never could be anything but beautiful warm spring days. The invalid was propped up upon the box bed eating her breakfast, and old Wetamoe was still cooking over the last embers. No one asked a question as Wenononee entered, for she was an Indian and they were Indians. They simply grunted the usual greeting, to which she responded, and Wetamoc put some food upon the corner of the hearth. But Weno turned away from it and silently threw herself upon a skin near the bed.

For an hour she lay there, and not a word was spoken in the cabin. The mother finished her breakfast and took from a pouch hanging beside her a piece of skin from which she was working a pair of leggings. The grandmother smoked her red clay pipe and braided the grasses.

From the council fires of the greatest chiefs and the powwows of the tribes to the lodge-fire of the medicine man, the pot-fires of the tepee and the hearth of the most civilized wigwam where an Indian ever was himself, it has always been in much this same fashion that the most startling and important revelations have been made. It was simple nature. Wenononee could not help it; and when at last she spoke, it was to repeat only four words:

"The master is dead!"

CHAPTER IV.

OSCAR'S FIRST DUTY.

OSCAR had not a near relative in the world. Both in England and America there were friends almost without number who were ready to extend to him their sympathy, but he had seen enough of the world to know that if he had been left destitute instead of "the young master" of so much property, he would not have received half so much sympathy. He did not feel competent to judge among them for some one to trust in his present emergency.

His father had rallied a moment before he died, but Oscar did not see him. His own life was hanging by a thread that night, and his mind was wandering. He only knew that they asked who fired the shot, and that his father replied, as he did on the yacht: "It must have been a mistake. The ball must have glanced." With that the people were satisfied, saying that it was probably some Indian hunter.

They asked Oscar the same question, but until he

could make up his mind why it was that his father insisted upon that reply he too said, simply, "I do not know." Then he would grind his teeth and say to himself: "But I will know; for it was not a mistake,

OSCAR'S TWO FRIENDS.

and it was not an Indian. That is my first duty, and I will do it."

Oscar had two dear friends. They came to him from Manitoba to Oxford, as a Christmas gift from his father, a year before, and now they had come back with him to Manitoba. One was a horse — the finest colt that had been raised upon a stock farm. The other was a dog which Oscar, at least, considered a match for any setter in the country. He was reading Don Quixote when they arrived, and he named the horse Sancho, and the dog Panza, after the famous esquire of that old Spanish satire. The boys laughed at him for his choice, but he said that whenever he spoke their names he thought of the jolly old squire, and it made him want to laugh, so he was satisfied.

Now they were dearer to him than ever, and the three were together almost all the time. They thought as much of each other and of Oscar as he thought of them. Panza would go to the stable for Sancho and take him back, and Sancho was thoroughly satisfied to trot away with Panza upon his back, holding the reins in her jaws. It was astonishing to see how carefully he would step, trying to keep the saddle steady, always holding his head on one side to watch and see that she did not fall. When they reached their destination and Panza jumped, Sancho would squeal and apparently do his best to nab her; but either he never really tried or Panza was always too quick for him, for he never succeeded. If any one else attempted to mount, however, Sancho began in right good earnest, and he must be an excellent horseman who could gain the saddle at all, much less keep it.

With these two Oscar started to perform his first duty. As he rode down the village street he was surprised at the cordial greetings he received from every one. They all knew him, and their eagerness to be friendly made him stronger and braver, even though he did not know them. When they were passing the log cabin he paused for a moment, thinking of the time when he had lived there. His eyes turned toward the shed almost as though he expected to find the little sign still hanging there. In a moment the oak door was opened and the old squaw appeared, bobbing and grunting a welcome.

"How do you do, Wetamoe?" Oscar exclaimed, riding up and offering her his hand. "I should know you anywhere. I used to be afraid of you, but I'm not afraid now."

"No, no!" she replied, taking his hands in both of hers. "No fear Wetamoe. Heap friend." Then she looked about her with a quick, half-frightened glance, to be sure that no one had heard her speaking English.

"Wetamoe's brave and her son were very kind to my father. I shall never forget it," Oscar said; and while the old squaw pressed his hand to her wrinkled cheek he asked, "Where is Mama, the young squaw? I remember very well when she was my nurse."

"Mama seek. Soon die," replied Wetamoe sadly; and then in the universal sign language of the Indians she asked him to come in and see her daughter. Quickly dismounting, Oscar threw the reins to Panza and hurried across the cabin to the box bed where the invalid sat.

She took his hand and kissed it, and the tears rolled down her sunken cheeks as she gently touched his brown curls and whispered, "Pretty! pretty! You pappoose me." Then she took a pair of leggings and moccasins from the pouch beside her and gave them to him. She had evidently worked them as a gift to

THE SQUAW'S CABIN.

the young master when he should come back, and she was celebrated for her beautiful handiwork.

Oscar realized at a glance that these were by far the finest he had ever seen. He tried to speak, but something choked him. He could only look his thanks and press his old nurse's hand. After waiting a moment he asked, "Where is the little one — the pappoose? I can just remember her."

The mother was too weak to call, but Wetamoc gave a shrill Indian cry and shouted, "Weno! Wenononee!"

Had Oscar looked directly above his head, through the hole leading to the little room under the roof, he would have seen one stray lock of glossy black hair and two bright black eyes appearing just over the edge. But he did not look, and as there was no response he took from behind his saddle (where he had bound it in the common custom of the country) a blanket robe which he had brought from England, gave it to his old nurse, and rode away to Wawanka's wigwam.

So far as an Indian could be, Wawanka was the village shoemaker. He had outlived his usefulness in the forest, and settled down near the village; for aside from his skill in making leggings and moccasins for his own people he made a strong, high-topped boot of tough, soft leather, which was popular among the farmers, and had invented a curious kind of iron claw, which he called slug-holds, and fastened on the heels of modern boots to prevent them from slipping when climbing over fallen logs or icy rocks, in the winter. They were in great demand among the hunters and lumbermen. When it was absolutely necessary, Wawanka would repair a strictly pale face boot or shoe, but he did not like to, and avoided it if possible.

Oscar sat down on one end of his bench and watched him for a time in silence. This was quite in accord with Indian etiquette. The more important the errand which calls one to another's wigwam the less inclined he is to make any sudden declaration, and Oscar's first five years with his Indian nurse had given him many a trait which he himself did not appreciate, but which was fully in accord with the established rites of the red men. The boys at Oxford always called him odd. It had troubled him, and he had tried to discover and overcome the oddities, but never once came near enough the truth to realize that they were only the intuitive instincts and traits of his Indian nurse transplanted into his own boyhood. So Wawanka grunted a welcome, brushed the dust from the end of the low bench where he kept his leather and tools, and silently went on with his work, and when Oscar sat down in silence and watched him it did not seem odd to either of them.

Wawanka was taking some well-worn slug-holds from a pair of boots. The summer had come in good earnest, and there was no more need of them.

"Those are great," Oscar said, at last.

The Indian grunted. "Pale face boots no slug, no good," he said, a little scornfully.

"Which are the best, Wawanka, boots made here or in the States?" Oscar asked.

"Both no good," replied the Indian, decidedly. "State boot heel no good. Heap no good." Wawanka was fumbling about under his bench, and now pulled out a pair of boots which he held bottom up, and Oscar's heart stood still as he looked at a pair of "State" boots with one missing heel. "Black-dog bring boot Wawanka's wigwam. Want slug. Pale face go hunting. Black-dog guide. Two days pale face come. Swear Wawanka heap big cheat. Take pair new Indian boot. No pay. Ugh!" and the Indian settled back to his work.

"Do you know the name of the pale face?" Oscar asked.

Wawanka grunted savagely, and finally replied: "No see just once. Heap bad. Good no stop. Heap big. Bottom part here gone." He took the end of his little finger between his thumb and forefinger, and then turned to his work again.

This was all that Oscar could get out of him, so he purchased the boots, much to the delight of the Indian, and rode away to the mines to find Black-dog. But Black-dog was not to be found.

"He's a slip'ry skunk, ef ever thar war one," said an old miner who had charge of the division where Black-dog was supposed to work. "Never wus a bad row in these parts but Black-dog was skulkin' roun' sumwhar on the outskirts, jest too fur away to ketch. He's lugged more dirt-mean whiskey inter these diggin's nor all the rest combined. The day afore yer father got — got — hurt," said the miner, trying in his rough way to speak as gently as possible of the sad event, " he wus here to the mines an' gin Black-dog a good lay out. He told him he wus goin' up the lake the next day fur to peck out a place fur a saw-mill, an' thet he might go up thar an' go ter lumberin' or leave the place altergether, es he wudn't hev him round no longer. I heer'd thet much myself; an' thet night he wus gone, takin' his hoss, but leavin' his cart an' his squaw. He allers takes them 'long with him when he's arter whiskey, so I reckoned he'd gone ter the woods; but next night she lit out. She'd be wuss'n him ef thet war convenient. Waal, she tuk the cart an' Ben Billin's's hoss. Got a big white face an' a chopped-off mane, an' one white foot. Ben don't say 's she stole et, but she borred et 'out leave or license, an' he'd be proper glad to git et back ag'in."

Oscar only waited for him to pause when he asked eagerly, "Had Black-dog's horse four white feet, a piece cut from his ear, and " —

"An' a hump on his hip? Thet's him," the miner interrupted.

"Do you know what firearms he carried?" Oscar asked.

"Reckon he hed an old navy — most on 'em do," replied the miner; "an' fur the rest he owned an ole double-barreled shot-gun."

" And an English rifle ? "

" Lord, no! He never went inter shootin' irons thet luxurious unless'n he stole 'em ; an' he hain't bin nowhar to steal one fur the last month ; an' he wudn't 'a' been two hours in swappin' et off ef he hed."

Here the miner stopped short for a moment, looked keenly at Oscar and exclaimed : " I say, young master, ye been't a-thinkin' et mought 'a' bin him es — es — fired, up in the woods ? "

" I hardly know what to think," Oscar replied. " His horse was left by a deserted tepee, and I saw it killed by wolves not over half a mile away."

The miner stood for a moment whistling and looking away over the lake, then he sat down on a rock and replied : " Look a-here, young master, you jest hold yer hosses or they'll run yer inter a detch on thet trail. Black-dog wus a pesky good trapper. He know'd them woods ef ever any one ded, an' he never lef thet hoss o' his'n war he'd be eet up by wolves. He was a tarnal coward, an' ef he'd know'd the master wus thar, es he ded, he'd never 'a' called attention to his wharabouts by shootin', countin' 'twus a mistake ; whiles ownin' to his hands a-shakin', frum suthin' like p'ralisis, he's sech an everlastin' poor shot thet he'd never 'a' dar'd ter resk tryin', hed he 'a' bin in arnest. He mought 'a' let his hoss out, or he mought 'a' gone es guide fur summon es ded, knowin' or not knowin', es the case may be ; but Black-dog never ded thet thing himself.

Ye kin sot yer stakes on thet claim, young master, an' be sure o' strikin' the right vein."

"Have you any idea where I can find him?" Oscar asked.

"Likeliest way is ter wait fur him," said the miner. "A bad penny's putty sartin' to turn up ag'in. The Injuns come outer the woods 'long in March, ye know, an' 'bout this time they've got their tradin' done, an' I hear thar's a big bunch campin' down nigh Neepawa, whar they'll likely be havin' their spring games 'bout now. 'Twould be jest one o' his dirty tricks to hustle a lot o' mean whiskey in amongst 'em, ef he cud steal or smuggle et."

"How does he look?" Oscar inquired, eagerly.

"Yer must wanter see Black-dog more'n most folks ef yer'd foller him to Neepawa," observed the miner. "But ye cudn't miss him ef ye once sot eye on him. He's the doggonedest critter thet ever ye see. An' his squaw's another jest like him. Yer'd know him by the hoss an' by his big fur cap. He wars et winter'n summer. They say et's 'cause he's pesky 'feared o' gittin' his skull cracked in some row."

This was all the information which Oscar could obtain, and with it he rode home to prepare for a trip to the Indian encampment on the prairie stretching westward from Neepawa.

CHAPTER V.

BAGATAWA.

FOR a guide and companion Oscar found a young fellow who had been in his father's employ for several years, watching cattle on the prairie. Before daylight they were on the way and with no roads or fences to help or perplex them, without even a trail in the direction they were going. They struck out at once over the open country; through the broad wheat-fields of the estate and then across the pasture-lands beyond. To the southwest lay the great prairie, stretching away to the foot of the Rocky Mountains. To the northwest were the wild and ragged pine-lands, with some of the grandest scenery in the world. A thousand lakes were buried there where the wild duck and the plover made their nests. For more than a hundred years hunters and trappers had been sending its treasures of fur by great shiploads all over the world, and yet the supply seemed inexhaustible. Some day the lumber would be called for, and after that even, those wild lands would still be some of the richest to be found, for the vast treasures of minerals which Nature hid in those fastnesses.

It would require nearly two days to reach the Indian camp, and they carried food and blankets, a cup, coffee pot and frying-pan strapped behind their saddles. They did not need them the first night, however, as the cowboy arranged to stop at a ranch that was a little more than half-way to Neepawa. Here they learned that the encampment, this year, was nearer to them than they supposed, and nearer to the hills.

As they were crossing the plain, early the next morning, they passed a little band of Blackfeet braves engaged in conversation with one of the mounted police of the prairie. The cowboy grunted a good-morning to the Indians and waved his hand to the soldier as they passed, but seemed to pay them no further attention. Oscar was much more interested, for, though they were conversing very eagerly, no one spoke a single word. They were using the universal sign language of the Indians. Oscar was saying to himself that it might do very well for an emergency, to ask for food or water, but he didn't believe one could impart much information, when the cowboy remarked, "Black-dog, the half-breed you're looking for, comes from the Peterson mines, doesn't he?"

Oscar assented, and the cowboy continued: "He's

got a squaw with him and a box prairie cart, and a pony with a white face and one white foot, and a bobbed mane?" Oscar nodded in astonishment. "He's got a load o' smuggled whiskey?"

"I presume so," Oscar replied; "but where did you find out about him?"

"That fellow was asking the Blackfeet if they'd seen such a turnout on the way to the camp. Smuggling cornjuice is bad business in these parts just now, and I'd ruther be a treed coon than a smuggler with them fellers after me. He was a big fool to tell those Blackfeet, though. If Black-dog is at the camp they'll tell him the first thing."

They reached the camp early in the afternoon. A thousand Indians had already gathered, and others were occasionally coming in. They were all in their happiest mood, having traded their winter's catch of fur for whatever seemed to them to be the best of good things, and they were bent upon making the most of them while the good things were new.

"Only keep your eyes open so as not to give them a chance to steal anything from you, and you are all right anywhere," said the cowboy, as they separated to search for Black-dog. Little clusters of tents covered the plain for a mile or more in each direction. Tepees, lodges of all sorts — anything that would make a wigwam — appeared, and every tribe that trapped or hunted in the North was represented.

A CONVERSATION WITHOUT WORDS.

Most of the families possessed one or two of the famous prairie carts, looking so much like the carts of the old Normandy peasants as to prove that the first French settlers had a hand in their construction. A plain, oblong box, with the bottom side-boards running straight out in two long shafts, was placed upon a heavy crossbar for an axle, connecting two great wooden wheels. There were no springs and no seats. The felloes were very broad, so that they should not cut through the turf, and the spokes very long to go safely through mud-holes. There was not a nail or bolt or anything but wood about any one of them, so that if a prairie cart broke down it was easy to repair. Sometimes poles were run up, making them look like hayricks. Sometimes long, slender poles were bent and fastened to the sides, making a frame upon which an awning could be drawn.

It was easy to tell when a cart was coming, for an Indian was never known to grease the wheels. The contents were always a jumble of dirty bedding and blankets, guns, axes and tent poles, canvas covers, skins and cooking utensils. If there was room left and the load was not too heavy, there was usually a basket of puppies to be seen. If there was still more room some of the babies were stowed away there. Occasionally a squaw would ride, and least frequently the brave himself would appear balanced on the cart.

It seemed to be a thoroughly manly occupation for

the brave to stalk along before the horse, wrapped in his long blanket and bright-red leggings covered with beads, which he had just purchased with skins; but he would never carry any burden. If there was too much for the cart or the pony the squaw must carry it, often with a pappoose beside, strapped over her shoulders.

Very often the aboriginal Indian vehicle was still in use. It was two long poles, fastened at one end and hung upon the saddle. Just behind the pony the two were again fastened, by a crossbar, about two feet apart, and the other ends dragged upon the ground far behind. The pony carried all he could upon his back, and as much more upon the crossbar. Even the dogs were sometimes harnessed in this way on a small scale; and Oscar laughed heartily as one big dog walked solemnly behind a cart, carrying a basket full of puppies tied to the crossbar behind her, and again when a knock-kneed, jaded little pony ambled along with two Indian babies all alone, tied to his back.

From the frilled poles of the canvas tepees, and bark wigwams and leather lodges that were already set up, little clouds of blue-white smoke curled slowly upward, indicating that housekeeping had begun. In other places the squaws were busy unloading and setting up the tents. This was evidently not a manly occupation, for the moment the little caravan reached its tenting ground the braves disappeared, and did not show themselves again till the smoke was rising.

With his eyes wide open Oscar rode about the camp, attracting little attention, for, from miles about, settlers came to these encampments to watch the games; but search as he would he saw nothing, heard nothing of Black-dog. Here and there he paused to watch a game that was going on, in which the contestants usually ended by coming to blows, but no one seemed particularly interested except those who were fighting, and they were always allowed to finish unmolested.

At one side of the camp the Indians were racing their ponies, and his love for horses drew Oscar instinctively to the spot. Sancho pricked up his ears and began to tremble as they approached, as though he would very much like to take a turn himself.

"You could beat anything they've got in this valley all to pieces, old boy," Oscar said, patting his neck. Then his entire attention was turned upon the field, for two of the finest ponies he had ever seen came dashing down the brown prairie. They were without saddles or bridles, except the usual Indian lip-rope. One was white, the other black, and neck and neck they flew along the ground, while their riders, almost naked, swung their long lashes in the air and urged them on.

Nearer and nearer they came, each muscle swelling, their nostrils dilated, as with every bound they seemed to throw new life to every nerve, and faster and faster and faster they swept along, still neck and neck, the white against the black.

Oscar sat in his saddle as restive as Sancho, and even Panza, with her ears pricked up and her eyes wide open, stood panting and quivering with excitement.

The only beings who did not seem to be paying attention to anything were a group of Indians seated opposite. They seemed more than half-asleep. Oscar wanted to shout to them to wake up and see the race, when the two beauties dashed madly between them, came to a sudden halt which threw them for an instant upon their haunches, and the solemn Indians opposite, declared that the white had won by half a head.

Oscar had not recovered from his surprise at finding that those fellows, apparently so sleepy, were really the judges and very wide awake, when he started as a hand was laid upon his shoulder and the cowboy's voice sounded, saying, "You'd make a poor hand in an Indian country if you forgot yourself that way," while with a laugh he handed Oscar his blanket, saddle, knapsack and rifle, which he had unstrapped from behind him while he watched the race.

Oscar laughed, too, acknowledging himself well-caught, when he noticed that the Indians opposite, were also laughing.

"I declare," he exclaimed, in a low tone, "I was just thinking that those fellows over there were sound

THE BLACK AGAINST THE WHITE.

asleep, when I suddenly discovered that they were the judges at the horse race, and I'm blest if they were not taking in the whole of this business, too, and no one knows how much more."

"That's the dif' between a pale face and a red," replied his companion. "When an Indian's acting he acts in every inch of him, and when he's not right in it he's so dull you'd think the crack o' doom wouldn't start him; but either way and all the time his eyes and his senses are just scooping in everything. An Indian will always come upon you when you don't expect him, and where you are not looking for him, but you can't get within a mile of one of those red putty-faces, unless he's drunk, without his knowing all about it."

"Well, I thank you for a very good lesson," Oscar replied, "and another time I shall try and keep cool and keep my wits about me. Have you any news from Black-dog?"

"He's here."

"Here!" Oscar gave such a sudden start that even Sancho jumped.

"There you go again," said the cowboy, with another laugh. "I'll bet there isn't an Indian in that bunch but knows, now, that we're here for something important. The next thing they'll find out what, if they can, and then try to balk us, if they're able. That's the nature of the beast."

Oscar's face showed his chagrin, but he simply said, " Where is he ? "

" Down at the medicine man's lodge," replied his companion. " I found his horse first, and then his cart. They were a quarter of a mile apart and a long way from the lodge. He's a sly skunk. He's lying low for great business to-night and to-morrow morning, when they have their big game of Bagatawa."

" Could I see him ? " Oscar asked.

" I doubt if you could get at him, or if 'twould do any good if you did," said the cowboy. " He'd be deuced up on his dignity, here among his friends. Best way is to watch and catch him when he's moving off. He'll not go to-night. We can roll up somewhere here and take turns at sleeping."

Oscar looked at Panza and was about to say something, when the cowboy continued: " She'd be all right if we were a mile away from everything, but right here in the midst of such a bunch any Indian could get near enough to fix her with an arrow before she opened her eyes. My advice is, that if you want to keep your horse you had better keep awake."

Oscar was rapidly learning much that proved invaluable to him before long. He saw that the cowboy was right, and though it looked like cowardice at first, he soon made up his mind that it was not.

They rode along the bank of the river till they found a good place on a little knoll. There they unsaddled their horses and let them feed while Panza watched them, and they built a fire and cooked their supper.

As they brought their horses in the cowboy said: "I reckon you'd better watch for the first half, 'cause it's new to you, and if you tried to sleep you'd only lie awake and make a whole night of it by the means. You watch till twelve, and you'll be tired enough to sleep anywhere."

He took the halter in his hand and very easily made his horse lie down. Then he lay down close beside him, all rolled up in his blanket.

"He likes it, and it keeps a fellow warm, cold nights," he added, seeing Oscar watching him. "Besides, it's harder to steal him this way, and he wakes a fellow up mighty quick, with his sniffing, when anything's wrong, if you're close enough to feel it."

Sancho had been watching very closely, too, and it occurred to Oscar that he would like to teach him the trick, so he took the halter just as he had seen the cowboy when, to his surprise, Sancho lay right down almost as quickly as Panza could.

Not to disappoint him, Oscar threw his blanket around him, and sat down with his back against Sancho's, and Panza curled up at his feet. He could not make up his mind whether it was a trick which Sancho had been taught before he was sent to England or had caught just by watching the cowboy's horse.

He was quite sure that Sancho was clever enough for either. Very soon, however, he gave up thinking to watch the Indians in the valley.

It was a beautiful moonlight night. A fire of pitch-pine burned upon the river bank not far away. About it the Indians were dancing, to the beating of drums and the rattle of dried gourds filled with pebbles, preparing themselves for the great game the next day.

After dancing for nearly an hour they stopped short, made a rush for the river and plunged into the ice-cold water.

Oscar had often heard of Bagatawa, but he had never seen the game played or witnessed the preparatory ceremonies which always take place through the night before the contest. Even the squaws were taking part, and the whole camp seemed awake and active. He had no idea what time it was when the cowboy opened his eyes, lifted his head just high enough to look quickly about in every direction, then sat up, turned his watch to the moonlight, and remarked, "Twelve o'clock to the dot. Now it's your turn."

"Have you been awake long?" Oscar asked.

"Not a second," said the cowboy, rising and stretching. "A fellow gets a sort of clockwork inside of him, lying round loose on the prairie for a living. Now you turn in quick, so's not to lose time."

Oscar was sure that he waked up several times, and thought he had not slept at all; but when he finally got his eyes wide open he was surprised to find that the sun was almost up, and that the cowboy had the fire kindled and breakfast cooking.

"I spoke to you a little while ago," he said, "but you were so sound asleep I thought it would pay you to take another turn. Pretty stiff in the joints, are you? Well, it won't last. Just run for all you're worth down to the river and back, and see how quick you'll forget it."

Oscar tried the experiment. At first it seemed as though he could not put one foot before the other but, though it was only a very short distance, by the time he was back again he felt a warm glow from head to foot, and was ready to enjoy any kind of a breakfast that could be eaten.

Indians from all sides were gathering about the place that had been selected for the game. They were all dressed in their holiday best, and bright colors flashed and merry shouts resounded everywhere. As the boys rode down among them Oscar thought he had never seen Indians look so clean in all his life.

Those who were to take part in the game were gathered at opposite ends of the field, entirely naked, except for the little breech-cloth, and a long wolf tail or fox tail hanging down behind. The height of fashion demanded that it should be a white horse-tail, but very few could support that luxury. Many were covered with bright war-paint and bands of eagle feathers about their heads, tossing in the air as they danced and laughed and shouted threats and taunts to the other side.

Forty or fifty men on each side were gathered about their respective goals, which were made by planting two long poles in the ground and fastening a crossbar at the top. Each player held two sticks, about three feet long, bent into a loop at the end and held there by a netting of leather cord.

A tall old Indian patriarch, all covered over with beads and feathers, and wrapped in a gorgeous new blanket, walked solemnly into the center of the field and gave a signal, at which all the players laid down their sticks and came together. Then the chief counted the sides and each man chose his antagonist. The chief made a short speech, the players went back and took up their sticks, a medicine man came forward with a large ball, the chief gave a signal, and the medicine man threw the ball into the air with all his might.

Up to that time everything had been as still as death. The players stood like statues. But the moment the ball went up, a shout rose from the crowd of spectators and every muscle of every player on the field seemed suddenly to start into action. From that instant the game went on without a moment's rest. The players would rush toward the flying ball regardless of any one about them. They would catch it if they could between their sticks or, if not, then strike it and send it as far as possible toward the enemy's goal. If they could not do, that they tried to prevent some opponent who was nearer from doing the same, and if too far away for that they did their best to prevent the enemy from getting any nearer than they were.

They were not allowed to touch the ball or other players with their hands, but must always use the sticks. Sometimes they rushed together with such force as to leap upon one another's shoulders, and carry on the struggle up there for a moment. They would dart between an adversary's legs, leaving him sprawling on the ground the moment he thought he had successfully caught the ball. They piled themselves up three or four deep over it when the ball fell and was lost for a moment in the crowd, but none of them wore shoes or even moccasins, so that there were none of the bruises of football as the result.

For some minutes the boys had been watching a tall, handsome fellow who had hung about the rear at the start, but had suddenly made a dive into the thick of the game. "He's got it! He's got it!" Oscar exclaimed as he made a bound and nipped the ball between the nettings on his sticks, several feet in the air.

"And he'll keep it, too, for one while," replied the cowboy.

It seemed impossible, but he sprang right over the heads of those about him and darted away like a deer, holding his hands high above his head. In an instant the whole band of players was after him, to help or hinder, to head him off, trip him up, knock the ball from between his sticks — anything to prevent his getting it to the goal.

Now he leaped into the air to escape a foot or a stick thrust out to trip him, then he sprang to one side to dodge a fellow who made a quick dive to run into him.

BAGATAWA.

He left him sprawling on the ground instead, for half a dozen to trip over, before they could turn, and a comically wriggling pile they made, each trying to regain his feet regardless of the others.

The runner was far away from them in a twinkling, making for the goal about as a yacht makes for a landing against a head wind. But dodging, leaping, running, turning, he was constantly coming nearer.

Suddenly the ball went out of sight, and with a groan Oscar exclaimed, "He's lost it!" But it was up again before he had finished. The Indian had not dropped it. He had simply ducked to avoid a sudden blow aimed by a player who sprang upon him from one side, and the stick whirled harmlessly over his head. The next instant he was darting on again with the ball high in the air.

It was growing desperate. Some of the players left the chase to gather nearer the goal by a short cut and intercept him. A dozen at least were close behind, and a dozen more running from the side when he sprang into a cluster of trees. The whole were after him in an instant, but they had no sooner entered the tangled grove than he turned upon them, shot back again directly through their midst, and was out of the grove, between the goal and his pursuers, with three or four yards of distance gained before they appeared. A tremendous shout rose from those who were watching the game as he started off in a direct line for the goal.

He seemed to be made of eyes, watching his opponents in front and behind and on all sides of him, watching his path over the rough ground, watching the ball that it should not slip from between the sticks, watching the goal for the best chance of reaching it, running at the top of his speed, with his hands all the time high above his head.

The players about the goal ran out to meet him.

Three of them came up directly in front, whirling their sticks about their heads. Two ran toward him from the side. He dodged to escape them, when one from behind quickly thrust a stick between his legs and he plunged forward at full length upon the ground. There was a groan from the spectators, and in an instant the whole party of players, of whichever side, came piling in on top of him.

Then everything was still, and all stood watching the struggling mass, when suddenly there was an eruption in its midst like a miniature volcano. Up, out of the center, the same fellow appeared, the players rolled this way and that, he sprang upon the top of the pile with the ball still firmly nipped between his sticks, and with one bound cleared the whole, leaving the struggling mass behind him, and started like the wind for the unprotected goal. Bound after bound was breathlessly watched and when, a moment later, the ball flew under the arch and the point was gained, the whole crowd sent up one Indian yell that might almost have split the sky.

"I tell you, but that's a game!" Oscar said, with a quivering breath, at the end. "And yet it's for all the world like Lacrosse."

"It's the origin of Lacrosse," replied his companion.

"Why, they told me in England that Lacrosse was a Scotch game," said Oscar, but the cowboy only laughed and shook his head.

BLACK-DOG AND HIS SQUAW.

"They'd rather do anything than credit a single good idea to an Indian," he replied. "But the fact remains, and you'll find that it is a fact."

"It's awfully interesting," Oscar repeated.

"I reckon Black-dog thought you'd find it so," said the cowboy, "for he and his wife lit out half an hour ago. I saw um starting up the mountain trail."

"Why didn't you tell me?" Oscar exclaimed.

"'Twould 'a' spoiled the game for you before you're used to taking in three or four things at once. We can catch him easy."

"Well, I wish I had your eyes," Oscar muttered.

"I couldn't spare them very well; but you'll have better ones of your own as soon as you've had to do some watching out with life and death at stake," he replied, as they started after Black-dog.

A half-hour later they heard a sharp altercation not far ahead, in which an Indian's voice was prominent.

"That's him, sure's fate!" whispered the cowboy. "The soldiers have got him. You want to put in your whack lively, for it's the last you'll see of him for some time to come."

They hurried on and soon came upon the scene. A soldier of the mounted police held the white-faced horse, and one sat on either side with a pistol pointed at Black-dog's head, while the poor half-breed, in his big fur cap, holding up his hand to surrender, was the very picture of despair.

After a little explanation Oscar obtained permission to speak with the prisoner for a moment, and crawled up to the seat beside him.

Black-dog's story was disconnected enough, but Oscar gathered from it that a stranger from the States had stopped at his cabin for a week. He said he was a miner and spent some time at the mines. He was inside the cabin when the master stopped at the door and told Black-dog that he was going up the lake to place a sawmill, and that he must either go to lumbering or leave the place. When the master left the stranger said he was going hunting, and sent Black-dog to Wawanka to have slug-holds put on his boots. He had a fine English hollow-ball rifle. He took Black-dog's horse, promising to bring it back the next day; but Black-dog was in haste. He did not want the master to force him to go into the woods, and he did want to secure some whiskey for the encampment, so he started on foot, telling his squaw to come on the next day with the cart. The horse did not come back, so she borrowed the first one she could find and followed him.

The story had some truth in it, at any rate, and, satisfied that, true or false, it was all he could get out of the half-breed, Oscar left him and with his companion started for home again. The cowboy left him at the Peterson Ranch, a few miles from the village, and, after dark, with Panza beside him, Oscar left Sancho at the stable and entered the house on the butte.

CHAPTER VI.

NOT FOR GOLD.

THE house was dark and still. The two servants had doubtless retired, and Oscar entered softly, that he might not disturb them. He heard a fire crackling and burning in the great, oak-finished room which, through the winter, was used as a reception-room and office, as well as dining-room, on account of its enormous fireplace. It had been raining hard through the evening, and saying to himself that the servants must have half-expected him that night and lit the fire for him, he hurried to his room, threw off his wet clothes, and in a woollen shirt, trousers and slippers came down to the great dining-room.

The table was spread with an elaborate meal, and set for three people. Oscar was perplexed, but hungry, and without waiting to inquire into it he sat down and ate a hearty supper. Then drawing his chair to the fire he began to think.

The doctor had extracted the fatal bullet, and he

had found the one buried in the wolf skins. They were the same, and came from a hollow-ball English rifle. The heel and the boots he obtained from Wawanka matched. Black-dog and Wawanka had described the stranger in almost the same terms. The man was conversant with mines and mining, and evidently went up the lake for the express purpose of firing that shot. Oscar remembered what his father said about the new mine in the States, and something forced the conviction upon him that the agent of whom he spoke was the man for him to find.

He turned to Panza, lying behind his chair, and said: "That is our duty, Panza. We'll stick to it till it is done. We'll need all the money that the estate can earn to help us, but we will do it."

Suddenly voices sounded outside the house. They were rough, strange voices, and Panza began to growl.

"Be quiet," Oscar said, sitting erect and listening.

They came nearer. Heavy footsteps sounded in the hall. The door burst open and with a boisterous laugh three men entered. One was an Indian and two were white men. They were all heavily armed, and all strangers. Panza was ready to spring upon them, but Oscar held her back and she lay down again behind his chair.

"Halloo, youngster!" exclaimed the one who seemed to be the leader, as he noticed the boy sitting in the great fireplace. "Be you young Peterson? Surely

"WERE YOU SHAKING YOUR FIST AT ME?"

thought you'd skipped. Couldn't find ye nowhar, an' been kinder makin' myself ter hum, meanwhiles, bein' I'm likely ter be ter hum here, fur the most part, frum now on; an' sence I found ye I mought's well sarve this slip o' paper on ye right now, afore we furgit it, ter show yer my 'thority."

Oscar had not been away from the refinement of civilization long enough to understand the roughness of frontier life, and his idea of dignity was so outraged that, irrespective of the man's mission or business, he was thoroughly indignant, and without touching the paper he turned deliberately away, resting his elbows on his knees, and sat looking into the fire.

"Stuffy, eh?" observed the man. "Waal, I reckoned yer mought be, but it can't be helped. An' sence ye won't look at the paper I'll take the liberty o' givin' ye the contents by word o' mouth. Seems yer dad gin a deed o' this property an' a bill o' sale o' what's on it, fur vallerble consideration, ter the man I represents. An' he's had 'em duly administered 'cordin' ter law, an' I 'pinted ter look arter the investment, git what I kin outer it — sell off as I have opportunity, an' so forth. Not findin' yer I've been round fur a couple o' days takin' possession an' straightenin' things out. Now I don't want no trouble, an' I ain't goin' ter hurt nobody ef I kin help it." He was becoming aggressive as Oscar refused to pay him the slightest attention. "I tell yer I don't want no trouble, an' thar won't be none unless'n you make it. But I'm here under bonds, ter do my duty, an' you've got ter git. Do ye hear me?" he exclaimed, bringing a chair about in front of the fire opposite Oscar, resting his foot upon it while his arms swung over the back; and the two who were with him edged forward, ready to seize the boy when he gave the word. "Do ye hear me? I ain't a-goin' ter draw on a kid, leastwise on one as hasn't his shootin'-irons about him; but you look a-here, youngster." He pushed back the sleeve of his shirt, exhibiting a brawny, muscular arm. "I don't need nuthin ter handle you with. Ef you don't git, in good peaceable shape, you know what that means," and he swung his arm about suggestively.

Like a flash Oscar was upon his feet. His chair fell with a crash behind him. His fists were clinched, his head erect, and Panza by his side his very counterpart.

"Were you shaking your fist at me?" he muttered, looking savagely across the hearth; for the chair upon which the fellow had been leaning stood empty. The two behind him had backed up against the wall, and the leader was as close to them as he could crowd.

"No, sir! No, sir; I wus not," he said decidedly. "I wus only tryin' ter explain how matters stood, an' if I did it wrong I 'pologize. Thar! Ef that's fair an' you'll excuse us I reckon we'll go now. Thar ain't no haste 'bout yer vacatin'. Take yer time. Fur's I'm consarned, I don't care if yer never go."

Oscar folded his arms and calmly asked, "Is what you have told me about this property true?"

"Here's my paper of authority, sir, signed by the holder of the deed, indorsed by the court at Winnipeg," the man replied, humbly.

"Do you claim everything?" Oscar asked.

"'Tween the deed an' bill o' sale, sir, it's pretty much all covered, I reckon, sir."

"You have been stopping here, I think?"

"Yes, sir; beggin' yer pardon, sir. Thar wus no insult intended, an' we kin jes' as well go summars else."

Oscar noticed the two behind him cast a longing glance at the table, and replied: "You may as well eat your supper here; it seems to be ready; and you may as well sleep where you have found beds before. You would be perfectly welcome, if I owned the property, so long as you were civil. I did not know that my father had deeded this property to any one, and I think there is some mistake; but I have no time now to consider the matter. I own a horse, in the stable, which I brought with me from England, a month ago, and I own this dog." For an instant his eyes fell and rested lovingly on Panza. The man cringed and muttered, "Yes, sir." Oscar continued: "Supposing that you are right, within an hour we three will leave here for — perhaps forever. If I should accomplish my business and return it may be that we shall discover some mistake. Come, Panza, we must be going."

"I say, mister," exclaimed the fellow in a very different tone, "thar ain't no need o' your goin'. I'm sorry I put it as I did. Is that thar hoss I see in the stable, the light-colored one, the hoss you speak of?"

Oscar was moving toward the door as he replied. "Well, sir," continued the man, "it's the puttiest piece of hoss-flesh I've ever sot eyes on, an' I'll tell yer what I'll do; I'll gin yer a clean deed o' this house an' all the land yer want round it in swap fur that hoss, an' I'll make it good with the owner."

"Not if you'd give me the whole farm," Oscar said, decidedly, with his hand upon the door.

"Ef yer'd druther have gold I'll gin yer five hundred clean, outer my own pocket," the fellow pleaded, coming a step forward.

"No; not for gold," said Oscar. "If you'd give me his weight in diamonds I would not part with that horse for an hour."

As Oscar opened the door the man added, "I'd treat him like a baby, sir. Thar shouldn't a har o' his hide be teched by nobody;" but he closed the door behind him and went out. As he climbed the stairs with Panza he heard the man's voice exclaiming, "By the great horn spoon! but that youngster beats a regiment!"

Going to his room Oscar put on his strongest hunting boots and a rough Manitoba suit, his cartridge belt and pistol. He took his rifle and blankets, and what was necessary that he could strap upon his saddle, and went to the stable with the intention of going back to the ranch and his friend the cowboy, till he could determine what to do. As he threw the saddle over Sancho he muttered, "Well, Panza, we have not got the property to help us, after all, but we three are left, and we will do it by ourselves."

The rain had ceased and the moon was bright as he rode slowly down the village street where everything was deserted and still. Only in the log cabin a faint light was still burning. There must be some trouble there. Possibly his old nurse was worse. The thought that in his own trouble he was about to leave, perhaps forever, without saying farewell to the Indians in the log cabin, disturbed him, and without a second thought he dismounted and knocked on the oak door.

It was opened by Wenononee, with Wetamoe close behind her, and as a flood of moonlight fell over them Oscar started back. For a moment he stood staring at the little Indian girl. Once before he had seen that face and though, in the sorrow and changes of the past few weeks, it had not occurred to him more than once or twice even to wonder whose face it was, that once was a moment and a face that he could never forget, and now the flood of moonlight brought it all back to him as vividly as upon the stormy afternoon when he looked up out of the water and saw the face of the Indian girl bending over the side of the yacht to save him.

Wenononee shrank back behind Wetamoc, but Oscar sprang forward and caught her hand. "Is this Wenononee? Is this Mama's little pappoose?" he exclaimed.

Weno bowed her head.

"It was you who saved my life out on the lake, and you who brought in the yacht, with my father," he

"WENONONEE!"

continued. "O, Wenononee! how much, how much I owe to you and to your mother for all that you and your people have done for me and my father! Some day — some day or other I hope I may be able to show you how I thank you. To-night I have nothing. I have no home, nor anything in all the world but my horse and dog. I think that some one is trying to cheat me, but I cannot tell yet. I only know that they have taken everything away from me, and I came to say good-by."

"Young master got no home! Young master go?" cried Weno, catching his hand in both of hers. "Oh! if Indian squaw had home young master should have all of it. But pale face come to Indian wigwam, too, and say Indian squaw no pay rent Indian squaw must go."

"He has turned you out, too?" Oscar stepped back aghast, and even in the moonlight his face was dark with rage. "Had he a right to do a thing so brutal? Wenononee, your mother is too ill to go. Your grandmother is too old. They must not! They shall not go. Wait a minute. I have one chance left. Tell them quickly that they need not go. The man who said so shall come, in the morning, and tell you to stay forever. There, there! Light the fire again. Put the things back where they belong. The wigwam is yours, and always shall be."

Weno was bending over to kiss his hand, but he drew it away, and leaping upon his horse without touching the stirrup, he rode swiftly back the way he came.

Oscar was too thoroughly occupied with his own

thoughts to look behind him, and even if he had he might not have seen the fleeting shadow that as silently as a ghost, but swift as Sancho, followed in his path as he climbed the butte again.

When he reached the house Weno was there. He did not see her, but she was watching him. She saw him dismount. She saw him put his arm over Sancho's neck and lay his cheek against his nose. She saw him go up and open the door, letting the bright light stream down the steps, and then turn back again to Sancho. She saw him stand for a moment with one clinched fist resting on the stone balustrade and one on Sancho as he looked into the open door. Then she saw him resolutely enter the house and she knew what it meant, though she was only an Indian girl.

Half an hour later Weno was still at hand. She was crouching in the shrubbery as he passed. Her face was very pale for an Indian, even in the moonlight, and her cheeks were wet with tears as she watched the young master. His head was bowed. His strong heart was almost broken. Even Panza felt the weight of the burden that bore upon him. Her head hung down and her step was heavy and slow.

Oscar had strapped the saddle knapsack and blanket upon his own back, and once more started upon his mission.

As he passed the spot where Weno was crouching she heard him say, " Well, Panza, you and I are left and we must forget everything but our duty and do it if we can."

He struck out over the plain, never dreaming that the shadowy form of a little Indian girl was hovering in the distance, always too far away to be detected, always near enough never to lose sight of him.

UPON HIS MISSION.

CHAPTER VII.

AT THE RANCH-HOUSE.

OSCAR entered the ranch-house without ceremony, and the dusky shadow which had been following him disappeared.

The house was a large and comfortable log cabin, fitted up for the cowboys and other ranch hands during the winter. It was surrounded by commodious out-buildings and corrals. A forest sheltered it upon the north and extended to the cliffs and foot-hills, a mile or more away.

The buildings stood upon the extreme eastern limit of the grazing lands, nearest the settlement, while the prairie where the cattle pastured stretched away to the west, only limited by the Rocky Mountains. The northern arm of the Assiniboin formed the southern boundary, and many little tributaries coming from the mountains watered the broad valley.

It was the ideal cattle range of Manitoba, and better than many even farther south than South Dakota.

From early spring till fall the cattle wandered steadily westward, with little opportunity to stray away or die of thirst, as is so often the case farther south. In the fall there was a grand round up, all along the line, and they were driven back to winter quarters near the ranch-house, where the grass had been growing all summer for their winter supply, and where they could find shelter from the snow in the forest, and from the fierce winds under the high cliffs.

The corrals were made of posts planted firmly and close together, entered by passages which gradually grew narrower till only one animal could pass at a time. These were used for branding, for every ranch from Manitoba to Mexico has its own brand to mark its property, and a calf following a cow is always branded with the mark of the cow. Then follows the sorting for market and the departure of the drove selected for the nearest railway station, and the merriest time on the ranch is over. Everything settles down, then, to make the best of the long, cold winter. A part of the cowboys turn lumbermen and trappers, for very few are needed upon the ranch. The cattle will not stray far, and wolves and Indians are the only invaders that must be kept at a distance.

All along the prairie, stretching westward, there were little huts, or dugouts, or bark lodges, at intervals of a mile or two, occupied, one after another, by the cowboys as the cattle moved westward, through the summer. They had already been away for nearly a month, and no one remained at the ranch-house but the keeper and an assistant.

Visitors are rare at ranch-houses anywhere, but especially so upon the comparatively few ranges of Manitoba, even in mid-summer.

At stated times supplies are brought by "Prairie schooners" — great covered wagons, drawn by long lines of mules or oxen, driven by bronzed and weather-beaten "bull-whackers," or "mule-skinners." Now and then parties of hunters stopped for the night on their way to the forests, and at long intervals a little band of emigrants would pass, on its way to search for some new home away toward the setting sun.

Mountain Charlie, the cowboy who accompanied Oscar to the Indian camp, had simply stopped at the ranch-house for the night, intending to join the rest upon the range the following day. He was an important figure among them, and had won his name by several exploits among the Indians in the mountains. His position was that of a sort of coast guard; not so much with the cattle, through the summer, as a free ranger among the foot-hills, keeping watch of Indians in the neighborhood of the cattle, and driving back the cows if any were found wandering too near to the mountains.

Very few cowboys ever hear their last names spoken by their associates. If the first name is not enough to identify them, some characteristic is added, or the brand of the ranch with which they are connected, or some deed which has made them famous. The brand of the Peterson ranch was a half circle and a dash — " (— ; " and if there had been no better name for him Oscar's friend would have been known as " Half-circle-dash Charlie." It was a much more honorable distinction which he had won, however, and he was justly proud of the name of " Mountain Charlie."

He was awake before Oscar had lifted the latch, and as the moonlight streamed through the open door Oscar saw him leaning on his elbow, on the edge of his bunk, with his six-shooter in his hand.

"It's nobody very fierce, Charlie," he said, softly, that he might not disturb any others who were sleeping. "You can put up your shooting-irons and go to sleep again. Panza and I have started out on another trip. I'm on foot this time, and we've run in to spend the night with you. Tell me where I'll find an empty bunk, and I'll go into particulars in the morning."

The cowboy had the good sense to accept the situation without making an ado. In simple frontier fashion he asked, " Had your grub ? " and receiving an affirmative reply added : " Bunks are all empty on that side. Pick the best." Then he laid down his six-shooter, and threw himself back upon his pillow with a sigh, as though he were already half-asleep again.

Oscar did not dream of the keen eyes that were fixed upon him from the shadows of Charlie's bunk as he laid down his rifle, unstrapped his pack and cartridge belt, took off his boots and trousers and lay down in the bunk.

With a contented grunt Panza stretched herself upon the floor beside the bunk and was asleep in a moment. Oscar watched her with envious eyes, for it seemed to him that after all he had passed through the last straw would surely break the camel's back, and that he could not bear the burden that was being piled upon him. He did not believe that he could possibly fall asleep, but he was mistaken. There was many a straw yet to be laid upon his back without breaking it. No one ever knows how much he can bear till he is tested, and there is a philosophy that if one is true to himself and his convictions there is no burden so heavy that he really cannot bear it.

Oscar Peterson had a brave heart, a healthy body that was thoroughly tired, and a clear conscience, and even while he was envying Panza he fell asleep himself, in spite of the changes which had taken place: taking the happy student, looking forward to a year's vacation with his father upon one of the richest and best frontier estates of America, and making a lonely orphan, lying on a blanket, in a borrowed bunk, without a possession in the world except his pack, his rifle and his dog.

Charlie lay awake much longer, looking steadily across the cabin toward Oscar's bunk.

"Something's going all-fired wrong with him," he muttered. "He's too good a fellow to be bucked before he gets his eye teeth cut. Whatever the muss is I don't believe he's having fair play. He's got the grit to fight and win, whatever's against him, and I wish I could lend a hand to give him a fair show. He wouldn't take help from anybody if he knew it, but I wonder if I can't work it some way so's he'll have to let me."

While he was wondering he, too, fell asleep again.

Still another heart was beating for Oscar that night.

As soon as the door closed behind him, and it was evident that he proposed to remain there till morning, at least, the shadowy form behind turned back again, the bright eyes looked toward the butte, and the silent feet flew almost as fast as a horse could run. There was no rest or sleep for Wenononee that night. All alone she had conceived an idea and plotted and planned its execution. She knew just what was before her, but with true Indian loyalty she determined to accomplish it, and she did.

Faster and faster her feet flew, for the task was long and difficult, and daylight was none too far away. Up the butte she went, like the shadow of a cloud swiftly and silently gliding over the meadow. The moon shone full upon the ragged face of the butte that looked down over the village. Every rock and ledge and cranny was visible. It was much shorter than the road which wound down the gentle slope to the south, and shorter than the foot path cut into the face of the ledge, and without a moment's hesitation Weno leaped from the upper rocks, and with bound after bound darted down the steep declivity. By that means it was only a moment later when she entered the little log cabin.

All was dark there now, but Weno needed no light. Swiftly and silently she crossed the room, climbed to her own little chamber under the roof, and threw off the loose dress which she wore. Out of a characteristic pile of everything in one corner she drew an English hunting jacket and put it on, buttoning it down to her leather trousers. It was the jacket which Oscar had thrown over his father, in the yacht, and left there. Weno found it the next morning. She was too much of an Indian to stop to think whether it was stealing or not for her to keep it; but no Indian ever took anything that did not belong to him with less thought of personal profit. She had never put it on before. She had never thought of using it in any way; but she valued the treasure more than all that she possessed — even the bear skin and the antlers.

As she drew on the jacket she whispered: "Heap good horse. He know."

Then she unbraided her hair, which she had plaited for the night when Oscar came to the cabin early in the evening, and tied it in a knot at the top of her head. She took off her leggings and moccasins and rolled them into a bundle with her dress and a bright Indian blanket, and with it hurried out of the cabin again as complete an Indian boy as ever ran barefoot over the mountain trails. She was exhausted and panting, and her heart was throbbing fiercely as she entered the cabin, but she was as fresh as ever when she left again and started on a run up the butte.

She did not go near the house, but kept well under the hill till she was opposite the stable. Then she threw her bundle into a clump of shrubbery and attempted to enter, but the door was locked. She walked slowly about the building till she found a place where she could climb to a ventilating window in the peak, and a moment later was pulling herself through the narrow opening. Then all was still till a door swung open that had been bolted on the inside, and Weno stood in the moonlight, covered with dust and hay.

For a moment her courage seemed almost to fail her. She looked quickly and nervously in every direction. She took a step forward, drawing the door after her as though she were coming out. With one foot over the threshold she hesitated, shook herself, stood very straight and, with a low laugh which made her white teeth flash and sparkle in the moonlight, she turned about, resolutely pushed the door open wide, and disappeared.

For a moment there was a commotion inside which would, at least, have brought Panza to the spot had she been upon the butte, but no one heard it, and presently Weno appeared leading Sancho who came with decided protestations. She had succeeded in getting on the bridle, but had evidently found it impossible to put on either the saddle or blanket.

Once out of the stable he made less noise, but it became almost impossible for her to manage him. More than once he lifted her off her feet as she clung to the bridle, and by slow degrees guided him down the butte toward the west. When he stopped, positively refusing to go farther, she patiently waited, patted him as he rubbed his nose over the hunting jacket, and with the same low laugh whispered: " Young master's coat. Weno say Sanch heap good pony. Heap good friend young master. Heap know young master's coat."

At last the foot of the butte was gained and Weno prepared for the last struggle. Many a wild Indian pony and unruly bronco had yielded to her. She was not afraid of Sancho, but she evidently realized that a difficult task was before her. She took off the hunting jacket and threw it on the ground, very gently sliding her hand along Sancho's neck till she fastened a firm grip of the dusky little fingers upon his mane just over the shoulder. For a moment Sancho seemed to have forgotten her. He was pushing the coat about with his nose, as though hunting for the master that should be inside of it.

Weno watched him for an instant, then she drew a long breath, the muscles over her bare arms and shoulders stood out and quivered in the moonlight, and the next instant she was sitting on Sancho's back. He

WENO AND SANCHO.

was taken completely by surprise, but had not the least intention of allowing the acquaintance to go any farther. He lunged, reared, kicked, snorted and plunged about. He tried to bite and tried to roll. He looked about for some tree or fence against which he could scrape off his unwelcome burden. Doubtless he had never learned the frontier art of bucking, for that was the only means he did not try; but when, at last, he was exhausted, and stopped from sheer inability to do anything more, he found Wenononee still sitting upon his back, holding the reins firmly in her hand.

Now it was her turn; and the moment Sancho paused she curled her feet under him, punching his sides with her bare heels. If Sancho thought himself thoroughly exhausted he must have been surprised to find how much go there was left in him after all, as, with a savage grunt, he shut his eyes, laid back his ears, and started at a wild run down the prairie. He ran as though it were an idea entirely his own and not at all what Weno wanted of him. With leap after leap he cleared the ground, hardly seeming to touch it. By degrees Weno worked him about into the direction of the ranch-house, but she did not try to check him till they were approaching the buildings. Then, just as she was preparing to make the attempt and wondering how she should succeed, something happened which entirely relieved her of the necessity.

The trail led directly to the cabin door, and instinctively Sancho had been following it. It was not a part of Weno's purpose to let herself be known, but she began to realize that possibly it might be very hard to arrange it in any other way, when suddenly, as they came within fifty feet of the cabin door, a sharp bark sounded from inside. Sancho stopped short. It threw him on to his haunches and very nearly threw Weno over his head. With his ears pricked up he

WENO PAUSED, TO GATHER COURAGE.

stood still and listened. A moment later the bark was repeated, though not so loud, and with a low, peculiar whinny Sancho started toward the door; but Wenononee was no longer upon his back. As fast as her Indian feet could carry her she was running along the trail by which she had just come. As she ran she said to herself: "Dat heap good pony. Know heap. Heap good dog."

Thus for the fourth time that night she followed the trail between the ranch-house and the village. It was a long distance, and though she hurried till her bare feet were cut and bruised, it was almost sunrise when she reached the butte and hid behind the clump of shrubbery near the stable where she had left her clothes.

When she came out again she was once more the little Indian girl, with leggings and moccasins, loose dress and flowing hair, wrapped in her bright-colored blanket.

This time she walked straight to the great house on the summit of the butte, but she walked slowly, for she was very tired and much more frightened than she was when leading Sancho.

At the steps she paused for a moment, just where Oscar stood during his last struggle the night before, waiting to gather courage.

It is very probable that her task was harder for her than his had been for him, but she faced it bravely a moment later, walking resolutely up the steps and entering the hall.

When she appeared again there was a peculiar light in her eyes and a proud smile on her lips. She was satisfied with what she had accomplished. She walked slowly down the butte by the longest way, that she might recover the hunting jacket, and then turned homeward, singing all the way; for her work was done.

CHAPTER VIII.

BRIGHTER PROSPECTS.

OSCAR was aroused from a deep sleep by the bark which Wenononee heard. He knew that it was Panza, but it mingled with his dreams and he was still only half-awake when he heard the second bark and answering neigh. He began to wonder where he was, and if he were awake or asleep, and how he came to be in that curious little bunk. Then he remembered his present position, and shut his eyes again, forgetting what had roused him, trying to go to sleep once more, if only for a little while longer to forget his troubles.

Charlie had been roused almost as quickly as Panza. He heard the approaching hoofs and lay in his bunk listening to know where they were going. He heard them come directly to the door and stop there, and wondered why no one entered. He watched Panza sniffing and whining at the door. He heard a horse pawing the ground outside, and very slowly rolled out of his bunk and went to the door to investigate.

Oscar, who had been gradually coming to consciousness, opened his eyes again as Charlie opened the door. In the gray light of early morning he saw Panza dash out before the door was half-open. He heard Charlie mutter some exclamation of surprise. Then he heard a whinny which brought him to his feet in an instant, and before he knew it he was standing at the door with his hand on Sancho's neck.

"For mercy's sake! How did you come here?" he asked in astonishment.

"He's had a tight lick of it, however he came," Charlie observed. "Look at him pant. He's beautifully blown, and he's just painted with lather."

"Do you suppose he broke away and followed me, like a dog?" Oscar asked, ready to believe Sancho capable of anything.

"Where did you leave him?" Charlie inquired.

"Safe in the stable, and locked in at that."

"With the bridle on?"

"Of course not."

Charlie pointed to the bridle.

"I'll tell you what, some one must have tried to saddle him and he got away," Oscar exclaimed. "A stranger would find it pretty tough work to saddle him, and harder still to ride him."

"Somebody has been riding him to-night," Charlie replied, running his hand along Sancho's back. "And what's more, it was an Indian."

"An Indian!" Oscar turned in still greater astonishment to examine the mark on Sancho's back where the moist hair had been matted down. "Some Indian must have tried to steal him."

"Well, that don't account for his coming here," Charlie said, shaking his head. "And no Indian would have brought a stolen horse near this ranch-house while Mountain Charlie was about, you can bet," he added, with true frontier pride. "But we'd better run him into the stable to dry off or he'll catch cold and die of pneumonia while we're settling how he came here. That would be a big lump out of your pocket besides all you think of him yourself."

"He doesn't belong to me any longer. I sold him, last night," Oscar replied, sadly; and as they walked toward the stable he added, "as soon as we've had breakfast, Charlie, I'll tell you all about it."

Oscar had reached a point where he must tell some one. The burden was fast becoming heavier than he could bear alone. His father had been very fond of Mountain Charlie, and he had found him a cool-headed, warm-hearted fellow. He was the most of a friend he had in Manitoba, and without waiting to consider the matter he resolved to lay the whole story before him, from the beginning.

The regulation ranch-house breakfast was quickly prepared and thoroughly palatable, if one had a good appetite and digestion, consisting of venison fried with bacon, oatmeal pancakes and coffee. The sun was shining when they went out of the ranch-house again. Charlie mounted the upper rail of the stable fence. Oscar threw himself upon a log lying on the ground, and with one arm twisted about a rail of the fence sat looking up at his cowboy friend and told his story, beginning with the day in the woods with his father.

Mountain Charlie did not speak a word till he had come to the end, in the finding of Sancho at the ranch-house door. Then he swung his foot deliberately over the rail, looked at his boot for a moment in silence and finally remarked: "Well, I call that a clean stampede. It's a wholesale washout if there ever was one."

Oscar laughed, for to tell the truth he felt much better now that he had shared his burden with some one. It did not seem half so serious and heavy with some one holding one end of it, and he replied, "I have been pretty well stampeded, you're right; and I feel pretty well washed out, though maybe that part of it will do me no great harm in the end; but what there is left of me is going ahead to put the fight through, hit or miss, neck or nothing, till I find that man and have him punished."

"You say he had charge of a mine at the Black Hills and another at Leadville?" Charlie asked.

"He had one of his own at the Black Hills, and the one of my father's which he was developing was at

Leadville. So I am going to the Black Hills on the way, and if he is not there I am going to Leadville."

"Are you expecting to get possession of a big mine?" Charlie inquired.

"No; nor a small one either," Oscar replied, decidedly. "In the first place, I do not care anything about it, and in the second place, if that is the man who shot my father he did it to obtain possession of the mine, and he certainly would not have left it open for me to get it back."

"It's about all a fellow's life is worth to make that trip 'twixt here and Leadville, running the risk of Indians alone, not to speak of an occasional drift of pale faces that's worse to strike than all the red skins in a bunch," Charlie said.

"Well, it's my duty, and that's all there is to it," Oscar replied, leaning back and supporting himself by the rail; "and I'd rather die doing my duty than live shirking it."

"A fellow's scalp is a mighty precious piece of furniture," Charlie remarked, suggestively scratching his head.

"Well, I don't mean to lose mine, by a large majority, if I can help it; but wouldn't you rather lose it than keep it knowing that it covered up a coward who didn't dare to do his duty?" Oscar asked.

"Put it that way and of course I would. Yes. But I'd a big sight rather walk a long way round to do it than ride the best horse in the country cross lots within gunshot of a bunch of Indians, if they meant business," Charlie insisted.

Oscar looked up in surprise as he exclaimed, "Why, I have heard my father say that you were worth any five men in Manitoba for fighting Indians."

"Your father always thought better of any one than he deserved," Charlie replied earnestly. "The fact is, a fellow will do lots of things when he's once got his foot in it that he wouldn't start out to do for the fun of it. Your father was always talking of a time when I happened on some twenty Indians running a bunch of cows up into the mountains. I saw the cows first, and never mistrusted that there were Indians behind them. That was what I was there for, and I went for them. Of course I was alone, and if I had known of the Indians at the start I'd have thought twice, at any rate; but when I saw 'um it was too late. Well, I brought the cows back, every head of 'um, though the skunks fought me clean to the open. My horse was hit once, and one ball lodged in the saddle and one went through that arm. I got my Winchester hot before they hit me, though, and after that I hauled out my six-shooters, one after the other, and let out what there was in them. When I came out of the woods there were but five Indians left to go back and pick up the rest. Such things are pretty enough to talk about afterward, and your father made too much of it. I tell you I would walk ten miles and sleep in a snowdrift, rather than hear an Indian whoop."

"Well, I've got to go, Indians or no Indians," Oscar replied. "And as that's all there is about it I may as well make the best of it."

"I'll tell you what it is," Charlie exclaimed, throwing his hat on the ground and leaning back against the post, "I'd never have punched cows up in this frozen-to-death country if it had not been for the liking I took to your father. I thought I'd hang on and do the best I could for you, too, but if that game's up I'm going to make tracks for the States again. I'd a heap rather have company than go alone, and if you'll let me I'll go along with you till — well, till I strike a job, somewhere. I don't believe it's straight business, this taking the property away from you. There's a clean fraud about it, I'll bet my best bronco; but except for horse-thieves and smugglers and sich, there's no great surplus of law in these parts. Possession is nine points of what there is, and whoever the other fellow may be he surely has possession. I'd like to skin him, and maybe we'll have a chance some day. I'm thinking that when you've found the man you're after you'll find that you've killed two birds with one stone. Never mind. What do you say: do you think that poor company's better than none?"

"Your company would be better than the best I know of," Oscar exclaimed.

104   BRIGHTER PROSPECTS.

THE INDIAN MESSENGER.

At that moment Panza gave her low, warning growl. They both started, listened for an instant, and then looked down the trail along which they soon saw a rider approaching.

"He's a red skin. How I hate the sight of 'um!" Charlie muttered.

He was headed for the ranch-house, and as he came nearer Oscar asked: " Do you think he can be the fellow who brought Sancho here? Maybe he was riding and got thrown, and has followed him."

" Not by a large majority," Charlie replied, decidedly. " In the first place, he wouldn't dare follow a stolen horse to this ranch even if he knew he was here; and in the second place, the coon that rode your horse last night was little. Don't you remember where the heel-marks were? He wasn't so tall as you into five or six inches, while this fellow is 'most a head taller. O, no! He is not the one."

" I know who he is!" Oscar exclaimed. " He's the Indian that the fellow had at the house with him last night."

He turned directly toward them, now, holding a letter in his hand. A few paces off he halted, grunting a salute, muttering, " How," and extending a letter toward Oscar, who rose from the log and received it.

He began to ask the Indian a question about Sancho, but the moment the letter left his fingers the fellow whirled his horse and rode away as though some one had fired at him.

" That's a rather queer performance," Oscar remarked, breaking the seal. Then he began to smile, as he read, and at last laughed outright. When he had finished he read the letter aloud:

Mr. Peterson.

Respected Sir: — Some one stole your hoss last night. I might uv thought you left the barn door open only I know who stole him and whar he is now. Don't suspicion that I think you had a hand in it for I don't. No more I don't want him back and won't take him. Though he's a dretful likely piece of hoss flesh and I wish you joy of him. I shall send his saddle and the rest of his outfit to whar you are now by the supply wagon going down from the store this arternoon, cause I hear they wusn't stole with the hoss. I don't want none of 'um. It's all right about the Injun squaws. I didn't understand when I told 'um to git. They can hang onter the cabin till the sky falls. I told 'um so this morning. Whatever it is you've got to do away from here I wisht you'd hurry up and get back, 'cause if thar's a mistake 'bout this business I want to know it. I don't want to wrong no kid like you. I won't change nothing but try to keep things going as they is, best I can, till you get back. You're a trump, you are, and I wisht I hadn't begun with you the way I did. I was drunk last night and I apologise. If you will excuse me sir and allow me to remain,

Your obedient servant,
Simon Brown.

"Now what does that mean?" Oscar asked, as he finished reading and sat down again on the log.

"It means that the coon has got some mighty good cows in his corral yet, and that he's likely to be as good a friend of yours as he knows how," Charlie replied. "If you should find out that there was a mistake or a fraud, and that you have rights there, he'll take your side against the other fellow, I'll bet. And he and not the other fellow has possession, so you may have the nine points of the law on your side, after all. Why don't you go back and talk it over with him?"

"I don't know as I really care to just now," Oscar remarked as he folded the letter. "This other work is much more important, and now that I have Sancho again I want to start at once."

"Perhaps you're right about not seeing him. He'll keep just as well without. But you can't start without your saddle, and Sancho isn't fit, either, after last night. We need some grub, too, to take with us. Suppose we go out shooting this morning, and start fresh at daylight to-morrow?"

Oscar readily consented; and as no time was to be lost they started at once for the foot-hills where, for the most exciting sport and the best game, they should have been waiting as the sun came up.

CHAPTER IX.

WITH SHOT-GUN AND RIFLE.

"THE best sport is to get out before daylight and wing the game in its first flight up the lakes," Charlie remarked as they trudged rapidly through the outskirts of the forest. He had hunted and fished and fought and ranged in those hills and forests too much not to know where game was to be found at any hour of the day, however. "There'll be brant up in that valley, and duck and plover in a line of little lakes running down that long gorge to the left. That's the spot for us to strike, I reckon, for we're liable to hit a flock of geese coming down the gorge. From ten to twelve, any day, you'll hear the old honkers away at the ranch-house. Crane are everywhere. We may run across a hundred of them; but you can't depend upon crane turning up where you expect them, later than an hour after sunrise, and again about sundown."

"I wish I knew as much as you do," Oscar exclaimed enthusiastically.

"If I was in Oxford and wanted some dinner I reckon I should have to depend on you to show me the way; and you'd be ashamed of yourself if you didn't know," Charlie remarked.

"I could take you to a restaurant or a hotel, of course," Oscar replied.

"Well, this is our hotel, restaurant, meat market, produce exchange and everything else," Charlie said.

"But the stuff isn't always hanging upon precisely the same pegs and down precisely the same streets, as it is in Oxford," Oscar argued.

"Yes, it is," Charlie replied. "It's only in a country that is settled up and hunted to death, where the game is born frightened, that you have to go prowling about to find it. Any man who knew ducks and deer in any part of the world where they are let alone, could find them here as easily as you could find a meat market in a strange city. They're always on the same kind of streets, and they stay at the same stands — hanging themselves upon the very same pegs, so to speak, year after year, unless they get so thoroughly frightened that they absolutely have to hunt up a new shop."

Charlie stopped short and looked away to the northwest, up the long and narrow reach between the hills.

"Get behind a bush! Be quick!" he exclaimed, setting the example, which Oscar followed, diving behind the nearest clump of shrubbery. "Those are crane, and they're headed to go straight over us if they don't change their minds. Ay, they're coming. We're in luck. Crane steaks are fine! Crane fly slowly, but they get there in time, and they are flying low. Hope they don't light. No; they're going for the wheat back of the ranch."

Oscar heard these low, half-whispered sentences coming from Charlie's hiding-place, while he almost held his breath and quivered with excitement as, through the branches, he watched the huge crane coming nearer and nearer, their long legs dangling behind them like streamers. His cheeks glowed as he lifted to his shoulder the shot-gun he had brought from the ranch-house.

On they came. They were so near now that he could distinguish their feathers and see the peculiar undulations of their heads and necks stretching out almost as far in front of them as their long legs trailed behind.

"Are you ready?" Charlie whispered.

"All ready," Oscar replied, running his eye along his gun with the inevitable nervousness of the real sportsman.

"Take the leaders. I'll wait till they turn, and try then," Charlie said.

Oscar waited an instant, to bring the flock as near as possible between himself and Charlie. They were great, gaunt, ungainly creatures, and there was something almost frightful in the flopping of their huge wings. It was a sensation which Oscar had never felt before, and at the very instant when he was prepared to fire his strength almost deserted him. Every hunter can easily appreciate it, but Oscar had not been a hunter long enough to know what it meant. Chagrined, he made a sudden effort to pull himself together, and fired.

The great creature instantly doubled over his sight, and before it was clear the entire flock was so demoralized that at the instant it would have been impossible to single out any one of them.

If Oscar had been a little better drilled and experienced in the higher art of hunting he might have waited for them to straighten themselves out, that he might know where he was shooting, but he was quite too nervous and excited to think of higher art in anything, and gave the full benefit of the second barrel at the mass of flopping wings and trailing legs and long necks and open beaks, not over forty yards away.

Another huge crane came flopping to the ground, however, and at the double report of Charlie's gun, a second later, two more fell.

"Pretty good toll from that bunch," Charlie remarked as the rest flew away, and he began deliberately to reload.

Oscar was too excited for that regulation precaution, and dropping his gun started for the game. The first crane fell near their hiding-place, and was stone dead. Oscar hurried on to the next. He, too, seemed dead, at least, and Oscar stooped down to pick him up and throw him beside the first, when, to his astonishment, with a furious flutter, the huge creature sprang to his feet, uttering a shrill hissing cry, beating the air fiercely with his wings, while the feathers on his neck and back were savagely ruffled for a fight.

For a moment the two stood looking at each other, wondering what it was best to do next. Oscar was afraid the bird was about to rise, and made a grab for his neck. Quick as a flash, the bird dodged and returned the attack by fastening its sharp beak in Oscar's hand. Then it struck for his face, and Oscar swung up his arm just in time to save himself.

The battle once begun, the crane did not propose to drop the matter, but with wings and feet and beak came at Oscar in a most scientific way, that did not give him a chance to do anything but defend himself. It was all the action of an instant, but as desperate as it was sudden; too quick even for Charlie to come to the rescue. Oscar thought of his gun lying on the ground twenty feet behind him. He turned to run for it, as he could at least strike with the stock from a safe distance, when, with a triumphant hiss, the crane started after him, jabbing him in the back of the neck.

At that moment Charlie came from his hiding-place, with his gun on his shoulder, and when the crane saw him it left the retreating foe and made for the cowboy. When he could safely fire, the crane fell dead, and Charlie rolled over and over on the ground, convulsed with laughter.

Oscar did not much fancy the part he had played, but he could not help joining in the laugh, as he real-

HE TURNED TO RUN.

ized how supremely ridiculous he must have appeared running away from a bird he had shot.

"It was the funniest thing I ever saw in all my life," Charlie gasped, and began to laugh again. "You looked so astonished when he jumped up. And the way he hustled you! Why, he didn't give you a chance to lift a finger on your own account. Then when you turned, and he thought he'd scored a point, and started after you with a crow, that just beat everything."

"Well, it was a pretty poor beginning, any way," Oscar observed, as he lifted the dead bird. "I'm afraid I should make poor work with Indians, at that rate."

"Now don't be ashamed of your antagonist," Charlie exclaimed. "A wounded crane is no mean thing to handle. If I had been in your place I should simply have turned and run at the start. A crane killed an Indian up here last year. They always strike for the eyes if they can, like the heron; and this fellow sent his beak clean through into the Indian's brain. I didn't laugh when you were facing him, now, I tell you. But when you started off, and he gave that crow, and put after you"—Charlie leaned back again and laughed. "Well, come on! Let's skin 'um and clean 'um, and cut off their heads and wings and legs, or we shall have more than we can carry before we get through."

"I wish they had not taken my dog out on the range with them," he added, a little later, as they approached one of the almost innumerable little marshy lakes that lie hidden among the mountains of Manitoba. "He's a little fellow, and no great breed any way, but he's mighty good with cattle, and a terror at hearing things in the night, or smelling an Indian. He hates 'um as bad as I do. That's why they snaked him out there to spend the summer with them in the bottom; but I told 'um I'd come for him and take him with me when I went into the hills. Now they can keep him. Yes; he's a beauty for offhand hunting, I tell you. There's not much science about him, but he can spot game just the same, and he can just everlastingly pick it up and bring it in. I've seen him fetch a goose that was bigger than he was — a regular old honker; and one that was only wounded, at that."

"I never trained Panza for shooting," Oscar said. "She'd be too big to be any good, and " — Before he finished speaking, a grouse flushed just upon his right, and the last word was lost in the report of his gun.

"Jiminy! That was a good shot," Charlie exclaimed as the grouse fell, and a long line of feathers floated away on the wind.

Frightened by the report, several more rose, but too far away, and there being no dog to indicate their whereabouts in advance, they succeeded in startling others without getting another shot. It was no great loss, however, for every muskrat dome along the marsh was made the sunning-place for mallards, widgeons and sprig-tails that had finished their breakfast, and were waiting till they were hungry enough for lunch.

"The trouble now is that they have nothing to do, and are on the watch. You can't wing 'um. You've got to sneak up and take 'um dead still. If you're only out to stock the larder, though, that's not so bad. I have filled her up with shot, and taken as good as five at one crack, that way. Just before daylight is the time for real sport," Charlie continued, as he tied the game they had bagged so far, and, slinging it over his shoulder, started for a new field. "When it's cold as it was a month ago, just come out here in the dark, and stand round in this mush till your blood is like cold molasses, waiting for light enough to sight your gun.

"Everything is on the wing, then. There's no danger of freezing to death, for between each shiver you hear the whir and the rush as a flock of ducks goes sailing over your head. Sometimes a zipping wing will go past within a few feet of your ear, and give you a good start; for they don't begin to climb till later in the day. You can't see a shadow of 'um, it's so dark, just before day; but you know they're there, and it sets your heart going. Then it lights up a little in the east, and you can see them plain against it as they come steadily sweeping up to you; but by the time they get here you're looking against a darker sky, and you can't see a feather of 'um, and that makes you mad. Next you know, you can pick out your birds overhead, and down they come. Then you get warm quick enough, I tell you, and — Hark! What's that?"

They both listened intently, and from far down the gap they heard a steady honking coming up the line of lakes.

"Geese! What luck!" Charlie exclaimed. "Stuff in a lot of heavy shot, and let 'um have it from behind these reeds."

Every moment the honking became louder.

"Geese fly fast, you know," Charlie explained in a nervous whisper. "You take the leaders again, and I'll follow. Give them a good margin. When you're sighted, follow along till you just lose sight of the beak. Keep your gun still moving, and let her go."

They could see them, now, and they did fly fast; but most of the flock had drifted too far out over the lake to get them without dogs. There were only three in range. It was a moment of intense excitement. Oscar had never shot at a goose before. He tried to follow Charlie's instructions, but his first shot missed. It brought the three honkers to a standstill, however, and while they were turning out over the lake he fired again and brought one down. Charlie had only time for one shot before they were too far away to recover.

"Well, two out of three is pretty fair toll," Charlie remarked as they dressed and skinned their game; and before noon they had a burden quite as heavy as they could carry between them.

As they were slowly making their way back to the ranch-house, Oscar caught sight of a pair of antlers above the reeds on the shore of a little lake away upon their right.

"There's plenty of those fellows around, this spring," Charlie remarked. "But these shot-guns would only frighten them, and we couldn't carry home a pound more than we have."

"Couldn't we come back for them with the horses?"

ON THE LAKE.

Oscar asked. "I never shot a deer, and I'd like to get one good pop."

"You never shot a deer!" Charlie, who was walking ahead, stopped short and turned round as well as he could, without dropping the pole. "Well, you'd be too great a curiosity to live long in Manitoba, at that rate. Of course we'll come back again. And come to think, a haunch of venison won't be bad to hook on to the pack horse, 'long with some of these birds. It'll enliven the outfit immensely. Morning's the best time for deer, too; but I reckon that along toward evening I can find a spot where some of 'um will be coming down to the lake for a nightcap."

They spent an hour or two of the afternoon in making up their outfit, and while the keeper of the ranch-house was preparing the best of the game for their pack, they rode into the woods again in search of deer. This time Sancho and Panza were along, and as they approached the spot which Charlie had selected, he said: "I'll hang round here with the horses, while you work your way up the lake. I don't suppose any one would trouble the horses if we left them alone. There are no bad Indians in the neighborhood that I know of; but no matter how good and peaceable he is, a member of the Lo family isn't to be trusted alone in the woods where a horse is handy, any more than a bank cashier in the States, if he's on the line of the night express for Canada. Just go easy, and work along the shore to the upper end of the lake. Keep your eyes peeled, especially where there are patches of moss. If I ain't more than mistaken, before you turn back you'll strike one herd at least. If you keep out of sight, and see them before they see you, you've got 'um; but if they show you their tails, just let them go, and try for more. A little noise will scare them quicker than anything else; but if you see them first, and run your handkerchief out on a limb, it will sometimes draw them down to you. There'll always be one big buck with the bunch. He's your man. Take him right behind the fore shoulder if you can; if not, then take the neck right behind the horns."

The sun was less than an hour high when Oscar started up the lake. He walked carefully, keeping as much out of sight as possible, and stopping occasionally to look about him. But the position was against him. The dry twigs would snap under his feet, and twice he had the chagrin of looking up to see the dark-brown figures disappearing, that told him how near he had been to the coveted prize.

He was nearing the head of the lake, and growing disappointed, when, in turning about a huge bowlder that extended into the water, he discovered, on the hillside above him, and less than a thousand feet away, four of those slender, graceful creatures, standing out against the glowing western sky as though they were drawn in India ink.

It almost took his breath away, and his fingers twitched nervously about his rifle as he stood riveted to the spot, admiring the beautiful picture.

They were slowly moving toward the water, cropping here and there a tempting bit of moss as they passed it.

From a sportsman's view his position was the most unfortunate possible. They were coming directly toward him. He could not move without attracting their attention. They were above him, and even while they were eating would be looking right toward him. The sun was behind them, and full in his eyes. But for

EVERY HEAD WAS LIFTED.

simple beauty, a better position could not have been found.

They saw him quite as soon as he saw them, for every head was lifted, and every deer stood like a figure in bronze, planted on that mossy knoll.

The old doe was in front, with the youngest of the family just behind her, stretching its neck to see what was moving down below. A two-year-old came next, and the old buck was behind, standing on the very brow of the hill, knee-deep in moss. He stood square to the front, with his head erect, and his graceful antlers sharp and clear against the sky.

For a moment Oscar forgot his errand. With the sun in his eyes, and the narrow front which the old buck presented, he would not have ventured to fire even if he had been nearer, and he stood watching the group with much the same interest that they stood watching him.

They did not seem much afraid, or at all inclined to move away; and as the hunter's nature began to assert itself again, Oscar drew back behind the bowlder so slowly and cautiously that he did not disturb them, and carefully picked his way to a position where he could watch them through the branches, without being seen.

They were evidently suspicious, and ready, very easily, to take alarm; but gradually ventured nearer and nearer to the lake.

At last the sportsman conquered entirely, and with every muscle strained and quivering, with his heart throbbing and his lips parched, Oscar knelt in the shrubbery and waited.

Three times they seemed more inclined to turn back,

and three times his finger trembled on the trigger. It was a bad position for a shot, but he was determined to run his chance and fire, rather than let them go.

With many a timid start and doubtful sniff they reached the edge of the grass by the lake, not more than a hundred yards away, and all the time the old buck had kept his face directly toward the bushes where Oscar was hiding.

Oh! if he would only turn. He must turn! It seemed hours instead of less than fifteen minutes since they started down the hill.

In his intense excitement Oscar moved one knee a hair-breadth for a firmer rest, to stop its trembling. One little twig cracked under it, and in an instant every deer had whirled about and started up the hill. Oscar sprang to his feet, aimed and fired before he really knew what he was doing, and it was with a peculiar sensation of surprise that he saw the old buck give one leap into the air and roll over on the moss.

Springing forward he cut the buck's throat to let him bleed, and standing back a step or two looked at his first capture with an exultant admiration which only a sportsman can appreciate.

The triumph was too great to keep to himself long, however. He thought of his friends at the opposite end of the lake, and dropping his rifle put his fingers to his lips and sent a shrill, sharp whistle, three times, echoing down the gorge. He stood listening intently for a moment till up the lake there came the response in a distinct but distant bark. Then he threw himself upon the moss beside his prize.

Mountain Charlie heard the shot, and after waiting a few minutes was preparing to work his way in that direction with the horses, when the distant signal caught his ear. He knew what it must mean, but he was not prepared to see Panza and Sancho understand it perfectly, too.

Panza was lying down, apparently asleep, and Sancho was lazily cropping the grass at a little distance. In an instant Panza was upon her feet, and Sancho's head was thrown high in the air, with his ears pricked up and his nostrils stretched. The moment the third whistle sounded Panza gave a sharp, fierce yelp which must have sounded along the water for a mile or more, and Sancho tossed his head and watched her while she hunted for a moment till she struck the trail.

With a low bay Panza indicated that she was on the track, and with her nose to the ground started along the lake. Sancho did not wait for an invitation, but trotted close behind her.

Charlie stood looking on in astonishment until they started, and then mounting, followed after them. He could easily have found Oscar by shouting or firing his pistol in the regular ranger's signal, but there was no need of it. No guide could have led the way more intelligently. Once or twice she lost the trail for a moment, but Sancho understood her actions as well as the cowboy, and they waited, together, till the path was found again.

They were not long in coming out upon the knoll where Oscar was sitting, but before Charlie could congratulate him upon his luck he gave vent to deeper feelings in the exclamation: "By Jiminy! That's a horse and a dog worth having, now I tell you. If nobody steals them before you finish your jaunt it's because they don't know what's what, that's all."

"Well, I'm precious sure they won't try to steal them if they do know what's what," Oscar replied, laughing; and a moment later they were busily engaged upon the deer, preparing to fasten to their saddles such parts as were best worth saving.

"It makes one think of the poor hungry creatures all over the world, to throw away such meat as that," Oscar remarked, as Charlie filled up the waste pile, where Panza was daintily munching.

"There's two or three ways of looking at that," Charlie replied. "In the first place, if those poor hungry creatures would only come out here and go to work producing something for themselves, the world they left behind them would be much better off for their going, and the world they came into would be much better off for their coming; and they could have all this waste stuff or better, and would no longer be hungry and poor. Then again, if they won't come and get it, it does not really go to waste, after all. You come round here in the morning and how much do you think you will find left of it? In the course of time it will all turn up somewhere, in the shape of furs and skins or something useful that it has helped to keep alive and fatten. Nature does not ever let anything go to waste, even up here in Manitoba."

While they were talking there was a splash in the water of the lake. Charlie started, and looked quickly and cautiously in that direction.

"Look there!" he whispered. "See that big buck taking the water? He'll round that curve in five minutes. Oh! if we only had a canoe now, we could head him beautifully."

At the extreme upper end of the lake the head and towering antlers of a deer appeared, gliding swiftly out over the glistening surface, leaving a trail of dancing ripples and a white wake behind.

"There is a canoe!" Oscar exclaimed. "I saw one pulled up in the cove as I came round the rock."

"Well, if that ain't luck and A1!" Charlie replied. "Can you paddle?"

"Of course I can," Oscar answered. "But it's your turn. Go for him!" he added nervously, without taking his eyes from the deer as it shot swiftly down the lake toward the narrow run made by the bowlder and the cove.

SIX INCHES FROM THE MARK.

"I've shot more deer than I can count," Charlie whispered. "Don't wait a second. If the canoe is sound get out to the edge of the cove. Wait there till he sees you and turns. Then go it! Get as near him as you can, and just before he strikes the bank let him have it in his neck, right behind the ears. Be quick!"

There was no time for argument, and Oscar did not wait for a second invitation. He was beside the canoe in an instant, and had it in the water without noise enough to startle a mouse; but it was heavy and old. It had been lying there all winter, and he had to kneel carefully to prevent going through. He had often paddled on Manitoba Lake, with his Indian nurse, before he was five years old, and often upon the Thames between Oxford and the Coltswold hills, but this was something very different. Now his loaded rifle was beside him, and a glorious big buck was gliding past him, while the canoe lay heavily in the water and wabbled till he could hardly manage it. Altogether he made poor progress. More than once the paddle splashed in the water in spite of him, and by the time he reached the edge of the cove where he was to wait, he found that the deer had already heard him and swerved away. There was a long half-circle of ripples bending toward the shore, and the buck, with his back toward the canoe, was making for the opposite bank.

It was the critical moment. Only a narrow line of

neck behind the antlers appeared, in that position, and as the deer was swimming faster now, his head swayed from side to side, and the long hair down his back floated in a constantly twisting line just upon the surface. The crank canoe would shift in spite of him, the muscles of his arms quivered, and his hands trembled as much from his eager work with the paddle as from excitement. He could even see the muzzle of his rifle wabble.

An older hunter would have given up, but to Oscar it seemed as though to try and fail were better than not to try at all, and aiming quickly he fired; but he had the cold comfort of seeing the splash as his bullet struck the water, less than six inches from the mark.

He paddled back to the shore disconsolately, but as he stepped out of the canoe where Charlie was waiting, he said: "I believe I am glad I didn't hit him, after all. We have more meat than we can use now, and what was the use? He was mighty handsome. Too handsome to kill for the fun of it!"

CHAPTER X.

OVER THE PRAIRIE.

BEFORE sunrise the next morning they were ready for the start. Charlie owned two horses, one of which they were to use as a pack horse. Upon a regulation pack saddle of the plains was strapped everything absolutely necessary for their journey, and a supply of meat carefully wrapped up in prairie grass.

As Charlie was laying out the load he remarked, "It makes a pile of difference, with the size, whether you take just what you need or only what you can't do without."

It seemed to Oscar at the time that they must be pretty much the same, but he had occasion, later, to discover that Charlie was right, and that between the two there was a very wide range.

Seeing the meagerness of what was going on to the pack saddle out of Charlie's private possessions, Oscar protested that in order to make room for blankets, food and other articles for him, Charlie was leaving behind a great many of his own things that were too valuable to abandon. "We can do without them well enough," Charlie replied, "and a pack horse always gives out the first of all."

"Then why don't you pack them in a box and have them sent to you when you locate?" Oscar asked.

"They're of no great value," Charlie answered, throwing another armful into his bunk, "and expressing is expensive in these parts. However, they'll keep in there as well as anywhere. No one will want to use that bunk before fall, and we don't know what may happen by that time."

Oscar was satisfied, and never dreamed that Mountain Charlie was making that journey simply to be with him; to guard him from dangers of which he knew nothing, and aid him in defending himself, in the firm conviction that, if they lived and accomplished their purpose, Oscar would yet return and recover his rightful position as the master of the Peterson Estate.

They mounted just before the first ray of sunlight shot over the prairie from above the distant butte. Panza bristled all over with pride as she was given the lead line of the pack horse to carry, and Oscar cast one sad farewell glance at the speck of black upon the summit of the butte, sharply outlined against the coming morning. To him it seemed beyond a doubt the last time that he should ever see that beautiful home on the heights overlooking Manitoba Lake.

It is true that he had not actually lived there many weeks, and that everything was so changed since his early boyhood that the sentiments and associations of those days could have but little to do with the present. In reality, however, he had lived there, and only there, through all his schooldays. Every letter from his father, describing the changes, had fastened them in his mind; every breath he breathed had been in preparation for return. The pride that he felt in the little sign that hung over the shed end of the cabin had grown as he grew, and the ambition that thrilled every hour of study or play had been to perfect his ideal of "Oscar Peterson: Ranchman and Ranger."

He only looked once at the dark outline on the distant butte. Then he turned his head quickly, and looked away to the south, where his duty lay; a duty that meant far more to him than any sentiment, hope or ambition. It did not blot out the ambition of his life. It only rose above it.

Mountain Charlie noticed the farewell glance and the sad face, and had the good sense to realize that Oscar would do better to be let alone, so they started in silence and sadness; a good omen, perhaps, for a different return.

For the first mile the horses walked, and Panza followed sedately, leading her charge. When the rest broke into a canter, if he did not follow quickly enough, she would drop the line for an instant, give his hind leg a nip, and, dashing ahead, pick up the line and hurry on.

They were able to keep up a fair rate of speed, for the way was generally open, and a part of the time there was a trail to guide them. There were opportunities enough for shooting, but while the stock of provision held out the time was too precious to waste. The first human beings they met were a small band of Indians, during the afternoon of their second day. Charlie talked with them for a moment in signs, and they rode on.

"That is a language which I must learn about as quickly as I know how," Oscar remarked.

"It's very easy. There's nothing to it," Charlie replied. "It's mostly a matter of instinct, and a good deal guess work, with just a few established signs for the most common things. I was asking them about the lower branch of the Assiniboin; whether it was high, and if there was a ford anywhere where we should not wet the outfit. They said there was a Blackfoot camp just this side of the river; that we ought to reach it to-morrow night, and that near the camp there is a trail leading to the best ford for several miles. It was easy enough to make that out; but I don't believe that even the spoken language of any Indian tribe is very clear. They use the signs almost as much when they are talking among their own tribe, as when they are talking with others who have a different language. I have often heard it said of the Arapahoe Indians, for instance, that they cannot make one another understand with any certainty in the dark. Their name is 'Good Hearts,' and their sign is touching the left breast. The Cheyennes are 'Cut Arms,' and their sign is this: drawing one hand across the other wrist. The Sioux are Cut Throats. Their sign you can imagine. They and the Blackfeet are the same, practically, and they are the worst set of redskinned devils anywhere in these parts."

"What are some of the other signs?" Oscar asked.

"Why, just as near the thing you mean as you can get. A tent, for instance, is like this: shutting all but the forefingers of each hand, and touching the tips of them, so. See? It is supposed, at least, to look like a tent. Then a lot of tents is made by opening all the fingers and just touching the tips together. A man on a horse is two fingers of one hand astride the other hand. Crossing the fingers at right angles means to swap or trade. Bring your hands together, this way, and cross them in front of you, with the palms toward your body, and you mean night. Just reverse the motion, and stop with the hands stretched out and the palms up, and you mean day. Point upward, and make a circle in the air, and you mean anything pertaining to Heaven. See? It's very simple."

"I should think there would have to be a good deal

more to it than that, in order to carry on a conversation," Oscar observed, but Charlie shook his head.

"It's just like selecting your outfit. If you've got a schooner along, you can fill it with what you need, but if you've only your pack horse, you can take all that you can't get on without. Take anything that you have ever got to say to an Indian, and signs are quite sufficient; but if you undertook to enlighten him about something he had never seen or heard of, and if you spoke his language like a native, to boot, you couldn't do it. We had a great time with the fellows one spring. We had taken a lot of skins, among us, at the ranch, during the winter, and thought we'd add a few more and make it an object to ship them; so we rounded up a bunch of Indians on the way to the trading-post, with furs, and began a trade. We agreed to give them so much a pound for their skins, and charge so much a pound for tea, blankets, ammunition and tobacco. Well, we weighed their skins, and then as they picked out what they wanted, we weighed that. Pretty soon we found they were getting ugly, and come to find out, they thought we were cheating them. We explained the scales, and the way to come at the amounts and values, over and over again, but we couldn't get the first idea of it into their heads. At last we gave up in despair, and told them to take their skins and go; but that didn't please them, either. Then we asked them what in the world they did want, and lo and behold! they wanted us to put the skins in one side of the scales, and what they had bought all in a lump in the other side. You had better believe we were quick to accommodate them, and it only took about half of what we had laid out for them, to weigh down the skins. Some of the fellows were for making them take the stuff that way, after they had insisted on it, but we finally gave them the whole, and let them go; and over in the village, the next day, one of the boys heard them boasting to some of the Indians there, about how they had cheated us and got almost twice as much as they paid for."

"You wouldn't think that Indians were such stupid things," Oscar remarked; and Charlie replied, quickly:

"I don't think it was stupidity at all! That's just what I mean. I think it was simply because they had no words or signs that gave a chance to explain a thing so entirely out of their sphere as a set of scales. And I think that accounts for more than half the trouble which the United States Government has with the Indians. They have a treaty and reservation scheme explained to them, with a lot of conditions and quirks that nobody fully understands, and they say yes, and agree, and every one supposes it's all right, till they find that the Indians haven't the least idea of abiding by the arrangement, and then there's a howl against the Indians, and a fight, and all that, when, in reality, I don't believe the fellows ever really had any more idea of the matter than they had of our scales. I don't believe they are treated fairly; but it's not that I think there is an honest Indian in the whole bunch of 'um, for I don't."

A moment later, Charlie continued: "The system of signs goes a good deal farther than this hand business. There is a rather elaborate system of signals by smoke from a hot fire covered with grass. They take a big blanket and hold it over the fire, shutting in the smoke, and letting it out in bunches to indicate what they want to say to people miles away. They use their ponies, too, and arrows and blankets, and all sorts of things in telegraphing messages. By the way, the system of signals by flash-lights and reflections which the British army has recently adopted, was caught from the Indians. In a battle, if a chief can get up on a hill where his warriors can see him, with the sun in the right direction, and where he can see the enemy, he will give his commands from there more successfully than if he was on the spot. He has something like a small mirror which he holds in his hand, and sends a series of flashes in a way to indicate what he wants."

"Do they really use poisoned arrows in fighting?" Oscar asked.

"Why, yes; sometimes I reckon they do. But I don't believe they do so often as in stories. They have a way of pinning down a rattlesnake, and teasing him with a piece of liver till he bites it, and fills it with poison, and then they make a mush of it to daub on their arrows, sometimes."

"I wonder whatever started them in that horrible trick of scalping and mutilating," Oscar said with a shudder, as he thought of the days and the miles that lay before him through the Indian country.

"I believe it was their theory of the hereafter — that a man who is scalped never comes to light again in the other world. When an Indian has killed a man, his theories of the happy hunting ground are such that he would rather not meet him there ; so he scalps him. He is precious sure to scalp a pale face at every opportunity, on the same principle ; and as for cutting him in pieces, I suppose it is only because he is constitutionally so mad with the pale face that he can't help it. I believe they are very apt, too, to leave the mark of their tribe on a victim ; cutting out the heart for an Arapahoe mark, cutting the wrists for a Cheyenne, and cutting the throat for a Sioux, and so on. Ugh! How I hate them!"

"That's why they are so careful to carry off their dead, isn't it?" Oscar asked.

"I suppose so. At any rate, they do whenever they have a chance, and they are very skillful at it, too. If there is one thing that an Indian can do to perfection, it is ride a horse. I have seen two of them go at full speed for a dead Indian, lean from their horses, each grab an arm, and, with one swing, land the body across the saddle, in front of one of them, without slacking up an atom. I wish they were all in Texas, if I am to live in Manitoba."

"I don't feel so hard toward them as you do; perhaps because I have not seen enough of them; one family, at least, was very loyal and true to my father, and I shall never forget that," Oscar said earnestly, "and I don't know of anything that to me is half so interesting to hear about and read about. But it's a fact, they are a big disappointment, in reality; all that I ever came across, at least."

With unusual energy, Charlie replied: "Right you are! They're a greasy, dirty, treacherous set, wherever you find them. If the Government only understood them, and could make them understand, and would treat them honestly and fairly, on that basis, they would be a great deal better than they are; and I don't believe in shooting a man at sight, anyway, just because he's an Indian. But I do believe that if you don't, and he ever gets a chance, he will shoot you just because you are a pale face. And you have got to treat him accordingly, or get left."

"He certainly has some excuse," Oscar remarked.

"Indeed he has," said Charlie. "When you are out of Indian country, and stop to think, you wonder that he ever lays down his rifle and tomahawk long enough to eat or sleep. But the fact is, he has abused

his excuse till there isn't enough of it left to swear by.
He has some of the best qualities that were ever stored
in human hide. Indian children mind as well as your
dog. You never hear a pappoose yell. I don't believe
that a murder or a theft in one's own tribe was ever
heard of, unless it was after they had been turned
into a set of drunken louts upon a reservation. The
squaws are what we call abused; but it's more custom
than cruelty. They expect it as much as other women
expect the civilities to which they are accustomed.
Three or four generations are often huddled into one
tepee, and there's not a set in the civilized world that
could stand it; but you never heard of a family
quarrel or a fight of any kind, inside the tribe. They
are quicker than lightning, and shrewder and sharper
on the war path than cats after mice. They are brave,
too, and they will fight like your crane, even after
they are dying. Why, if they had the white man's
possibilities, I believe they could drive us out of the
country, even now. But just look at them. A full
stomach is the only thing they care for, except fire-
water. They are lazy, and dirty as hogs. They will
lie and cheat when you'd think it to their immediate
advantage, and more convenient, to be honest. A wolf
isn't more cold blooded. A fox isn't half so treacherous. I pity them, I admire them, I despise them,
and I am mortally afraid of them. I wish I might
never see another Indian as long as I live."

"It's a very funny thing," Oscar observed. "I've noticed it everywhere. The best sailors always seem to be the most afraid of storms. The best scholars in my class were the most afraid of examinations. Our bronco buster on the farm told me that he would about as soon have a finger cut off as break an ugly colt; for he was sure, every time, that he should come out of it with his own neck broken, instead, and wished he might never see a horse or a saddle again; yet that very day we watched him break the wildest colt I ever set eyes on. He saddled him with a pully line, while another fellow held him by a long lip-rope, pulling on it with all his might. It took a half-hour to get the bridle on. Then he mounted, and put a silver half-dollar under each foot. The fellow cut the lip-rope, for he could not get near enough to slip it. The colt lunged, reared, plunged, squealed, kicked — did everything he could think of; and between whiles, while he was thinking of something new, went tearing like mad round the corral. Twice he stumbled and went almost down. Once he jumped clean over the corral fence. Well, when he was completely tuckered, and gave up, the buster rode him up and down, a little, just as easy as you please, and then came up to where father and I were standing, and there were the half-dollars, still lying in his stirrups. Why, if I could ride a horse as well as that, it seems as though I should be crazy to bust a bronco every day of my life."

"I reckon that's the very secret of it," Charlie replied. "You can't. If you could, you'd find that it wasn't so easy as it looks. You know Pope said, 'For fools rush in where angels fear to tread;' and wasn't it Longfellow who wrote, 'Only those who brave the dangers comprehend the mysteries?' It's only by handling Indians or colts that you find out what hot potatoes they are, and how carefully you've got to touch them, or get burned."

"I never had much time for reading poetry," Oscar remarked, diverted from his theme by the surprise at finding such a thing hidden under the rough exterior of his cowboy friend. "I like it, and it does one good to read good poetry, and I mean to take up a regular course of it, sometime; but so far I have always had to work too hard at my regular studies. I should think that ranch life, especially in the winter, would give one just glorious opportunities for such things."

"Well, I suppose that if you really wanted to read, you might work in a little now and then; but I reckon that the fellow who takes to ranching, is not one who is overfond of books. There's plenty to do on a ranch, now I tell you, and as a fact, beyond newspapers and the Bible, I don't believe I have read a chapter a year since I came West. I got most of my poetry when I was studying English Literature, and when I left college I left books pretty thoroughly."

"College!" Oscar looked up in blank astonishment.

Mountain Charlie laughed and laughed, until the tears rolled down his cheeks, and Panza looked up with wistful eyes, as though she were wishing that she could laugh like that. When he could speak, Charlie gasped : " That's for all the world the way that you looked at the crane. But it's a fact! Just thirteen years ago this summer, as green and proud a boy as ever you saw, I stood up in Harvard College and received my diploma and degree of Master of Arts. I don't blame you for jumping, though, when you come across the fact out on this prairie."

"That's hardly fair," Oscar replied, slowly, thinking out his way as he went. " When I first met you at the ranch-house, the day I went down there with father, I thought you as perfect as a picture. Why, I could hardly even understand what you said, you talked so funny; and I was astonished when father told me that you were at the head of that whole department of the estate. Then, on the way home he told me about your bravery with the Indians, and I made up my mind that that must be your strong point, and that you must be a sort of a terror that had better be kept away from. Ever since we went to the Indian camp after Black-dog, you've been so different that I knew I was mistaken, some way, and I've been wondering how. Now I know."

Mountain Charlie laughed again till the broad prairie resounded, and Panza went so far as to bark, in a struggle to join him, though she had to drop the lead rope to do it.

"It's all in where you are and what you're doing," he said, at last. "If you're in Rome be a Roman, or get out. It's just as instinctive to be a cowboy, on a ranch, as it is to use signs with an Indian. There's just one lingo that fits a cowboy. Some of his words you couldn't use anywhere else if you tried, any more than you could find other words to take their place with him. The miner has his own lingo, just the same, and every man, coming from North or South, drops into it as easily as he does into appropriate boots and hat."

Oscar found the long days in the saddle materially shortened by such conversations, aside from the amount of information he received upon points that were to be of living interest if he ever entered upon the life which all his dreams had painted for him.

Before sunset on the day when they passed the Indians, they came upon a cowboy's dugout, in the side of a low range of hills, where Charlie thought they had better spend the night. It was only a hole dug into the hillside, with a log front in which was an opening for a door. Above it rose an old powder keg for a chimney.

"It hasn't been used since last summer," Charlie

remarked, "and it isn't particularly inviting; but if those clouds should turn out rain we might be very glad of the shelter."

"Why not stay outside, unless it does rain?" Oscar asked.

"That's all right," Charlie replied; "and it's a pity for either of us to keep awake. We might tether the horses pretty close in, and with nobody round to mix her up, I reckon Panza would let us know in time."

They placed most of the outfit in the hut, built a fire, and hung their kettles upon a cross-stick. Oscar was rapidly learning the ranger's art of cooking, as well as many other of his arts; but hardly an hour passed that he did not thank good Fortune that Charlie was with him; for the more he learned, the more he realized how much he did not know. After such a supper as only a ranger could either prepare or appreciate, he spread his rubber blanket, took off his boots, and rolled himself in his wool blanket as scientifically as any cowboy, and with his feet to the fire, and his saddle for a pillow, he stretched himself as contentedly for a night's sleep as though he were in his little room, with solid stone walls, and a deep-set window and comfortable bed, upon the banks of the Thames.

Charlie piled up the fire with what he could find that would be apt to "hang on," left a little pile of dry sticks beside it for cooking breakfast, tethered the horses less than twenty feet away, and lay down on the opposite side of the fire. By way of good-night, he said :

"Don't forget that if you grow chilly toward morning, it will make a pile of difference if you pull your blanket up over your face."

The moon was just above the foot-hills, ready to set, behind them, when Oscar woke. He was quite cold and stiff, but looking at his watch he found it was after four, and, instead of trying Charlie's experiment, which he afterward found to be a very valuable hint, he thought he would quietly get up and try his hand at getting breakfast all alone.

As soon as the fire was burning well, he cut the last of the meat from a venison joint, and threw the bone to Panza to keep her quiet, put on some beans and coffee, rolled up his blankets, set the horses out to get their breakfast, and knelt before the fire, with a knife in one hand and frying-pan in the other, to prepare the deer steaks.

Suddenly Panza dropped her bone and sprang to her feet with a low growl. With the frying-pan and knife in hand, Oscar started up. He was sure that Charlie was sound asleep a moment before, yet as he gained his feet, he saw that he had already thrown off his blanket; he heard the click of a hammer, and, glistening in the moonlight, saw his big six-shooter all ready for action. For a moment he forgot the possibility of danger, and realizing his own position, in contrast, was ready to burst out laughing at the ludicrous figure he must present to an approaching enemy, when Panza, dropping her fierceness, calmly trotted out into the darkness, turning to the right, along a line of shrubbery growing at the base of the hill.

"That's rather odd," Charlie muttered, as he lay looking after her.

"It's the oddest thing I ever saw," Oscar replied, decidedly, and laying down the knife and frying-pan, he picked up his rifle.

"Go easy, now," Charlie warned him as he passed, and cautiously crept out of their sheltered corner, keeping close under the bushes.

The three horses were quietly feeding within a hundred feet. It was growing darker as the moon went down, but he could easily distinguish their outlines and see that nothing else was near. One of them, not satisfied with his night's rest, had lain down again, and was eating in that position, which would certainly be impossible if he had been startled, and Panza surely was not with them.

He crept on a little farther, and was on the point of whistling for Panza, in the fear that by some mysterious means she might have been enticed away to be killed, when he saw, not far before him, the form of an Indian pony, as white as snow.

He dropped upon one knee, with his rifle at his

shoulder. The pony stood close to the line of bushes; but closer yet, in the dark shadows, he was sure that he saw something move. He was afraid to fire at random, and he did not dare to speak, but with his rifle ready, he watched intently, till his eyes became better used to the shadows, and he distinguished Panza's form, with her back toward him. Yes; and the movement that he saw was nothing else than Panza's tail, contentedly wagging.

What could it mean? A moment later he distinguished another outline, beyond. Some one was bending over Panza. He was completely puzzled, and, as if to bewilder him yet more, the figure stood erect, with one leap landed on the pony's back, bent forward to give Panza a parting caress, and was away like the wind, into the darkness beyond, leaving on Oscar's mind nothing but the certainty that it was an Indian.

"What do you think of that?" a voice asked, and turning quickly, Oscar discovered that Charlie was close beside him.

"I'm sure I don't know," he replied, as Panza came slowly trotting up to them, evidently unharmed, and quite unconscious that she had done anything at all surprising. "A week ago I would not have believed that any one could have come near enough to Sancho to mount him, or near enough to Panza to touch her; least of all an Indian. I wonder what he was doing to Panza?"

"Stealing her collar, perhaps," Charlie suggested, with a low laugh.

"No. Hold on! But what's this?" Oscar exclaimed, as he felt for Panza's collar, and his hand

IT WAS AN INDIAN.

came in contact with something that was fastened to it.

"It's a piece of bark, with something written on it," Charlie replied, holding it up in the fading moonlight. "I reckon we'd better pull the horses in, to have them ready, and then see what it is. It's a warning of some sort."

There was an air of mystery about it which, in that darkest hour before dawn, and in their uncertain surroundings, made Oscar move nervously as he hurried to act upon the suggestion. He did not feel so sure of Panza either, as he thought, and wondered if there were not other Indians lying about in the bushes, ready to spring upon them? He began to realize what a comfortable thing it is to have a companion at such a time.

When everything was within touch about the fire, Charlie knelt down to secure the best light from the blaze, and examined the warning. It proved to be a strip of shaving instead of bark, and with a charred stick some one had written upon it: "Blackfoot tepees by river, heap bad place. Pale face no stop, no eat, no sleep. Blackfoot steal horse, steal all. One mile more good place cross river. Six mile more heap pale face tepee. Heap good pale face. Pale face go there sleep, eat."

Oscar had learned enough of the uncertainties of signs like this upon the plains to refrain from forming any opinion, and quietly waited for Charlie to speak. He sat by the fire in silence, for some minutes, turning the shaving over and over, reading it again, and investigating in several ways which Oscar could not understand. Suddenly he looked up and asked:

"Have you any particular friend among the Indians — some one for whom you have done a great favor?"

Oscar only laughed at the idea, and replied that he had not been in Manitoba long enough even to know a dozen Indians by sight, much less to do a single act of kindness, large or small, to any one.

He was a little disappointed when Charlie simply remarked:

"Well, let's have breakfast over, and get packed up and ready to start as quickly as we can. I am losing my appetite."

He hardly spoke another word till all was ready for the start, but obviously kept the sharpest lookout in every direction, with one eye constantly on Panza, and his rifle always close at hand.

CHAPTER XI.

OSCAR HAS A PERSONAL EXPERIENCE.

THEY stood by their horses ready to mount. Charlie looked anxiously along the low line of hills, then at the eastern sky that was beginning to brighten.

"I don't like to run along beside those hills in the dark," he muttered; "but it's high time we were on the way if we must make that extra seven miles and a ford before night."

"Do you take much stock in that message?" Oscar asked, at last.

"Why, yes; in a way I do," Charlie answered, deliberately. "There's certainly some Indian around who knows quite as much about our business as we do, and that alone is disagreeable and dangerous. The Indians all hate me as much as I hate them, and there's no danger of it's being any one laying himself out on my account. If you had some frantic friend in a red skin, that would make all as clear as day. I rather think it is connected with you, any way, and that it is the same fellow who brought you your horse. You may have done something for him and forgotten it. But I may be mistaken, and that's where the trouble comes in. That Blackfoot camp that those Sioux told us about yesterday, ought to be just a good day from here. I was planning to stop there, to-night, for it is much safer to sleep in an Indian camp than anywhere in the neighborhood of it. There are precious few Indians who can write in English, and those who can are usually the biggest scamps in the bunch. This may be a Chippewa, who is death on a Blackfoot, first, last and always, or maybe there's an opposition bunch across the river that would like to get us over there after dark. The white settlement he speaks of, across the river, is Mennonite, and they are good people, any way. The country from the river on is as flat as a pancake, and if we can cover it by daylight, we're all right. I don't see how a Chip or any other stranger could make so free with Panza, though. She seemed to recognize him at sight, and I rather think you'll find it's a friendly Indian who has met her before. But come on. We'll know by night if he spoke the truth. Keep your eyes peeled, and we'll keep up a pretty good pace till we leave the hills."

If there were Indians about they made no demonstration. The sun came up and the trail led away from the hills, and over the broad plain toward the river, but they still kept on at a slow canter till nearly ten o'clock, when they stopped for half an hour to let the horses rest and feed. Far as the eye could reach, not a living thing was in sight. Away behind them the hills they had left were only a low, irregular ridge upon the horizon, and farther away in the opposite direction a dark shadow indicated the line of trees bordering the river.

At noon they stopped for dinner where the trails divided into three.

"I wish some one would show up to tell us which of these to take to strike the ford," Charlie remarked as he sat eating and studying the three. "I believe we had better keep the middle one, but I'll bet my boots it goes past the Blackfoot camp."

"What's the harm if it does?" Oscar asked.

"There's no harm, only that I am so constituted that the sight of an Indian takes away my appetite," Charlie said, with a laugh.

He was right in his conjecture, for by the middle of the afternoon they found themselves passing within a quarter of a mile of the Blackfoot encampment.

"I call this pretty good going," Charlie remarked with satisfaction. "Now the ford can't be more than a mile away, and if we can strike it first shot, without wasting time running up and down the river, we're solid."

"I wonder if these fellows wouldn't tell us straight if we rode over and asked them?" Oscar suggested.

"They might, possibly, and even if they didn't, it would do no great harm. I don't feel much like taking the pack horse out of the way, for he's pretty well tuckered, now; but I could lead him while you and Panza run over, and meet us again a half-mile below," Charlie said.

He said it so carelessly that Oscar did not imagine how carefully he had thought it out, fearing that the outfit might tempt the Indians, and wishing to have Oscar out of the way of any shots that might possibly be fired while he was taking it past the encampment. If he had suspected such a thing it would have seemed to him a curious place to send him for personal safety, but as a rule the safest place about an Indian encampment is right among the tepees.

They were following a trail made by the dragging ends of tent poles fastened to the backs of Indian ponies. It led directly toward the highlands that fenced in the river, but that alone was no evidence that it led to the ford. Leaving the two horses plodding on, Oscar and Panza struck out for the camp, with the parting admonition from Charlie, "Don't fire unless you mean to kill, and then be sure you do it."

They were not long in reaching the little cluster of tepees. It was the most quiet spot imaginable. "It's all humbug about these fellows here being dangerous," Oscar said to himself. "Why, there are not a dozen tents in all, and there's not a single soul in sight." When he came a little nearer, however, the silence at least was well broken by the barking of a small army of dogs of all sorts, colors and sizes, the moment they caught sight of Panza. They jumped up from the grass where they had been sleeping, they came from behind the tepees, they poked their way out under the sides of the tents.

The tepees were most of them canvas, though there were two or three of skin, with grotesque attempts at outline drawings in bright colors, on the sides. Even the barking of the dogs had but little effect. Here and there a squaw appeared in the shadows, sitting on the ground inside the tent, or a pappoose lifted his little head, somewhere, while Panza, in sublime disgust at the ovation she was receiving, showed a vicious row of teeth, and walked on close behind Sancho's heels. A half-dozen horses, without saddles or bridles, stood nodding in the shadow of one of the tents, and one of them whinnied to Sancho; but receiving no response apparently went to sleep again.

Oscar began to suspect that this was about all the welcome he was to receive. He rode through the camp without finding anything but an occasional squaw, and whether he spoke or not he received only a guttural grunt or a muttered "How," by way of greeting. Apparently they not only did not understand anything more, but had no notion of trying to. He was about to give up in despair and ride away, when a withered old medicine man appeared in the door of one of the tepees.

The medicine man is a chief of grave importance and great influence in his tribe. His work of healing is only a very slight part of his professional duties. Unless he is called upon to administer to some trouble that he thoroughly understands, where his golden-rod, arnica, wet blankets, blisters or sweat-house, or some of his innumerable combinations are an established remedy, he goes to the patient with a drum and anything else which will help to make a noise, and either kills him outright, or frightens him into pretending, at least, that he feels better.

An Indian's constitution is very apt to aid such theories and practice of medicine, by naturally making a quick recovery or a sudden death, and in either case the medicine man is held very little accountable. Everything that is profound or mysterious in nature, art or science, however, comes under the Indian term of medicine, and the medicine man is the scientist, the astrologer, the prophet and the priest of his tribe. If they want more rain the medicine man must bring it. If the floods rise he must stop them. Every brave carries about with him his little medicine bag, which contains, not a cure for anything, but a little ounce of prevention for everything, and the medicine man must prepare that.

A WITHERED OLD MEDICINE MAN APPEARED.

In these ways, where there really ought not to be any responsibility at all, the medicine man is held very responsible. Many a poor medicine man has been tortured, and even put to death by his tribe, for failing to bring rain, when they only honored him for frightening to death some sick man whose trouble he did not happen to understand. The fellow who appeared in the tent door to see what Oscar wanted had been not only very shrewd, but fortunate to reach that shriveled and withered age in such precarious service. He greeted Oscar with a grave and dignified wave of his hand, and spoke English well enough to make himself easily understood by the aid of signs.

The old chief appeared to answer the questions put to him to the best of his ability, and Oscar was surprised to see how easily he could understand the signs, and how natural it was to make them while trying to put his questions in the simple and direct Indian form.

After thanking him for the information, Oscar rode away in the opposite direction from which he came, for, if the chief had told him correctly, Charlie was upon the wrong side of the camp, and would reach the river nearly a mile out of the way. Before he accepted the statement, however, it occurred to Oscar as a good plan to ride out in that direction and judge a little, if possible, for himself.

Following the medicine man's directions, he struck for a low line of knolls which he said bordered the river, and were not more than half a mile away. For a time Panza seemed greatly relieved at being out of the Indian village, but before long Oscar noticed that she was again showing her teeth and savagely licking her chops, while she bristled all over, and kept up a low, deep grumble. He looked about for the cause, but as they were gradually climbing the knoll he was too eager to see what was beyond to think of looking back, till, finally, Panza turned clear about and gave a fierce and decided growl.

Then Oscar glanced over his shoulder, and a cold shiver ran down his back as he discovered a half-dozen mounted Indians dashing toward him from the village. He could distinctly see the camp, too, and see that the horses by the tent had disappeared.

It seemed cowardly to be afraid of them, so he spoke to Panza, and went on, muttering: "So those young bucks were hiding in the tents all the time I was there. I wonder what they are after now?"

A moment later he looked back again. They were nearer and less careful. He could easily hear the sound of their horses' hoofs on the soft turf.

"I could outrun them, fast enough," he muttered, looking ahead, "but I don't know where I should fetch up."

He looked off to the left. Charlie was a mile or more away in that direction; but to reach him would be to give the Indians the benefit of a short cut to overtake him, "as well as a broad side to sight on if they meant business," he added, without carefully considering the mathematical facts of the case. Then he remembered that he had not yet accomplished what he started for, and to give up anything was so much against the theories and practices of his life, that he was on the point of starting again, when the Indians saw that he was watching, and with a wild whoop they started forward at a quicker pace, swinging their guns in the air and shouting to their horses.

Panza drew her tail between her legs and skulked back into the grass. Sancho threw up his head, laid back his ears, and seemed ready to break and run. Oscar felt it, too, for if there is anything that can always make the blood of man and beast run cold, it is an Indian yell. Even in the excitement of the moment, Oscar thought of what Charlie had said about walking ten miles and sleeping in a snowbank rather than hear that whoop. He had thought it almost silly at the time, but he suddenly realized what it meant.

There was only one thing of which Oscar felt sure: after being so thoroughly frightened by that yell, he did not propose to close the scene by running away. To convince the Indians of this, he deliberately turned Sancho half-about, and sat looking at them as they came on.

He had not waited long before a shot was fired, and

the next instant his rein parted, cut by the bullet, half-way between the bit and Sancho's throat.

Oscar bent forward to be sure that Sancho had escaped, then, quick as thought, he slipped from the saddle, and making it a rest for his rifle, stood with a bead drawn on the foremost of the band. He remem-

"THAT WILL DO."

bered Charlie's warning. He aimed to kill, and did not propose to fire until he had to.

The effect was like magic. The Indians stopped short, and scattered in every direction, like a flock of ducks that had been fired into. Suddenly each rider disappeared behind his horse, and nothing was to be seen of them but feet clinging to the saddles and heads peeping under the horses' necks.

If they had been in the forest they would at once have dodged behind the trees, and running from one to another have made a circle about him, gradually closing in till they succeeded in shooting him. If it had been upon the open plain, they would have separated and, at a distance from one another, have ridden round and round him, firing at every opportunity, clinging to the horse's neck and back, and hiding behind his body whenever there was danger that Oscar might return the shot. Unfortunately for their tactics, however, it was not in the forest or on the open plain. Wholly unintentionally Oscar had chosen the best position possible, almost at the summit of the knoll.

Constantly moving about, to prevent his obtaining a good aim at any of them, the Indians held a council for a moment; then the leader, appearing above his horse, threw his rifle on the ground, waved his blanket over his head, and the rest of the Indians appeared. Holding up his empty hands the leader shouted:

"Indian no mean shoot. Heap bad gun shoot self. Me good Indian. Heap good friend. Come say 'How,' pale face."

"You can say 'How' where you are," Oscar called. "I don't want you here, and I'll kill the first Indian who comes a foot nearer."

"No kill! Pale face no kill good friend," replied

the Indian; but he did not come any nearer. "Me come show pale face right trail over big water."

"That will do," Oscar retorted. "I am not hunting trails this minute; I am hunting Indians, and you go back to your tepees or I'll have you. Now! One! Two!"—

That was all. With a wild yell, a parting shot which did no harm, and a volley of curses in English, they rode away.

It had all happened so quickly that Oscar had acted with very little time for thought or discretion; but to say that he was not well frightened would be to say that he was not a sensible boy of sixteen. He was in his saddle in an instant, with a hasty knot tied in the broken rein, and he let Sancho move as quickly as was in any way convenient. He was determined, however, to see over the top of the knoll, and he went first in that direction, keeping a sharp lookout on the Indians behind him.

They did not attempt to return again, and when he reached a point where he could overlook the valley beyond, he was hardly surprised to find that he was even farther from the river than he had been at the village. The path which Charlie was following was too far to the right if anything, and turning to the left he rode rapidly along the brow of the high land till he caught sight of his friend.

"The old sinner!" Oscar exclaimed, as he told

Charlie of his adventure. "He sent me out there just to get me into a trap."

"That's only saying that he was an Indian," Charlie remarked a little scornfully. "But they were too smart for themselves, that time. They thought that by separating us they could skin us both easier than if we were together, but when half went your way and half came mine, they didn't have men enough to skin either of us. Don't forget the lesson, though, and don't ever let a red skin send you off on a wild-goose chase again. If I'd dreamed of your going on such a jaunt I'd never have thought of your starting at all."

"Do you really think there was any actual danger?" Oscar asked.

"Of course there was. Very decided danger. You never can tell what those young bucks will do when they start out for a summer's stealing. They are all very well on the reservations if you keep your eyes open or have company, for they are not going to do anything that will get them into trouble with the Government if they can help it; but what witnesses would there have been against them if they had killed you? Probably all they really cared for was your horse and outfit, but, mind you, so far as conscience is concerned they would just as soon kill you as you would kill a fly that bothered you. That's the difficulty."

"What would they have done if I had let them come up with me?" Oscar asked.

"Why, just whatever they pleased," Charlie replied, with a laugh, though his face was very earnest. "If they can't use a thing they can swap it at an agency for something else. Horses and rifles and cartridge belts come in very handy to an Indian, and you will never find a red skin refusing to help himself to anything that is within reach, whether it is any good to him or not."

"I don't wonder that our people are down on the Indians," Oscar remarked, with the fresh prejudice gathered in his bit of personal experience.

"Well, I don't wonder that they are down on the pale face, either," Charlie responded. "If I were an Indian I'd scalp every pale face I met; and being a pale face I'd like to see every red skin blown to blazes. It's a pity, but it's human nature, I reckon."

Oscar was still thinking over the matter when they reached the river.

"Here's luck!" Charlie cried, as they found a large boat with three sturdy fellows ready to push off, and easily secured transportation for themselves and the pack saddle.

"I don't suppose it's much over knee-deep along the bar," Charlie remarked to Oscar as they seated themselves in the boat, "and we'll have to do a good deal taller fording, without any help, before we get through; but a horse is very apt to stumble in the water, and just at this season it is precious cold and wet."

Panza was given the lead line of the pack horse, as usual, and Oscar and Charlie sat in the stern to lead their horses.

"She'll have to swim," one of the men remarked, nodding his head toward Panza, as they pushed slowly out. "Ye ain't afeared she'll git drownded havin' ter keep her mouth open?"

Oscar had not thought of that, nor had Charlie, but before they could decide what to do Panza, who still stood on the shore, studying the situation and waiting for the other two horses to get into the water, gave one bound and landed on Sancho's haunches, with her fore feet on the saddle, as she had so often ridden from the stable. There she sat, high and dry out of the water, till they landed safely on the other side.

"That dog knows more than a dozen men," Charlie exclaimed enthusiastically.

"Leastwise she knowed mor'n ter git drownded towin' a horse that was walkin'," the fellows replied, with a laugh.

As they were about to start again one of the men remarked:

"Yer a heap safer this side the river than t'other. Thar's a squad o' Blackfoot Injuns campin' up the trail, thet's come over frum the States ter see what they kin scoop in through the summer. They've done consider'ble killin' as well as stealin', an' d'rectly they'll git the sogers arter 'um in good shape. Ef ye'd 'a' come in sight on 'um they'd 'a' helped 'umselves to your kit, live or dead, bein' only two on ye. Yer lucky crost the river."

Charlie did not seem inclined to speak of the attempt they had made to help themselves, so Oscar followed his example, and bidding the men good-by,

PANZA SETTLES THE QUESTION.

they started on with the sun still nearly an hour high upon their right.

"Well," Charlie said, as they dropped into a walk to rest the horses after a canter of a mile or more, "the warning on that shaving was all right. It was either a Chippewa or some good friend of yours. If it was a friend we shall very likely hear from him again, and if we do we can probably believe him in advance."

Oscar, who was bent upon gathering all the points

he could upon any matter he did not understand, asked, "What was the reason you did not tell those men about the Blackfeet?"

"Only general principles," Charlie replied. "In the first place, it's never safe to tell a stranger in the West all that you know about anything. Then every frontiersman seems to have a mania for boasting of his prowess with Indians, when nine out of ten of them would run like a fox from the shadow of a chief's king feather. If a stranger begins upon you that way set him down as a liar, and expect every one else to do the same by you. And chiefly, I rather suspect that those men are officers in disguise, on the lookout for people who will give evidence against those Indians so that they can order them back over the border on to Uncle Sam. We hadn't time to hang round here a week to testify about what we are not sure of, and besides, we're going right through the Blackfoot lands in the States, and an Indian never forgets a grudge."

"I thought the fellows must belong to the settlement we are headed for — what did you call them?"

"Mennonites? O, no! They were not Mennonites."

"It's a queer name. I wonder how they came by it?" Oscar said.

"I don't know much about them," Charlie replied, "but I do know that they are mighty good people. I stopped with a set of them a little way from here, over one night, as I came up. They're a religious sect

— at least they came by their name that way. Those in Manitoba are a sort of cross between Russians and Germans. A Roman Catholic priest named Menno, was their Martin Luther. About four hundred years ago he began preaching in North Germany and Holland. There was a good deal that was Quakerish about it, and he founded quite a church, that has kept growing ever since; but they won't go to war, and they won't fight at home, which doesn't work well over there. There were Mennonites among the first Dutch settlers in New York, and I believe there are over sixty thousand in the States to-day. These fellows here are a later edition. They told me that some hundred years ago their ancestors went from Germany to Russia because the Tzar promised that if they paid war taxes they should not be called upon to fight. Well, the present Tzar took it back, and told them to go into the army or get out; so a lot of them went to the States, and about seven thousand of them came here. The Government gave them half a million acres. Look! There is the settlement."

CHAPTER XII.

THROUGH THE WHEAT FIELDS OF DAKOTA.

OSCAR looked eagerly forward and discovered a little cluster of cabins, far in the distance, hardly distinguishable from the gray hills and the brown grass. They were all built upon the same plan, with low thatches and holes in the center instead of chimneys, on the principle of the smoke hole in an Indian tepee. They were of rough hewn boards, very strong and substantial looking, with small square windows, and were huddled together, in an irregular cluster, like a settlement of tents.

Oscar had studied German in Oxford, but he found that a hundred years in Russia had demoralized the dialect of the good Mennonites. However, they received a very warm welcome, and got on well enough with what they could understand of one another.

It was very evident that they would have got on and received the same hospitality if they could not have exchanged a word, for the warm-hearted

"Quakerish" people knew what hospitality meant; but they were overjoyed to find a wanderer from the plains who could talk with them, even if they did have to try hard to understand him and make themselves understood.

The very first settler whom they met insisted that they should stop with him, and at once led the way to his *isbar*, as he called his cabin. He helped them un-

OSCAR LOOKED EAGERLY FORWARD.

saddle their horses and put them in a shed at one end of the cabin, giving them such a supper of oats and hay as they had not had since leaving the ranch. Then he watered them and locked the door, putting the key in his pocket with the remark that they had been greatly troubled by Sioux of late. He said, with a broad smile, that his own horse was only a mule, and a poor one at that, so he left him in the corral; but thought that good horses should be kept under lock and key to prevent tempting the red men.

There was a broad, smooth stone for a step in front of the cabin door, and inviting his guests to sit down there he soon appeared with a bowl of milk and a large slice of rye bread and cheese for each, "to encourage them till his wife had prepared their supper."

While they ate he sat beside them smoking a huge Russian pipe, and asking all kinds of questions about the world at large, as though having come from somewhere besides that little settlement they must know just what was going on everywhere.

A wagon track was the village street, and the cabins stood at irregular intervals on either side, while the farms which the villagers had taken up in homestead claims stretched out in every direction. Just opposite was the sawmill and grist mill combined, and further down stood a cabin larger than the rest, but in the same shape, which was used as the schoolhouse and church. The old man had only been over for a few years, but he said that his only regret was that he did not come before. He wore heavy homemade boots reaching to his knees, and homespun trousers only coming down to meet them, tied just below the knees;

a dark shirt with a loose collar, a little jacket reaching to his hips, and a curious skin skull-cap.

Four barefoot, rugged and solid little boys and girls were working or playing about the house, and often appeared around the corner for an instant or thrust a frowzy head through the half-open door, to disappear the moment that Oscar looked at them. They were as much like the old man as the little cabins were like the church, and Oscar tried to make their acquaintance, but he could not even obtain a good look at one of them till they went in to supper.

While they were on the steps two or three of the neighbors came up, and stood leaning against the cabin or sitting on the grass, as anxious as their host to learn the news. The arrival of strangers in the isolated settlements of the frontier is always a signal for a general gathering, and as Oscar sat in their midst he could not help comparing those strong, sturdy fellows, brimful of honest good nature, with the Blackfoot camp, a few miles away, where they should have been cooking their own supper, then, if it had not been for the mysterious warning.

Indians was the great topic in which they were all most interested. They said that since the spring opened there had been no end of trouble with the Blackfeet, over in the States. They had left their reservation and literally covered the whole northern part of Dakota, murdering and robbing not only travelers, but settlers, and burning their homes. There were several Mennonite settlements across the border; but of late attempts to communicate with them had been entirely abandoned. They understood that United States troops and a company of Pawnees were after them; but one old fellow remarked, "The Indians are very hard to find, except when you don't want them."

Several bands had already crossed the border to escape pursuit, and they asked particularly about the band that had encamped a few miles to the north. It had passed the settlement a week before, taking several horses and mules and a few head of cattle as toll.

"They went by in the afternoon," said their host. "We gave them some food and tobacco, but they were not satisfied with that, and in the night came back for more. He heard them at it," he added, pointing to a broad-shouldered Mennonite, "and going out with his shot-gun he followed them till he was near enough to shoot, and then he let both barrels go. They scattered in every direction, and he got the horses and mules and brought them back, all but three that they were riding."

"If I had had any more powder and shot to load again I would have followed on till I'd got the whole," he muttered, with a vindictive nod that sent the ashes tumbling from his pipe.

"Wouldn't that be fighting?" Oscar asked before

he thought, remembering what Charlie had told him about the Mennonites.

With a curious, rippling wink, that spread over his whole face, their host replied, "Oh! he's a Buttoner;" at that they all laughed.

The wife came to the door to announce that supper was ready, and as it was growing dark the neighbors went away, giving Oscar an opportunity to ask, " What is a Buttoner? "

He did not fully understand the reply, but made out that some of the Mennonites had grown more strict and Quakerish than Menno himself, and some of them less so as time went on, till the final separation came when buttons were invented to take the place of hooks and eyes for fastening the clothing. The strict ones held that buttons were an introduction of the evil spirit, and would have none of them. They were called Hookers. The others were called Buttoners. By degrees it came to be a name applied to any Mennonite who fell away a little from any of the dictates of Menno.

The room they entered comprised the entire interior of the cabin. It was very much upon the plan of the squaws' cabin, only that the logs had been split into rough boards, and instead of a chimney there was a large fire basin in the floor, in the center, whence the smoke found its own way to the hole in the roof. The two ends of the room were occupied by bunks.

There was a work bench at one side, which boasted a very fair assortment of tools that had evidently produced every article of furniture which the house contained. Standing upon the bench, in process of construction, was the latest product: a quaint, old-fashioned cradle, looking as though it had been modeled from a cut of cradles of five hundred years ago. There was nothing quaint or ancient about its future occupant, however; a fat and rosy little urchin only a few weeks old, jogging about the room upon the broad hip of his fat Dutch mamma, while she spread upon the plain wooden table a supper as warm and hearty as her husband's invitation had been.

Early in the morning they started on their way southward, bearing the earnest God speed of their host, who stubbornly refused any remuneration for his hospitality, and of the whole settlement, in fact, for they all turned out to see them off.

"How strange it is to find two sets of people breathing the same air, living on the same soil, so different as the Indians and Mennonites," Oscar remarked.

Charlie thought the matter over for a moment and replied: "It's the nature of the beast. Skunk cabbage and forget-me-nots always grow in the same mud holes." He had another matter on his mind, however, and after riding a little way in silence began: "I've been thinking about what they said of the Sioux uprising. They are the worst set of devils on the plains, even when they are at their best on the reservation. If they've left it and spread out over the north of Dakota there's no telling where they'll fetch up, or what they'll do when they get there. There's not one chance in ten that we shall meet a single party going this way between here and Bismarck. There are precious few forts and less settlements, while it's a perfect Blackfoot hotbed, and there won't be a mile of the way that Indians won't know just where we are and what our outfit is worth. If there is anything to be gained I am ready to go on in a bee line for Bismarck, and fight our way as far as we can; though I very much doubt the possibility of coming out alive. If we do, we shall reach Bismarck pretty well tuckered, as well as our horses, with the worst of it all still ahead of us. Now if we go over east a little way we shall strike Pembina, on the Red River of the North, and can go by rail to Casselton, and then west by rail to Bismarck, getting there about as quickly, entirely fresh, and in all probability alive. What do you say?"

"The only way I can do it is by swapping Sancho for a cheaper horse to pay the fare," Oscar replied.

"Bosh!" Charlie exclaimed. "I've got money enough with me to take us that far and still have enough left for a while. I surely don't need it now. If we don't get through alive I sha'n't ever want it. If we do, and you ever strike it rich, somewhere, you can pay me back."

Oscar saw the necessity of consenting, and late that evening they entered Pembina, on "the American side" as it is called, and for the first time Oscar found himself in the United States.

Pembina was one of the first trading posts established in this region, and had made very little progress. Indians still flocked about the town, but the fort on the west bank of the river made them "heap good friend of pale face" while they were in the neighborhood.

Red River carts were in their glory here. Steamers for Winnipeg were supposed to leave every day. Hundreds of people were coming and going through Pembina, but the people who staid there were in the minority. It rained during the night, and in the morning the mud was ankle deep as they made their way to the railway station. The high and narrow wooden sidewalks were crowded with people of every stamp and every nation. The cars and the steamboats brought them from all parts of the world, upon every conceivable mission, and carts and oxen, mules and horses added to the motley crowd. There were swells, from distant cities, in white shirts and polished boots; bull-whackers and mule-skinners in broad-brimmed hats, woollen shirts open at the throat, high-topped boots heavy with red mud, and bull whips tied over their shoulders; Chinese, just like Chinese everywhere; Blackfeet and Chippewas, Indian from king feather to moccasin, and Pawnees, all paint and feathers above the shoulders, then calico hunting shirts and blue army breeches, to indicate that they belonged to the Indian scout department of the regular army of the United States, then moccasins again, suggesting that in head and heels, at least, they were still Indians; cowboys, as there are cowboys everywhere, for one purpose or another, in every frontier center; emigrants, starting for imaginary havens, their promiscuous outfit packed in Red' River carts, prairie schooners or jiggers, or tied on the backs of bony mules or jaded horses; immigrants with dilapidated outfits, coming back from unveiled havens; farmers, miners, ranchmen, going and coming with their various outfits or hanging about the stores; porters, bronzed and toughened by their long journeys with skins and preparing for return trips with the products of civilization; women who had been out of society so long that they had forgotten how to comb their hair; children at a loss to find out what they were made for; people in all stages of intoxication, in all stages of desperation, and in a lank and gloomy fashion in all stages of satisfaction, all set off by a background of irregular shop windows where everything useful or rudely and glaringly ornamental was huddled together in a thoroughly promiscuous but not thoroughly picturesque confusion.

Oscar hardly spoke from the time they left the hotel

till they reached the railway station, where they placed their horses in a box car, seated themselves by the open door, in order to be near them in case of accident, and the mixed train started for the south. Then Charlie laid his hand on Oscar's knee, remarking:

"You're pretty blue, my boy, and I don't blame you."

"I believe I'm a little homesick," he replied, and tried to smile, but his lip quivered in spite of him.

Charlie said nothing for a moment, but presently, leaning back against the side of the door, he began:

"It's a funny thing, but I think a fellow never feels half so much alone out upon a prairie, a hundred miles from a human being, as he does in such a place as that. They do make a fellow homesick, awfully homesick, there's no mistake. And yet there is something about them that you come to like, in spite of it; and if they don't please you themselves they do spoil you for liking city life in the East, if you once get accustomed to them. In college I was crazy over mining, and struck out for Leadville the moment I had my diploma packed away. It wasn't very ideal there, now I tell you, and I came up to the Black Hills over the same path that we shall follow, only the other way. Well, that didn't pan out for me, either. Everything was every which way, and nothing as it should be. I lost my money and didn't make more. I didn't strike it anywhere, even to grub stakes, say nothing of millions. Oh! I got desperately homesick, you can bet. I was just a wreck. I couldn't stand it any longer, and I lit out for Boston. Before I was half-way back, however, I was tired of seeing everything so law and order, spink and span, and I felt like one in a dream, finding himself somewhere where he doesn't want to be, and wondering why in the world he came there. I kept on, but I didn't feel right and I was ashamed of myself from the moment I landed. It wasn't the place for me, and in less than a month I borrowed money and came back. A trail is a good enough street for me, and my six-shooter is better than a whole squad of policemen. I have made money enough since then. I've corraled quite a bunch in Winnipeg, and rounded up a good lump in Boston, but now I have no use for it. I very much doubt if I shall ever touch it. I would not lie awake five minutes to learn that the whole was swept away. Look at these homestead claims we are passing. See those little shanties, ten by ten, with one door and one window in front, a roof with a single slant, nine feet high in front, seven behind, and a chimney. Stable's the same, only without the chimney and window. Maybe those folks are sad, but if they are it's something wrong. They have a right to be happy, and most of them are; but I reckon you could not say so much of the homestead claims staked out along the swell streets of Boston."

They found these homestead claims all along the banks of the Red River, with here and there a settlement of more or less importance, which had sprung up like magic, for some slight excuse, grown like a weed in the warm sun of future promise, often come to a sudden standstill, when the promises were postponed, or dropped into a forlorn collection of dilapidated huts, half of them deserted and already falling to ruin, where the promises had failed or been transferred to some other locality. It did not require much time or labor to build up a settlement, and hundreds were ready to undertake it if there seemed to be a future before it. There was not much of real value to leave behind, and the hundreds were again ready to leave it the moment they saw a brighter outlook somewhere else.

Wheat was everywhere. Every little claim and larger farm was raising it. They were entering the great wheat fields of Dakota, where the Sioux and the Chippewas chased the buffalo and fought each other till the buffalo ceased to be altogether, and the Sioux and the Chippewas became only desperate, isolated fragments of what they had been, and the Star of Empire came and stood still over an undeveloped country where summer wheat could be raised; so wide and so far reaching that it possesses the capacity for supplying the whole world with summer wheat for ages to come.

Large and small farmhouses constantly increased. Piles of lumber and long lines of farm wagons were at every station, ploughs, seeders, reapers, harrows, threshers, were waiting to be carried away to the farms.

They stopped for a day at Casselton, to rest their horses before starting on the road running west, which

A RUN TO THE DALRYMPLE FARM.

would carry them to Bismarck, where they were again to take the trail for the Black Hills.

To occupy their time they rode out to that world-famous combination of four gigantic farms which originated under the shrewd and practical management of Oliver Dalrymple.

The town itself was far superior to Pembina, with as much activity and much more system, but with a curious disproportion between the large wooden stores and the homes which at irregular intervals lay along the few streets stretching out over the level plain. It was such a condition as might in a few years produce a rival for St. Paul or Kansas City, or might in less time degenerate to a freight depot and a few crumbling memorials to prospects that had failed to materialize.

Oscar and Charlie were not there to speculate in real estate, however. They only looked about them to see what was to be seen, and rode away to the great wheat farm.

"I worked here for one season, while I was making my way north," Charlie said. "There were seventy-five thousand acres then under cultivation, and I presume there's twice that now. It was surely the best-conducted farm in the world. The worked part was divided into quarters and each quarter was a separate division, with its superintendent, a complete set of buildings — a house for the superintendent and a big boarding-house for the hands, a stable, granary, machine shop and blacksmith's shop. It is just a regular army, divided into gangs of twenty teams with a mounted foreman for each gang, who has a mounted staff of two machinists with him. I have forgotten how many hundred horses and mules are employed, but every piece of farming machinery run by man, horse or steam, that is any good, is at work here."

It was a beautiful day. There was not a cloud in

the sky or a fence or hill to break the perfect level of the prairie. Far away to the south the course of Maple River was marked by a dim fringe of trees, but in every other direction the prairie made its own horizon line against the sky. The divisions could easily be distinguished by the clusters of buildings, and everywhere gangs were at work as they rode about watching the various operations.

"It's not much like the old days that poets wrote their pastorals about, is it?" Charlie asked. "Why, I can remember my father breaking new land upon our farm. The plough was made by the village carpenter and blacksmith. It was a solid oak beam twelve feet long, with a natural wind helped out by the adze. It was shod with cast-off horseshoes and any old bits of iron we could save up, and the share was a strip of iron tipped with steel. They would sometimes hitch in six yoke of oxen, with two drivers, for new land. Then a fellow had to sit on the beam to keep it down and another work like grim death to steer it, while another followed behind with a mattock to turn the turf, and all together, if they had good luck and almost killed themselves, would get over an acre and a half of new ground in a day. Now just look at that gang in the new ground over there. There are twenty sulky ploughs in a line, drawn by two mules each. Nobody has to hold them. A ten-year-old boy could drive as well as any one. They are going at a good sharp walk and ploughing two or three furrows each. They break new ground that way this month and let the sod lie and rot till fall. Then they backset it and harrow it with machines which run just as easy, and leave it till spring when it is ready to seed. They put in the seed, sometimes, as early as the middle of March, in spite of the cold winters, and that is a great sight, too. It wouldn't be so wonderful to you as it was to me, for when I was a boy I many a time tramped along the furrows dragging a chain to mark the line for some one to follow with a big basket strapped to him, throwing the grain right and left and wasting more than half of it by sowing it too thick, or where it got covered too deep or lay on the top for the birds. All that these fellows do is to put the seed into boxes, on wheels, regulated to scatter it just as thickly as they wish and absolutely alike, everywhere, and cover it just so deep every time. Then with a couple of good horses in front of them they start off for all day. I don't know but the harvesting is the greatest thing, after all, when you think of the old sickles and cradles, and binding sheaves with wisps of straw and then threshing it out sometime in the winter. On this farm they do the whole thing inside of three weeks. They take four mules instead of two, for the machines do more work, and the extra man walks behind. The machine cuts the grain in front of it, gathers it up in bundles, twists a wire about it, binds the wire and tosses the sheaf out behind, for the man who is following to set up to ripen. Then the threshing machine is put to work and turns out at least seven hundred bushels a day, works night and

"THAT'S WHAT I CALL FARMING."

day, burns up the straw for fuel, and the work is all over by the last of September."

"That's what I call farming," Oscar remarked, as they rode back to take the night train to Bismarck, where they replenished their outfit.

"Did you see that Indian boy watching us and following us all the while we were in Bismarck?" Charlie asked, as they started again upon the trail.

"Watching us? Nonsense!" Oscar replied.

"No; it is not," Charlie insisted. "I tried to call your attention to him two or three times, but each time he vanished before I got a chance. Panza knew him. That was what first attracted my attention. She was trying to speak to him, but the moment I looked he turned away. I remembered seeing him around before, and I saw him two or three times afterward."

"Well, if Panza's getting to make friends that way, I'll teach her better," Oscar exclaimed.

"She was not making a new friend, she was greeting an old one," Charlie observed, and immediately changed the subject.

CHAPTER XIII.

A DOUBTFUL HOST.

OSCAR found his spirits rising again the moment the open country lay about him, though the path was very different from that which they had followed through Manitoba. It was more a wild and broken table land. The stage road, with its established stations, was not so well patronized as it had been when Bismarck offered the nearest railway connection to the Black Hills. Thousands upon thousands had been over that trail, but the thousands had dwindled now to a very few, and with the decrease trouble from restless Indians had increased. In the busy days only an occasional stage that chanced to be alone, or an isolated party, was ever disturbed by highwaymen. Everything was isolated and solitary, now, and as the result an attempt at least was made to hold up pretty much everything that went over the road. Little by little the road agents had been shot off, captured or driven away, or had left on account of dull business; but the few that remained had baffled every attempt to trace them, and had been growing more and more daring and desperate.

There was another trail, more of an Indian trail, that was shorter, leading very direct to Deadwood, through the badlands and reservations, and the country that had recently been opened. It occasionally touched the stage route, and a part of the way was the same.

There was little prospect of their having company by either trail, and considering that the advantages offered by occasional stage houses were less than the disadvantages of running into road agents as well as having more miles to go, they chose the shorter trail.

They were not disappointed in the prospect of being alone. Indians occasionally passed them, but seemed to be peaceful enough, and after they were beyond the immediate influence of the outlying farms and ranches of Bismarck, which were very few on that side of the river, they saw no signs of life except the omnipresent prairie dog and his associates.

As they sat before a fire cooking a rabbit which Panza had brought in, Charlie remarked: "If we don't strike larger game than this to-morrow we shall have to tie up and go hunt for it. We're not likely to strike many restaurant stations on this road, and the beans and flour and bacon in the pack will give out before we get to Deadwood, without help."

"Don't forget the box of crackers," Oscar said.

"No; I sha'n't forget that when I am hungry, I tell you," Charlie replied, with a laugh.

It was growing dark, and they were anxiously watching for some favorable place to spend the night, when Panza began to show decided signs of disturbance.

"What has she struck now, I wonder?" Charlie said, dis-

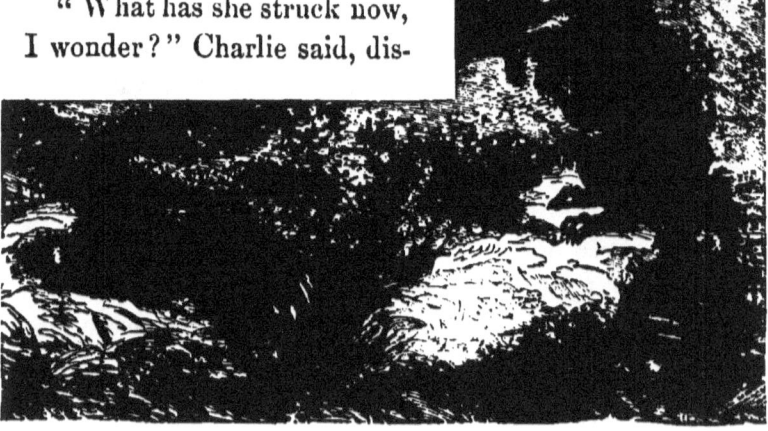

OLD SETTLERS.

mounting and taking the lead line, to set her at liberty.

"Something has been along there that she don't like; that's all," Oscar remarked carelessly.

"Well, the question is, what was it?" Charlie replied; "for there is an even chance that it may have been something that I don't like, either, and it is getting too near dark for that. This trail is so heavy and dry that I can't see a track. Hold on! She's struck it again in the dust. Oh! it's nothing but a wolf."

"No; it is not a wolf," Oscar said, examining the track which Charlie had found. "It's a dog, Charlie. I know a wolf's tracks — I examined them carefully in the snow, that day up in the woods with father, so that I should be able to tell them from Panza. A wolf's foot is larger and spreads out more, and has sharper claws. See? These are not so large as Panza's. It's a dog; an Indian dog. That's what's the matter with her. Do you suppose there are Indians round?" he added, with a quick, nervous glance about him.

"There'll be Indians round all the way to Deadwood. Bother their painted hides!" Charlie muttered. "But the dog is as likely to belong to a squatter as to a red skin. At all events, I should like to find out before we unsaddle. Put Panza on the track, and let's see where it goes, but stop her quick if she strikes toward the rocky land to the west."

Panza did not much fancy being put to trail another dog, but when she realized that it must be done she led away, and after they had followed for half a mile they discovered a low building, just where the stage route and the trail met for the second time. It was the first sod house which Oscar had ever seen.

It was larger than a log cabin, low and long, with walls of sods, laid like bricks, and the roof of sods, supported on corner posts and cross bars. There was one door and one window visible, a stone chimney built outside, and an empty powder keg on top.

"A squatter," Charlie muttered.

"We're in luck, then," Oscar said.

"We're liable to be," Charlie replied; "but it depends a good deal on who and what the squatter is. You stay here with the pack and Panza and I'll go up and find out."

He had not been gone long when the savage barking of a dog sounded, and Panza looked up with a low growl which very plainly said, "I told you so." Then the door opened, and a moment later Charlie called and Oscar rode up to the cabin.

The squatter still stood in the door with a heavy double-barreled gun under his arm. He was a powerful man, with grizzled and bushy beard and a mass of long and tangled gray hair. His motions were dull and slow, but even in the fading twilight it was easy to see that the eyes were quick and keen.

He did not seem particularly glad to see them or even passably civil, and had Oscar expressed an opinion, it would have been to stand upon his dignity and take his blanket out upon the open prairie; but seeing Charlie making the best of things as he found them, he quietly followed his example.

The end of the sod house was a stable. The squatter silently led the way, unlocked the door and sullenly stood there while they unsaddled their horses, fed and watered them and found places for them out of reach of the heels of two mules which were already stabled there. When all was ready for the night Charlie took a box of ammunition and a piece of bacon from the pack saddle, and the squatter locked the door behind them as they came out.

It was evident to Oscar that there was something seriously out of order in their present position. Charlie did not speak a word to him, but kept singing snatches of cowboy songs, and when he spoke to the squatter it was in a tone and dialect which Oscar could hardly imagine as pertaining, in any way, to his friend of a half-hour before.

There was a large trough at the stable door, supplied by an artesian well. As they passed it Charlie said, "Make a good livin' outer this hole in the ground, waterin' stage hosses?"

The old man grunted, for all the world like an Indian.

"They tell me biz hes lit out some, frum these parts," Charlie added, and the squatter gave a savage grunt.

"Bottom fell clean out, or will she strike a fresh vein later on?" Charlie asked; and the squatter shrugged his broad shoulders and answered with an

Indian's grunt of uncertainty, as he led the way into the cabin, leaning his gun against the wall just inside the door. Charlie set his rifle down on the opposite side of the door, and Oscar followed his example.

The only light in the room came from a fire which had recently been kindled. The only occupant was an Indian squaw seated on the floor before it, preparing some supper for the guests, and the dog, skulking away in one corner, savagely grumbling at Panza's presence there.

Charlie handed the box to Oscar, and walking across the room hung the bacon upon a nail in the rafter near the fire, at the same time saying: "The kid's got a box o' gun-fodder there. I s'pose ye kin make it work in somewhere?"

The squatter grunted. Oscar laid the box on the table.

"How's shootin' in these parts, pard?" Charlie asked.

"Good 'nough ter what et mought be," the fellow muttered, as he scraped out an old pipe.

Charlie tossed a piece of tobacco on the table, pushed a stool into a convenient position with his foot, and sat down, leaning back against a tier of bunks and balancing his feet on the table, as he continued, "Fact is we're flyin' light for fresh, an' ef ye've got a good buck handy, that we could drop 'out gittin' our scalps lifted, 'twould stock up the larder in good shape."

The squatter bobbed his head in acknowledgment of the tobacco, which was more than he had done for the bacon or ammunition, and while he cut and prepared a pipeful of it replied: "Injins is everywhar, an' fightin' drunk. I don't make no promises 'bout scalps; but arter grub we kin go up a piece an' scoop some deer on shares."

Charlie took his turn at grunting, and stuffing his hands deep into his pockets, threw his head back against the bunk and began to whistle.

Oscar was thoroughly perplexed, but realizing that it was a game of grave importance which Charlie was playing, he did his best to follow the lead, and made himself thoroughly at home. Not knowing what it would be best to say, he very wisely said nothing. For some minutes he sat watching the curious picture, and all the time not a word was spoken in the sod house. Charlie was whistling and dreaming, with his eyes apparently shut, as though he were alone in the universe. The squatter puffed upon his pipe and drowsily watched the clouds of smoke as though no living thing were near him. The fire crackled and the frying pan and kettle bubbled and hissed, while the squaw watched them, apparently unconscious that there was a mortal behind her. Only Panza and the yellow Indian dog seemed not to have forgotten each other's existence. Now and then a whining snarl would come from under a bunk in the distant corner, and in response

Oscar heard Panza, lying beside his stool, give her chops a quick, savage lap, and the click of her teeth as her jaws came together again.

Oscar began to dream, himself. A curious atmosphere pervaded the sod house, in which each occupant seemed too deeply engrossed in his own problems to be aware of anything else. Oscar gave up trying to understand the situation and began to recall old märchen stories, with the squaw before the fire for the witch, and the grizzled squatter a grim giant, waiting to have his table spread with victims. The longer he thought of it the more real it grew, till it seemed to him that he and Charlie were the little mortals who had fallen into the giant's clutches and were about to be served on his table. There are people — who really know no more about it than other people — who will say that it was a wave of thought-power creeping over him from an intense mental activity, any outward expression of which the two men before him were so successfully concealing, which was really going on behind the whistling and the smoking. At all events the dream had its effect upon Oscar. It made an impression which did not wear away, but influenced his actions throughout the evening and even longer.

At last the squaw broke the spell with a grunt which signified that her preparations for supper were complete. She rose from the fire, and Charlie brought his feet down from the table, remarking, as if in answer to the last words of the squatter, " I don't lie awake nights spoilin' fur a fight with red skins nor white stuff, nuther, but 'twould take a stiffer breeze nor has blow'd so fur ter snow Mountain Charlie in, ef it cum ter straight biz."

The surly host made no reply, but stuffing his pipe in his pocket pushed his chair to the table with his foot. Oscar did not wait for an invitation, but gave his stool a shove and lounged along after it in a way that won a glance of hearty approval from Charlie.

For a squatter's sod house, with a squaw at the helm, the supper was decidedly good. They all ate heartily, helping themselves, without invitation or ceremony, with their own knives and forks. The moment he had finished, the squatter lit his pipe again, spoke to his dog, took up his gun and bobbed his head toward the door as he opened it, by way of indicating that he was ready to start. Charlie deliberately stretched, yawned and replied:

"Kid's goin'. He kin knock the head off a pin fur's he kin see it. Two's 'nough fur deer. One's none too many ter hang round sech hoss-flesh as our'n."

A frown shot across the squatter's forehead. An involuntary motion of his hand toward the door showed very plainly that his first intention was to close it and abandon the hunt. Without seeing through it Oscar realized that their host was in a disagreeable box, where Charlie had intentionally placed him. He covered it well, however, and a moment later muttered: "Good 'nough! Come on, youngster," and started.

"Better leave yer dorg behind," Charlie called to Oscar as he turned to follow him. "She don't hitch hosses with t'other one."

The hint was enough. Oscar went out alone, with his strange companion. He was not particularly alarmed for his personal safety, for he had unlimited confidence in Charlie, who evidently grasped the situation and knew what he was about; but he was only a boy of sixteen, after all, and this was his first experience of frontier life. There was something uncanny about it, at the least, that constantly recalled the giant and his feast.

The man went to the stable, took out one of the mules, and with the lead line over his shoulder and the dog at his heels started for the rough land rising in broken buttes and low hills and knolls a little distance to the west. He had already disclosed the fact that he was not an expert conversationalist. Oscar expected nothing, and having enough to do on his own account without talking, he did not try to tempt him.

They went on in absolute silence till the dog began to sniff in a suggestive way, when the squatter at once tethered the mule, and leaving the dog beside it struck a more cautious pace and crept onward, followed closely by Oscar. A moment later he dropped upon his hands and knees and Oscar followed his example.

The moon rose without a cloud, making the smooth surfaces almost as distinct as by day, while the shadows seemed all the blacker in contrast. They were creeping toward a fantastic pile of bowlders, surrounded by scraggy cedars, upon the brow of a butte, and as they climbed higher, nearing the summit, a grand scene beyond gradually unfolded before Oscar's eyes. Wild and magnificent Nature stretched away in an opening panorama so sublime that, forgetting everything else, he stopped more than once to admire it.

Beyond the bowlders a hill evidently fell away into a ravine, neither of which could be seen, as yet, but beyond them stretched snow-white ledges and black gorges, out of which came the rumbling of cascades, and here and there a cloud of mist rose like white smoke in the moonlight, marking some headlong plunge which the stream was making among the rocks.

A few feet more and they were crouching behind the bowlders. As Oscar gained his feet the squatter touched him on the shoulder. It was only to point through a cleft in the rocks, but it sent a cold shudder over him — as though the man had stabbed him with a knife — and for an instant the märchen picture flashed before him again. He was ashamed of it, and resolutely turned and looked through the cleft at a sight to thrill a sportsman's heart.

In a smooth slope, only broken by a few moss-covered bowlders, the hillside stretched down into a deep valley. The silvery moss and dew-covered grass gleamed in the moonlight, and wherever his eye rested over the entire knoll, dark heads were thrust up above the grass, broad ears were turned full toward the bowlders, delicate pointed noses were sniffing suspiciously, and in the immediate foreground, less than a hundred feet away and not twenty feet apart, two magnificent pairs of antlers, looking as if they were crusted with snow, tossed in the moonlight above the heads of two large bucks, suddenly roused from sleep by some suspicious sound or odor beyond the bowlders.

It was such a sight as Oscar had never seen before, and might well have obliterated everything else for the moment, at least. Even while he looked Oscar wondered that it did not absorb his entire attention, and that he turned, almost instantly, to look back at the man beside him. He wondered, while he was doing it, that, instead of preparing at once to fire, where he was, he motioned the squatter to keep the place, while he quickly and noiselessly crept away to the farther end of the bowlder, keeping his eyes more intently upon his companion than upon the deer. He was certainly acting more upon instinct than reason, but if the most profound reasoning is not founded on instinct it is in great danger of leading even the wisest men astray.

Upon the side of the rock which he approached the bowlder shelved in at the bottom, leaving a deep crevice, absolutely black, under its shadow. The change of position had required but a moment. Not a deer had risen from the moss. Oscar could easily have started them and fired from where he stood, looking over the edge of the bowlder, but all the time his thoughts were bent upon something else which he did not himself begin to comprehend. As his eyes fell upon the black shelter under the rock, he slipped down into it with a sigh of relief and muttered: "All ready. Start them up."

There was no need. The sound of his voice was quite sufficient. The two bucks were on their feet in an instant. Taking the one nearest his end of the rock, Oscar only waited for him to turn for a fair position, and fired.

Many a wonderful story has been told of the amount which the brain can accomplish in dreams, in a moment's time; but there is something much more wonderful in the amount which a wide-awake brain can accomplish, if put to the test and all that it does is traced.

It was the first time in his life that Oscar had made a moonlight shot at a deer. It required a cool head and a steady hand. He saw the deer leap and drop, and knew that he had killed him. All over the hillside he saw others springing to their feet, and thought how easily a band of Indians instead of deer, might have lain hidden there till one had walked right into the midst of them. He knew he had not heard his companion's gun, and to see if they had possibly fired at the same instant he glanced at the other buck, just turning away with a bound, and knew that he had not fired at all. His ear caught a faint sound, as if a twig cracked behind him. Without looking he knew what it meant, and his rifle was empty. He remembered a statement Charlie had made way back in Manitoba, that one rarely needed a six-shooter, even upon the plains, but when he did he needed it quicker than lightning and sure to a pinhead. He thought how he had practiced the cowboy's art of pulling a six-shooter, cocking and firing all in one motion. He remembered that he was sheltered by the shadow of the bowlder and that as long as he kept in it he had at least that protection. All this flashed through his mind and, careful that his pistol did not strike the rock, he caught it from his belt and cocked it as he turned, like a flash, exclaiming:

"That'll do, now! Drop that gun or I'll fire!"

It was all so quickly done that as he stood with his revolver leveled at the crouching form of the burly squatter, saw the big double-barreled gun for an instant aimed at him, then dropped to the squatter's knee, he noticed the smoke of his own rifle drifting above the fellow's head.

With a grunt the squatter muttered: "You there! I couldn't see nuthin' an' I mought 'a' blowed daylight through ye, drawin' on that buck. Wall, he's went, now, an' ye kin give me half o' your'n fur gittin' in my way. Yer'd better go down thar lively an' cut his throat, ter let him bleed."

Oscar was perplexed. He knew very well that the man was aiming at him, and would have fired before if he had seen him, yet it was quite possible that he was simply crazy. He could not think of any other reason for his shooting him. At all events, there was no sense in discussing the matter, so he simply said: "You can do that better than I. You are more used to it. Drop that roer of yours and go down to the deer." The man's only response was to clutch the gun more firmly. He even made a slight motion, as though he were ready to throw it to his shoulder again. Oscar took one quick step forward, bringing his pistol into the light, saying sharply, "Drop it! and do as I tell you, or I'll" —

"Put up yer shootin'-irons!" the fellow shouted savagely, throwing his gun on the ground. "I'll cut the buck's throat fur ye, an' yours, too, ef et'll 'blege ye any."

"Not to-night, thank you," Oscar replied. "I am not so sure of you as I might be, but I am sure of this shooter; and from now till we reach your cabin it is going to cover your heart. Do you understand? It goes off mighty easy, and if you make one false move I shall pull the trigger, and pull it quick. Hurry up, now!"

Without another word the squatter moved slowly toward the deer, drawing his hunting knife as he walked, and running his thumb along the blade with a suggestive grunt.

Oscar picked up the gun and his rifle, leaning them against the rock, keeping his eye carefully upon the squatter, when he heard a low whisper pronounce his name. With a start which betrayed his strained nerves and showed how thoroughly frightened he really was, in spite of his calmness, he looked over his shoulder to see Charlie with Panza at his heels, creeping from behind the shrubbery.

Grasping Oscar's left hand he whispered in his ear: "You did that nobly, old fellow. I was afraid he'd cook up something, so I followed close behind. I had a bead on him, but I waited for him to put his gun to his shoulder to be sure. I was just touching the trigger when you spoke and he flopped. I never fired at a white man yet, and, thank God, I didn't have to begin to-night. I tell you, you did that fine."

"Are the horses safe?" Oscar asked eagerly.

"I reckon so," Charlie replied. "I only told the squaw that I was going out to watch round the place; and he has the key in his pocket. Keep your eye on him for a minute more. I'll come up from the other side. Don't act as though anything had happened."

Charlie disappeared, and Oscar leaned against the bowlder, with the pistol still in his hand; but his hand was trembling so that he could scarcely keep it from falling. Help had come lifting the burden from his shoulders, and he suddenly realized that he was only a boy of sixteen, after all, frightened almost out of his senses.

If he had stopped to consider the two sides of himself portrayed in the last five minutes, under the shadow of that rock, he would have found an explanation of the peculiar condition he had described to Charlie on the Manitoba prairie, and have realized why the best scholar dreads the examination, the best sailor the storm, the best bronco buster the unruly colt, and the best Indian hunter the red man, for he would have seen a boy, who, in an emergency, faced down the giant squatter and his double-barreled roer, shaking like a leaf at the very sight of the unarmed man, kneeling with his back toward him, a hundred feet away.

Oscar was not philosophizing at that moment, however. He was upbraiding himself for being a coward, struggling to stop his hand trembling, pressing his knees against the rock to keep them from shaking, vacantly staring at the squatter while he cleaned the deer, cutting away the waste parts and angrily muttering: "He could cut my throat with a feather if he should come back and try. I wish Charlie would hurry up."

Suddenly the Indian dog began to bark in short, sharp yelps. In an instant the squatter was upon his feet, and turning toward the bowlder said: "Them's Injins! Gimme my gun!"

"Indians!" The word sent a cold shiver through Oscar's relaxed muscles; but in spite of what he had been saying of himself his fingers tightened about the revolver. His wrist and arm were strong and steady. He stood as firmly on his feet as ever in his life, and calmly and sternly replied: "You stay where you are! I can empty your gun as well as you can."

"Ef they lift your scalp 'tain't none o' my funeral," he muttered, and at that moment Charlie's voice sounded in a boisterous "Halloo!" as he came over the brow of the hill, leading the mule.

"Is that all you've struck, pard?" he exclaimed. "I thought ye must 'a' hit out a schooner load an' wus waitin' fur help. Whar's the kid?"

"Watchin' out," muttered the squatter, bobbing his head in the direction of the bowlder.

While Charlie and the squatter were placing the deer on the mule's back Oscar removed the cartridges from the double-barrel, loaded his own and joined the rest as though he had really been on guard for Indians.

Sullen and silent as usual the squatter led the way back to the sod house, with the lead line over one shoulder and the empty gun over the other. His dog kept at his heels, snarling every time he caught sight of Panza. Charlie walked beside him, making an occasional remark, and Oscar followed a few feet behind the mule, his rifle over his shoulder, but cocked and ready to be brought into position on the slightest provocation. Panza brought up the rear.

All was safe at the stable, and seeing the door locked again they entered the house. The fire burned low. The squaw sat on the floor before it. A candle, stuck in the neck of a bottle, stood on the table. The squatter left his roer as before, beside the door, but Charlie kept his rifle in his hand, and walking across the room threw it into an upper bunk directly opposite the door, following it himself without taking off his boots. "Hop up in the top one, kid," he said to Oscar, pointing to bunks nearer the fire, and turned over as though he meant to be asleep in an instant.

Oscar took his rifle as Charlie had, and was very glad that it occurred to Panza to follow him, and lie on the outside edge of the bunk. He did not believe that he should be able to shut his eyes all night, but there was a sense of security in the big shaggy form and regular breathing of Panza, and the next thing Oscar knew Charlie was saying, in a sharp, decided way, "Look a-here, pard, ef yer goin' ter take a look at yer mules, I reckon me an' the kid'll have a squint at our hosses, same lick."

Oscar was wide awake in an instant, and out of his bunk ready for action, almost as soon as Charlie. It was still dark, but he could distinguish the burly form of the squatter by the door, with his boots in one hand and gun in the other.

"Hain't no great need o' turnin' the hull camp inside out," he replied, laying down his gun. "Thought I heered a sound as mought be Injins. But ef ye're so anxious to do the lookin' fur yerselves, why, I'll turn in ag'in."

"Ef it's Injins, pard, yer kin rest easy. We've got a cur along as hates 'um like pizen, an' smells 'um a mile away ag'in' the wind. But I say, pard," Charlie added, lighting a match and looking at his watch, "ef the sun's on time this morning she'll be along in an hour. Jest shy over the key afore ye drop off, an' we'll be fixin' up ter light out."

The mere rude frontier combination of dialects which Charlie had assumed was so thoroughly consistent with the surroundings, that after his first surprise Oscar could easily have forgotten that it was not his natural mode, and could very easily have fallen into it himself; but what won his constant surprise and admiration was the cool and dictatorial way in which Charlie deliberately took the management of everything into his own hands. There was nothing in his tone or manner that could provoke such a reply as the squatter had made to Oscar, when he ordered him to cut the deer's throat, yet with every sentence there was something which said as plainly as a loaded six-shooter, "This must be done, and done quickly, or" — and it was done.

The old fellow threw the key on the table, gave the squaw a savage shake, told her to get up and build the fire, and then got into the bunk again and pulled the blanket over his head.

As they went out Charlie motioned to Oscar to remain by the open door, just out of range from the bunk, while he went to the stable, fed and watered the horses, saddled them and strapped their share of the deer meat upon the pack.

Breakfast was a silent act of duty, and even long after they were on the trail again Charlie was absent-minded and constantly looking back.

"You don't think he will follow us, do you?" Oscar asked, with a decided shiver.

"I am very sure that he will," Charlie replied. "He did not say good-by, which looked very much as if he intended to see us again. He has set his heart on having these horses, and it is my opinion that he will get them, too, before to-morrow morning."

"He will get them! How?" Oscar gasped, clutching the rein and instinctively laying his hand on his revolver.

"I don't know. I wish I did," Charlie replied. "Trade is dull on the trail now, and three good horses are not going to be let slip. There's a ranch somewhere or other, for there's a prairie post-office, there where the trail leaves the stage route again. If we should strike that we might work it all right, but if we don't we shall hear from him before this time tomorrow in a way that means business; for he knows us, now, and he'll be prepared."

Oscar looked ahead where Charlie pointed, but the only sign of humanity which he could see was a post, set in the ground, with a small box, apparently, fastened to the top.

" A prairie post-office?" he repeated.

" Yes," Charlie replied. " Maybe the ranch has moved away. Maybe it's for some squatter out on this trail; but that is the nearest that the stage goes to something or other, and if there are any letters for that point the driver leaves them in that box."

"If it should be another squatter we're not much better off," Oscar added a moment later.

"That depends," Charlie replied quickly. " They used to say at home that it never worked to judge of a church by the man in the pulpit or the fellows in the best pews. Squatters are all of them a rather solemn set, especially when they have Indian squaws. The life they lead is solemn; but you'll find many a true man and a good friend in a squatter's shanty. What's that on the top of the post-office?"

" It's something hanging on a stick."

"Yes; it's a signal of some sort," Charlie added, giving a searching glance in every direction. He

THE PRAIRIE POST-OFFICE.

hurried forward, and Oscar, following close behind, heard him exclaim, "By Jiminy!" as he rode up and pulled it down.

Oscar knew Charlie well enough by this time to be sure that his favorite expletive was caused by a pleasant surprise, but when he looked over his shoulder he found him examining a square piece of bark, containing only some rude figures roughly drawn by an Indian. He passed it to Oscar remarking, "This is addressed to you, and I suppose I should not have read it."

"To me!" Oscar exclaimed, looking up in astonishment. "What do you mean?"

Charlie turned the bark over, and on the opposite side Oscar saw a half-circle and dash plainly drawn with a charred stick. "That was a very wise precaution," Charlie observed. "To people in these parts not familiar with the ranges, it means nothing. To you and me it means 'Mr. Oscar Peterson, Ranchman, of Manitoba.'"

Oscar stared in blank astonishment; for if there is an incident more startling than hearing one's name pronounced when hundreds of miles from any acquaintance, it is to find a letter addressed to one's self out upon a prairie trail, under similar circumstances.

Seeing his surprise, Charlie continued: "Have you forgotten what I told you — that you had a loyal Indian friend who was keeping track of you, and that you would probably hear from him again? Much as I hate them I will say that a better, truer, more reliable and self-sacrificing friend cannot be found than an Indian who feels that he has a debt of gratitude to pay. This fellow is all-fired smart, too, I tell you."

"But, Charlie, I tell you I have no such friend, any way," Oscar insisted, "and if I had, what does he mean by this?"

"That's the question. Let's give it another look," Charlie replied. "I'm not much on Indian writing, but I reckon I know as much about it as an Indian. He knew your name, and could write in English if he wanted to, but this was to be left where it might be seen, so he put it Indian fashion, which shows that the people he was afraid to have see it were pale faces and not Indians. That's meant for a tomahawk sticking in a stump. That is a danger signal; as common as a red light on a railroad. Then that crossed line, open at the top, means a white man, and those three mean there are three of them. Those wiggled lines are trees. That's an open eye, and that circle means the Great Spirit. That line under the trees I'm not sure — yes, that means a gulch. There! That's all I can make out of it."

"Does it make any sense?" Oscar asked.

"Why, certainly! Don't you see? There is danger ahead, in the shape of three white men, in a patch of woods, running through a gulch. Their eyes are open; that is, they are on the watch, and our only hope is in God."

"That sounds pretty serious," Oscar said.

"I reckon it sounds about as it is," Charlie replied. "But come on. It will not help the matter any to stop here."

"Indians are bad enough. I don't want to meet any more white men on the war path this trip," Oscar muttered, as they started on. "It is simply outrageous! With all respect for you, Charlie, I believe the cowboys, as a class, have demoralized the whole frontier life of our continent."

"You're snapping just about the same kind of judgment that you did at squatters because you came across a fellow who looked like a squatter and lived like one and aimed his gun at you," Charlie replied, with a little show of dignity. Changing his mood in an instant, however, he continued: "Well, Oscar, you're only making a mistake which hundreds of wise men have made before you; the mistake of thinking that every fellow who has a slouch hat and open collar and wears spurs and carries a six-shooter is a cowboy. Whatever such a fellow does is always charged to cowboys. If a drunken bully loses his head in a barroom and sets his gun going, it is cowboys for sure. If a bunch of rascals gets into a gulch in Dakota and holds up everything that comes along, why, they're cowboys, even before you've set eyes on them. Even if a tenderfoot gets himself mixed up with them sometime, and is treated like a gentleman, whether he is one or not, and discovers for himself that in reality, as a class, the cowboys of the West are the best set of fellows on the face of this earth, loving law and order as much as they do a roaring good time, and hating rascals — 'specially horse thieves and Indians — when he gets home again what does he do ? — tell the truth about them ? No. He just goes about boasting of what a marvel of courage he is; that he dared to beard the lion in his den; that he has grubbed and bunked with real live cowboys, and still lives to tell the tale. Take that gentleman who entertained us last evening. You'd say he was a cowboy who had grown old without making his pile; that he was ashamed to go back to civilization a pauper; that he had let his beard grow, taken an Indian squaw to his wigwam, and settled down for the rest of his days as a typical squatter. Hundreds of 'um have done just that, but if you are to sample the lot you must at least have one specimen. That fellow never drove a cow or lived a day by farming or trapping. He's an old buffalo hunter, and they are the worst set of fellows the West has produced. You see, they lived the roughest, wildest, most reckless life that a human being knows, while the buffalo lasted. They made money fast and spent it all each time they took a let up. When buffalo gave out there was nothing the country could offer that was wild enough for them. Some of them turned scouts and are running after Indians. Some gave up, clean, and are still lying round cattle towns — what there is left of them — keeping themselves drunk and making all the trouble they can for cowboys, and a lot of them drifted into the highway business and became professional road agents."

"What does the fellow we met last night do for a living?" Oscar asked, and Charlie looked up in astonishment, exclaiming:

"You don't mean to tell me that you did not see through him?"

Oscar shook his head, and Charlie continued: "Well, upon my word! You couldn't have done better if you had. You took hold so easy that I thought you not only caught on at sight, but must have met some friend of the family before."

"Well, you haven't told me what he was, yet," Oscar remarked, a little impatiently.

"Why, a road agent of the road agents, my dear fellow. A man who lives by robbing at sight, and killing as quick where it is the easiest way to come at the property," Charlie replied. "He keeps that watering-trough for the stage horses, and any other prairie joggers, which is enough to cover up his tracks. While they are watering up he doubtless takes his inventory. He's one of a gang — I reckon the boss —

and has a telegraph wire running somewhere, I presume to the gulch this warning speaks of. It's the biggest scheme I ever heard of. I struck the ticker just after you went out last night. I staid behind to get a chance to look round. It was behind the upper bunk, where I lay. That's why I took that bunk. It is an underground wire, and he can keep his pals posted right up to date. See? I didn't know where it went, but I was bound he shouldn't get a chance to use it. Halloo! What's that?"

"A signpost, I should think," Oscar replied, looking forward to where a trail crossed the one they were following at right angles, and a post had been set up with a board across the top.

Charlie laughed. "Signboards would be a new luxury in these parts. I reckon Uncle Sam don't waste that much lumber to tell the Indians the way to their reservations."

"What is it, then?" Oscar asked.

"Time enough to see when we get there," Charlie replied, "and it's high time we took a rest and grubbed up. We sha'n't be troubled till we get into the gulch, I reckon, and we might as well lay in one more good feed while we can; but let's be quick about it, for I should dreadfully like to get through those woods before it's pitch dark."

"What's that in the grass by the post?" Oscar asked.

Charlie shaded his eyes and looked for a moment, then muttered: "An Indian. Bother their red skins! It's a little fellow, though. I wonder if his pa is round," and he looked carefully in every direction. "I don't see any signs of more, but, plague take them! a whole tribe will hide behind a grain of sand or a single stalk of golden-rod."

There were no more about, however, as they drew nearer. The little fellow was simply lying in the grass, idly sunning himself, and a moment later their attention was absorbed by the board nailed upon the post.

"Look at that for a sign, will you?" Charlie said, as they rode up to it. And Oscar did look, with all his eyes.

CHAPTER XIV.

DEAD OR ALIVE.

"Dead or alive!" Oscar read with a shudder, as he wheeled his horse about in front of the sign they had been watching.

"Dead or alive," Charlie repeated as he came into position to read.

Seeing that there was to be a halt, Panza started at a furious run after a rabbit, the moment she could drop the lead line, and no one paid the slightest attention to the little Indian who was lying in the grass beside the post as they approached.

It was the first time that Oscar had ever seen such a sign, or been brought face to face with a grim offer of gold for a human body, dead or alive. With quivering breath he read the description of three desperadoes who had been the terror of the district so long that this measure was at last resorted to, and dead or alive one thousand dollars in gold was offered for each of them, with five hundred extra for the leader.

"I should hate to be in one of those fellows' boots," Oscar said as he finished reading, "and I should everlastingly hate to meet them. Do you suppose there's any danger of their venturing within a hundred miles of this sign?"

"I'm sorry to take away your appetite," Charlie replied, "but perhaps it will help you to appreciate how I feel about Indians. I am inclined to think that these are the very fellows who are waiting for us in the gulch."

"Can't we go round it some way?" Oscar asked, feeling his heart throbbing as he spoke.

"It's probably some gulch where there isn't much show to go around," Charlie replied. "If a stage should come along we might get through all right, but to tell you the honest truth I don't believe that there is one chance in ten for us, if we have to try it alone."

"You don't think the fellow at the sod house had anything to do with these, do you?" Oscar asked.

"It is my impression that he is the fifteen hundred dollar man, himself, if any one only looked into the matter," Charlie replied.

For a moment it almost took Oscar's breath away, but recovering himself he said, "Well, I can tell you one thing: he's a big coward, any way."

"That's true enough," Charlie remarked, in an absent-minded way. "All road agents are cowards. It takes a coward to go into the business, in the first place, and it is a kind of occupation that would make a coward of a man precious quick if he wasn't one at the start. But the meanest and most dangerous skunk that crawls is the coward who has the best of you and knows it."

"Then what are we to do?" Oscar asked.

It was some time before Charlie replied; then he simply said: "I do not know. You have a mission to perform, and a long and useful life ahead of you. It is outrageous to run the risk that we shall have to in that gulch, against such contemptible odds, and all to no purpose. If we turn back, there is the sod house to pass again. If we go to the west on this other trail there will be nothing but Indians. The trails east and south both lead through the gulch. You must take your choice, and I am with you for all that I am worth, the moment that you set the course."

Oscar thought it over for a moment, and very earnestly but calmly replied: "We started for Deadwood, and Deadwood is that way. Let's have some grub and go on."

"Good enough!" Charlie responded, with an enthusiasm which showed that he was much better satisfied with that decision than any other. "When they overhaul us, if we have the shadow of a show we'll make the most of it. If not we'll give in so quickly that it will take their breath away, and see what that will do."

DEAD OR ALIVE.

"You don't mean that you would give in to them while you had a breath of life left, do you?" Oscar exclaimed, indignantly.

"With all my heart, I do," Charlie replied, with a smile. "If they get a bead on me and my shooter isn't handy, they have the drop and can do as they please for the time being. It's my only show for presenting a bill of damages later on. Now let's eat something and feed the horses quickly. We shall need every glimmer of daylight before it is done."

"Where's Panza?" Oscar exclaimed, dismounting, looking about in every direction and whistling.

"I saw her start off after a rabbit as we came up. She's all right. Her nose will bring her back," Charlie remarked, carelessly, and then looking quickly about him, he added: "Where is that Indian boy? Seems to me he's cleared out in a rather sudden way. Plague take the red skins! We don't want any more of a muss than we're in now. I'd like to kick myself for forgetting to watch him."

"There's only one way he could have gone, and that's into those low hills. If Panza were here we'd soon find out," Oscar replied a little reproachfully, and whistled again, but there was no response.

"If it wasn't that the horses have got to eat, we wouldn't stop," Charlie remarked as he took his rifle from the saddle and leaned it against the post. "We won't take off the saddles."

Oscar mechanically followed his example. He was too anxious about Panza to think what he was doing.

The horses quickly took the hint and began to feed. The lead line of the pack horse was dragging. Charlie took it up and was throwing it over the animal's neck when he exclaimed: "Halloo! What's this?"

Oscar turned in nervous haste to see him pulling a strip of shaving from the rope, where it was fastened to the horse.

In dark red letters, plainly traced, they read: "No stop minute here. Heap bad pale face close by. Woods empty. Hurry fast."

"That's blood, and it's still wet," Charlie muttered. "To your horse, Oscar. Be quick."

He caught the lead line in his hand, but before either of them could move, a deep voice, not far behind them, shouted:

"Hands up, or you drop!"

Oscar's hand made a dash for his pistol, but quick as thought Charlie caught it with a grip like iron, and forced it up, saying in a low, stern voice, "Hold up your hands and keep still, or we're gone."

It was in that peculiar tone which, irrespective of grammar or dialect, demanded obedience, and Oscar obeyed. Charlie's hands were up, too, but Oscar noticed that he had dropped the shaving and was grinding it into the earth with his foot.

The voice had sounded from behind, and as they

turned, with their hands up, they discovered the masked heads and the shoulders of three men, ten feet apart, less than a hundred feet away from them, half-hidden in the grass, and evidently protruding from holes dug for the purpose. In a line from each one, through the grass, there shone the subtle shimmer of a rifle.

"See that double-barrel on the right?" Charlie muttered in a low voice. "That's our friend. I thought we should see him again." Then aloud and with a reckless laugh he shouted: "Halloo! there, coyotes! Come out o' yer skunk holes an' scoop yer boodle. Our arms ain't much 'customed ter hangin' toward the sky, an' they'll git ter aikin' bloomin' quick an' may drop on our shooters."

The voice of their late host sounded in reply, "Jest you shift yerselves over so's we kin blow daylight through ye, 'out stuffin' the horses."

With a boisterous laugh Charlie leaned back against the pack horse, calling, "Fire away! Don't be skeered! I'm tougher'n ye think fur, an' you hain't got no gun-fodder thet kin find its way through me ter start a hoss t'other side. But yer want ter look alive, now, fur we ain't a-goin' ter hold our hands up all day, not fur a regiment sech es you. You kin jest dispense with further preliminaries an' git in yer licks pesky lively. Ef it's the outfit yer arter you've got the bulge on us, an' we hollers, so take it an' be gone.

But ef it's target shootin', we're with ye. Empty them four bar'ls ye've got atween ye, an' see whar yer fetch up. If thar's ten seconds o' breathin' space left in eraone o' us, it's mighty likely ter be the last time thet some o' you fellers runs his eye along a rifle bar'l. Speak up quick, now. Biz is biz, an' it's gettin' late. Will you take the outfit an' leave us without a scratch, or will you clean yer guns an' take the consequences?"

For a moment there was a consultation in a low tone, when the voice replied, "Well, pard, sence yer make the offer, p'raps we'll put up with the outfit."

"Do ye gin yer word of honor, not a scratch?" Charlie asked, in the same cool, jovial way.

"Honor bright," the man replied, and Charlie called:

"Let her go, then! The outfit's yours."

One of the men came out of his hole, and deftly and swiftly relieved them of their pistols, cartridge belts, knives and watches, laughing and joking with Charlie all the time.

"Got some rope handy, pard, thet I kin use ter anchor ye onter thet hitchin' post?" the man asked, nodding toward the post which held the notice offering a thousand dollars for his body, dead or alive.

"What do ye take us fur?" Charlie responded. "Think we're bull-whackers, ter carry a rope on our saddles? Mebby ye'll find a piece on the pack saddle, but ye'll want ter save out 'nough ter tow the youngster's hoss with, fur thar ain't none on ye kin straddle him."

Oscar's heart seemed ready to break as he stood there holding up his hands for that ruffian. He was acting under Charlie's orders, without any cowardice in his nature to help him out. He thought of Panza and Sancho, and of his own bitter humiliation, and it required more courage and self-control to stand there than it would to have caught his pistol and faced the whole of them.

"Hurry up, now," Charlie exclaimed, as the other two men came up. "It's more than a feller's life is worth ter hang round this way too long. Farsten us onter the post an' git out. I'm in a hurry ter be on my way ag'in."

The men all laughed at this; and as they tied their hands and feet, and then tied them back to back, with the post between them, one of them remarked: "I reckon ye won't travel fur from here fur one while. Folks isn't frequent goin' this way, these days, an' yer'll have ter wait till some one comes along."

"What 'bout Injins?" Charlie asked.

"Don't know nor care," their host replied, with a surly grunt. "We hain't made no promises fur nobody but ourselves."

"Thar, Capt'n Bill," said one of the men, when the work was finished and they stepped back to look at it, "that's a putty pair o' witnesses ter the above-mentioned notice. It'll look well in Eastern papers, won't it? 'Two fellers cleaned out, an' lef' tied to a notice offerin' three thousand five hundred dollars in cold cash, fur the heads o' them as did it.'"

They all burst into a loud laugh, and the one addressed as Captain Bill, the man who carried the roer, took a quid of tobacco from his mouth and threw it at the notice, saying, "My compliments ter the men as backs it with their gold."

"Good shot," muttered another man. "It struck clean on yer own pictur. Be keerful ye don't go throw it in yer own face instead o' their'n, by some slip."

With that they turned away.

Three times one of them tried to mount Sancho and failed. Then he gave up in despair.

"Never mind," said Captain Bill. "Straddle the other one and lead the two. We'll go down an' git the mules an' meet yer by the brook."

Sancho still rebelled, but as the other two horses moved away he reluctantly yielded. The man was careful not to injure him, for he thought much more of the value of horse-flesh than humanity. Oscar ground his teeth till the men had turned away. Then great, bitter tears came crowding from his eyes and down his cheeks to fall upon his shirt. He was glad that Charlie's back was toward him, so that he could not see him cry. He would have been more astonished than he was by the rifles of the highwaymen, if his own back had not been turned; if he could have looked behind him and seen the blood-shot eyes and the bronzed cheeks wet with tears on the other side of the post.

Charlie's voice was husky, but Oscar did not suspect the cause, as he said cheerfully: "Well, we're much better out of it than I expected. I didn't suppose they'd keep their promise after they'd once got our guns, and I surely thought they'd take our coats and boots; I reckon they have another job on hand and were in a hurry. Tell me when they're out of sight, and we'll begin."

"For mercy's sake, begin what, Charlie?" Oscar asked, in a choking voice.

"Begin getting ready to recover our outfit, and collect a bill for damages," Charlie muttered.

"Do you suppose there's any way that I can ever get Sancho back?" Oscar asked, wholly unable to comprehend Charlie's words.

"Keep up your courage, my dear fellow," Charlie responded. "I don't suppose anything about it, now. I know that if I live to see you reach Deadwood, it will be on Sancho's back, with three thousand five hundred dollars worth of human flesh rounded up, alive or dead, in front of you. Now then. Can you push against this post without hurting you?"

"Of course I can, but I can't do anything else," Oscar replied.

"That's enough for now," said Charlie, cheerfully. "I will count 'One, two.' You push on one and I will push back on two. We'll work the post loose in no time and lift it out from between us, see?"

"What fools those fellows were!" Oscar exclaimed, as they stood, at last, free, hand and foot. But the moment so much was gained, he thought of his two friends again, and anxiously asked, "Do you think that they killed Panza?"

"We can look around their holes and see," Charlie responded, walking out in that direction. "If they did it was with a knife, and she'll be close by. I rather think, though, that your little Indian was at the bottom of that."

"Who was he, any way?" Oscar muttered, thinking of a possibility that the Indian had carried Panza off, and forgetting the rest.

"You'd know, Oscar, if you'd put on your thinking cap," Charlie replied; "but look at those holes. They're the neatest idea I ever struck. They've been used before. I tell you that gang has got things down fine. No; Panza is not here. That settles that, any way."

"I tell you, Charlie, that I don't know anything about that Indian. What makes you keep saying so?" Oscar exclaimed.

"Why, it's this way," Charlie said, lying down in the grass. "That piece of shaving was precisely the same as he used for the first message, and the writing was the same. He wrote it with his blood, this time, because he was in haste and had no burned sticks handy. He did it himself, and after we came up, for it was wet when I found it. He left the message this morning, thinking that the fellows would be in the gulch. When he discovered that they were here, there was nothing for him to do but lie round and warn us, if we were fools enough to stop over that notice. Jiminy! what a nerve that little fellow had to lie down and wait right in range of three rifles, when he knew he wasn't wanted, and that those fellows would have shot him as quickly as they would a rat. He knew we had the dog along, and that his smeller might work the mischief, for our only chance was to slip by in a hurry without noticing them, so he caught that rabbit over in the hills, and the moment we stopped, let him loose under Panza's nose. That disposed of her. I thought it was a queer place for a rabbit to be roosting, and I wondered when he started up that he hadn't left before. Now I have studied it out. Well, the next thing was to warn us. If he had done it openly it would have been sure death to the whole of us, without a whisper, just as bad as if Panza had struck on them. He did the best he could, and if we had found that notice before we had laid down our rifles and left our saddles, I think we should have escaped. Now he is no friend of mine, so he must be a friend of yours. And all I've got to say is that one such little hero is enough to lift the whole red skin race more than one peg in my estimation. I shall think twice before I shoot another Indian, God bless him!"

"Charlie," Oscar said earnestly, "I know you're wrong, some way, for I haven't got such a friend, and I don't deserve one. I never did a real kind turn for any one. But I will, if I live. You see if I don't."

"Just now I'm more anxious to see something else," Charlie replied, rising and walking toward the post. "'Captain Bill' is what they called the fellow from the sod house, and they said he hit his own picture with that tobacco. I'm ready to bet my boots that I was right when I told you he was the fifteen hundred dollar man. There! Look at that! There's no guess work about it now. Let's set her up again. It'll make good reading for others, and literature is scarce in these parts."

As they dropped the post into the hole again Charlie added, "To-morrow at this time, that offer will be obsolete, or I shall have handed in my checks." Then throwing himself on the ground beside the post, he stretched, yawned, and smiling at Oscar's anxious face said: "Sit down and take life easy while you can. There's no use watching out when we've nothing to fight with. There's no good in being hungry when we've nothing to eat. There's no sense in anything but being tired when the only thing you can do is rest; and without one atom of slang, I can very truly say that those fellows made me tired."

"I wish I knew about Panza," Oscar said as he sat down.

"Well, I wish I was half as sure that you would reach Deadwood all right as I am that she will turn up," Charlie replied. "To tell the truth, I'm rather glad she stays away, for I'm pretty sure the little Indian has got her, and if he has, he's hunting for some way to lend us a hand. I'm not particularly good natured with myself for hating his folks the way I have."

"Supposing you're right, Charlie, how could he have got here? He surely didn't follow us by rail," Oscar said.

"Well, if the Mennonites told him we were going to Bismarck he might have thought that he could help us through the Indian country and started in. Then if he found we left the trail for Pembina, the amount of common sense he has displayed would have suggested that we were going by rail, and if he was tough and his pony tougher, he could have cut across and reached there before us. Don't you remember my speaking of a lank little Indian boy who kept dodging us at Bismarck " —

"And how Panza knew him, and I didn't believe it?" Oscar interrupted.

"Look there!" Charlie whispered, suddenly lifting his head and pointing down the trail which led into the hills, in the only direction where the prairie was broken; for in spite of his apparent carelessness the habit to "watch out" was strong.

"A horse!" Oscar exclaimed, springing to his feet. "An Indian pony! Without a rider! And — Charlie! For mercy's sake! It is — it's Panza leading him."

"God bless that little Indian!" Charlie said earnestly, as he rose to his feet. "Yes; I thought so. That's the same white pony that we saw in Manitoba, only he's pretty well jaded now, for he's seen hard times."

Panza had become an expert leader, and was soon beside them. She had evidently been restrained by force, for her collar was torn and scratched, but she was beginning to comprehend, and very humbly licked Oscar's hand as if to atone for bad behavior.

Upon the pony's back was strapped a simple Indian blanket, and fastened to the strap were a rifle, six-shooter and double cartridge belt.

"Those were my father's," Oscar cried, as he caught sight of them. "See! His initials!"

"Well, what do you think about your Indian now?" Charlie asked. "And here is something," he added, pulling a folded strip of brown paper from a slit cut in the blanket. "The dear little thief stole this from the wrapper round our cartridge case when he was at the pack saddle. How did he come by a pencil? Oh! I see. He wrote it with a bullet. There's where he wiped off the wax," and leaning back against the pony he read: "Heap bad pale face gone woods. Eat. Sleep. No watch to-night. Indian pony heap strong. Two can ride. Ride fast. Dog find bad pale face. Kill. Kill. Tie Indian pony where water cross trail."

As he finished reading Charlie brushed his hand quickly across his eyes and muttered, "Mountain Charlie's spoke his last hard word ag'in a red skin, so help me!" Then he gave a little start, as if to shake himself from the mood that was upon him, and carelessly inquired: "How are these irons for aim, Oscar? Have you ever tried them?"

"I have snuffed a candle at thirty paces, with this rifle," Oscar replied with pride.

"Good 'nough," Charlie observed. "Then you keep that. Let me give this pistol a try. Take that *o* in the 'or' up there." He tossed the heavy six-shooter with a twirl into the air, and as it came down, turning over and over, he caught it, cocked and fired it, before his hand had hardly seemed to touch it, and Oscar looked in blank astonishment at the notice, where a bullet hole appeared in the very center of the *o*, between "Dead" and "Alive."

"That'll do," Charlie remarked, as he returned the

pistol to its case, put a few cartridges in his pocket and gave the belt to Oscar. "Now for the gulch. 'Twould be kind of mean to make that little pony carry both of us, but here's an Indian trick." He took the rope which had bound them, made a fast collar at one end and a loop at the other. He threw the collar over the pony's neck and the loop round his own body under his arms.

"Now, then," he said, "put Panza on Sancho's track, hop up and ride after her as fast as you can get over the ground. We sha'n't be a minute too soon. If I get tired running behind I'll change with you for a while."

It was after sundown when they saw the irregular outline of trees ahead, with rugged, rising ground on either side, and knew that they were approaching the gulch.

They were walking, leading the pony, keeping Panza close between them as they entered.

"It's death or victory this time," Charlie whispered. "If they see us first and give us the hold up just get a bead and fire, quicker than lightning. There's always a chance that they may miss or not kill, at any rate. Take advantage of it in advance."

"I'll do my best, Charlie," Oscar replied earnestly.

They reached the brook, crossing the trail, and on the other side Panza seemed at a loss. She could not find the track again.

"That's all right," Charlie said, in a low voice. "It's another little game that those fellows work. They leave the trail here and go up in the middle of the stream. They are somewhere on this brook. This is where the Indian wanted his pony left, but I wouldn't tie him yet. You may need him. Keep close to him and keep Panza with you. If I want you I will whistle three times. If there's shooting and it's all right but I don't need you, I'll whistle once. But if you hear a shot and I don't whistle, just follow this trail and make for the other end of the gulch as fast as that pony's legs can fly; for there'll be nothing you can do for me."

Oscar caught Charlie by the shoulder. "Do you mean that I am to sit here while you go in?" he asked.

"It's the best way. We can't talk about it now. Remember what I say, and fire to kill if any one tries to stop you," Charlie answered hurriedly, trying to push off Oscar's hand.

"Do you think I will save myself that way?" Oscar muttered.

"It's the only way, just now, Oscar," Charlie replied. "Your life is much more valuable than mine, and there is no sense in your running this risk."

Charlie was turning away in spite of him, but Oscar whispered: "Very well. You take one side of the brook and I will take the other. I am going in there with you, Charlie."

Charlie saw that it was useless dissuading, and waited till the pony was tied, and with Panza again between them, they crept along the brook.

Any one who has ever made his way through a strange and rocky forest, so dark that he could not see his own hands, can appreciate the difficulty which greeted them; added to which was the constant possibility of stumbling upon a party of sleeping outlaws or walking into their midst to find them wide awake and watching. They did not dare to move out of reach of each other or speak, even in a whisper.

For fifteen minutes they made their way as rapidly as possible. Many a noise caused Oscar's heart to throb violently, but his hand was steady upon the rifle, and his foot was firm.

Suddenly Panza began a low growl. Oscar stopped her instantly, and pausing for a moment they listened and looked about them. They had kept by the brook, guided by the sound of the water; but now, above it, they heard the faint sound of voices, laughing, a little to the right. There was a dense growth of foliage upon that side, but looking into them they could distinguish the glow of a fire dimly reflected on some of the leaves.

In five minutes more they were beyond the bushes and a wall of rock which inclosed a natural fortress; a great corral which nature had built there for some better purpose than sheltering desperadoes. Neither spoke. It was no time for words. They were in the secret den of the outlaws, and life and death hung upon a single blunder. There was a flat surface two hundred feet in diameter, surrounded by the great wall and hedge. It was completely covered with large trees, and in the center a bright fire was burning. Upon one side of the corral they saw the indistinct figures of the horses and mules, and Oscar had hard work to prevent Panza from making a dash, as he would have been glad to himself, to those dim outlines, knowing that Sancho must be there; but sitting on the ground, all on one side of the fire, were the three outlaws. A cold shiver ran over Oscar as he looked at the grim and ugly unmasked faces. The litter of a camp was scattered about them. They were eating. Captain Bill sat at one end.

Oscar fell behind to follow Charlie's lead, and cautiously and noiselessly they crept forward among the trees till they reached a point directly opposite, where the three were sitting, with the fire between them.

"Are you all right, Oscar? steady and firm?" Charlie whispered.

"Yes," was the quiet reply, though in his heart Oscar knew that he was trembling and shivering with fear; and every time that he looked across those glowing coals at the savage faces, illuminated till they seemed to glare and flash with the fire, he felt the cold perspiration gather on his forehead.

"There's no danger of their seeing us. They can not see five feet beyond the fire. Can you do some fancy shooting to show off?" Charlie asked.

Oscar could scarcely control his lips to whisper, "I'll do my best."

"All right. I'll make them think we're a squad of Government scouts. Draw a bead on Captain Bill. You'll find you can line as sure in this light as by the sun. If he goes for his gun when I speak you will have to fire, and fire to kill. I'll look out for the other two. Have an extra cartridge ready to slap in quick if we put in a fancy shot. Are you ready?"

"All ready," Oscar gasped, as he stood with his rifle resting against the tree to steady it and his eye along the sight upon a point just below the shoulder of the outlaw. He was stifling — choking. His heart, with heavy throbs, seemed to shut his throat so that he could not breathe.

"If Charlie knew what a coward I am," he thought, as he stood there, quaking, waiting for the fatal word that should disclose their presence, sure that if Captain Bill should so much as look at him he would be utterly helpless.

Hark! Was that Charlie's voice? Clear, firm and loud it shouted:

"Now then, gentlemen, hands up!"

Captain Bill's hands went up like a flash, one of them still holding a tin coffee cup, with a long ladle handle. The man next him followed as quickly, dropping a knife; but the third man made a sudden move and caught a pistol lying beside him. Oscar saw the act, saw the man's thumb cocking the revolver, heard the crash of Charlie's heavy six-shooter, saw the pistol fall and heard a groan and an oath as the man's hands went up, one of them covered with blood.

"That thumb will never lift another hammer, sir," came in cool, clear tones from Charlie. "Sorry you obliged us to spoil it, but another motion on your part and we shall be obliged to spoil you, too. To convince you, gentlemen, that there is no mistake about this, I will ask you, Captain Bill, to hold that cup steady, on your life. I am going to knock the handle off, and one of the two men who are now covering your heart, will empty out the coffee through a hole in the bottom. Steady, now; one, two, three!"

While Charlie was speaking Oscar raised his rifle till it covered less than two inches of the cup which flashed in the firelight under the outlaw's hand. He noticed that the hand was trembling and aimed as low as he dared. When he saw the flash of Charlie's pistol he pulled the trigger; then, quick as thought, discharged the empty cartridge, slipping in a fresh one, and as he lifted his rifle again glanced across the fire to see the handle of the cup dangling in the air, and the bottom completely blown away. Charlie called:

"You held that well. I think you are not hurt."

"P'raps I ain't," growled the squatter, with a savage Indian grunt; "but I don't keer ter hold no more targets fur your fellers to fool away gun-fodder on. What do yer want, any way?"

"In the first place," Charlie replied, "I want to say to all of you, gentlemen, that two dead shot cover each one of you, and that if you move one hair you drop, without a word of warning. You understand me, gentlemen? You are worth just as much cold cash dead as alive, and it will be easier to transport you dead than any other way. Now I have a young man here, Captain, who was coming from Bismarck with a friend, when you and your associates overhauled him, this afternoon."

"Curse the kid! I wish we'd killed him as I said," the outlaw interrupted.

"Another time, Captain, another time," Charlie responded. "At present he will examine you and your associates and recover his own property and that of his friend. And while you are about it, young man, you may take charge of whatever weapons you come across."

"Yes, sir," Oscar answered, in a loud voice, and handing Charlie the rifle and some cartridges he started quickly toward the trio. As he stepped into the light his heart failed for an instant; only long enough to recall the fact that the last time he thought of himself he was calling himself a cringing coward, steadying his hand against a tree and saying that if Captain Bill should look at him he would be utterly helpless. From the moment Charlie's voice sounded he had so entirely forgotten himself that he did not know whether his heart had beat or not.

He began with Captain Bill, for he knew that he should feel much easier to be sure that he had no weapons about him, and he felt the words of encouragement that were intended for him as Charlie's voice sounded, commanding the imaginary squad:

"Stand steady, boys, and drop the first man who moves. It's money in your pockets to accommodate them, if they want to die."

With the second man Oscar found that the work was much easier, and by the time he had relieved the third he even stopped and carefully bound up the wounded thumb with his handkerchief.

It required several trips to carry everything to where Charlie was standing guard. When he came with the last Charlie said: "You did that well, young man. A little experience of this sort will not hurt you if you expect to grow up in these parts. The sergeant has a coil of rope and some line. Tie these gentlemen's hands behind their backs, and tie them together by their necks, four feet apart."

As he spoke he handed Oscar the rope which had already played so many parts that day, and a ball of strong twine from his pocket.

Returning again, when this was accomplished, Oscar took the position of guard while Charlie with Panza, went in search of the horses. He found them carefully corraled and well fed. The moon had crept over the mountains and now shone into the gulch, and by the help of an occasional match, for an instant, he soon had them ready to start; the mules and pack horse tied together; the captured arms and ammunition rolled in blankets and strapped upon the saddles. He brought up a pail of water and took the box of crackers from the pack; a most welcome sight, for they had eaten nothing since breakfast, and when all was ready, with eyes and ears upon their prisoners, they began their lunch.

"What are we going to do next?" Oscar asked.

"Get out of this gulch right away, if you think you can stand it," Charlie replied. "The fact is, we have not struck their headquarters. This is only a way station. I don't know whether they intended to spend the night here or are simply waiting for some one. It's likely enough there's more than three, you know, and it would be too bad to have another fellow drop in now, and turn the tables back again. They are too easy for men going to the gallows. They expect to get off in some way, and the quicker we are out of this gulch the better."

"All right," Oscar replied, grasping his rifle and mounting.

Charlie took the rifle and belt which the Indian had sent them, with a piece of bacon and some crackers rolled in a blanket, to leave on the pony as they passed. "They must walk first," he whispered, as his last instructions. "You ride about twenty feet behind. I'll be close after you leading the pack. Remember life depends on being quick and sure if there is the shadow of a necessity to fire."

They filled their shirt fronts with the remaining crackers to eat on the way. Charlie tied the lead line to his saddle and mounted. It was already so light from the moon that had it not been for the fire directly in front of them, the men must surely have been able to see them; but they had comparatively little to fear from that immediate quarter now. Only on the chance of carrying out the illusion a little farther Charlie called:

"Attention! Boys! All ready! Now then, gentlemen, I must trouble you to stand up."

They made very slow work of getting on their feet; but when they were standing at last, Charlie continued: "We are going down the brook to the trail. If one of you speaks or the slightest thing occurs that is out of order, or we have any trouble from outside, you three men will drop in a bunch, before you draw a second breath. Those are orders. Now then, forward!"

They reached the trail, and turning to the right they followed it all night, at that dragging pace which the prisoners, with hands tied, necessitated. Every shadow seemed some friend of their captives coming to rescue them. Every sound suggested Indians ready to murder the whole of them. It seemed to Oscar the longest night he had ever known. It was almost morning when they emerged from the gulch upon a broken prairie land, and even then the lagging daylight would not come. There was not a cabin, hut or tepee anywhere, or any sign of life; nothing but the twisting trail, forever winding away in front of them, as far as the eye could reach.

At last the sun came up, however, and far ahead of them Oscar saw a better beaten path joining the trail, and knew that it must be the stage route they were looking for. By the time they reached it the prisoners could scarcely stand or drag one foot after the other, and humanity forced Charlie to abandon the wisest course, and call a halt.

It was the first word which had been spoken since they left the brook and took the trail. The men were thoroughly exhausted, and instantly dropped upon the ground, while Oscar quickly untied their hands, and tied their feet together instead. They might have refused to go farther long before, but for the reminder that the price upon their heads was "dead or alive," and the impression that their captors needed very little excuse to take advantage of the fact; in which they were judging others by themselves.

Charlie sat in his saddle, rifle in hand, while the work was going on, then said, "Now, Oscar, you did it all last night, and if you'll stand guard this morning I will see what I can do."

A fire was soon burning, venison was roasting, coffee was boiling, and bacon frying, and half of their remaining supply of flour and meal was mixed for prairie pancakes. After breakfast Charlie took the

THEY EMERGED FROM THE GULCH.

watch, telling Oscar to roll up without delay and sleep. For a moment he demurred, but he did not realize that Charlie had lain awake all night in the sod house as well, and he easily yielded, for his eyes would hardly keep open, even for breakfast. As he stretched out upon the ground, with his rifle beside him, and drew a blanket over his face, he heard Charlie say:

"Well, fellers, the best I kin do for yer is ter say flop over on yer backs and go ter sleep," and he felt a cold shiver as Captain Bill's voice sounded for the first time, asking:

"Whar's the rest o' yer regemunt?"

"There's enough of it here ter manage you fellers," Charlie replied, with a laugh.

"Do you tell me that you two kittens wus alone, and bagged us three old rats?" the squatter asked, in blank astonishment.

"That's about the size of it," Charlie answered.

Oscar was peeking from under his blanket, and in spite of his tired muscles and sleepy eyes he laughed aloud as the sullen old outlaw gave one powerful grunt and lay down.

Charlie began his watch, and a tough one it was. Every one about him was soundly sleeping. Even Panza was stretched at full length on the ground, and the horses and mules were all asleep. The sun was hot. The sky was without a cloud. Sometimes it seemed utterly impossible to keep awake, and as he walked steadily up and down beside the prisoners he more than once stumbled, and roused himself to find that he had been tramping in his sleep.

At last he yielded to the temptation to look at his watch. Four hours had dragged themselves away since Oscar lay down. He made up his mind that he must call him at the next turn. There was no help for it. But one of the prisoners started up, with a cry. He was simply dreaming, but it roused Charlie from his stupor in an instant, and he found that he could give Oscar a little longer rest.

Another half-hour wore away, when he caught himself yielding again, and turned to take one careful survey of their surroundings before waking Oscar and turning in.

"What's that?" he muttered, as his eye caught a speck, a dark shadow, in a cloud of dust, moving along the side of a distant knoll. "If it's Indians, or friends of these fellows, we're done for. But it's long past time for the Deadwood stage." He shaded his eyes, and watched till the shadow disappeared behind rising ground; but his eyes were too tired to serve him. He could make nothing out of it.

He woke Oscar, and started Sancho and his own horse to their feet.

"There's something coming from the north," he whispered. "You'll see it, presently, right there. If it is Indians, or anything doubtful, we had better leave and light out for Deadwood, for these fellows are in with the red skins, and they may have no end of friends about."

The object came in sight again. It was nearer, and in a better position. Oscar looked carefully, with shaded eyes, while Charlie watched the prisoners.

CHAPTER XV.

DEADWOOD.

"I SHOULD think it was a stage coach," Oscar whispered.

"Don't make a mistake, now," Charlie said, in a voice that was almost pathetic. "I don't feel much like fighting Indians this morning."

"I am not mistaken," Oscar said slowly. "It's not Indians, sure. And it is a stage coach. There are four horses ahead, and people sitting on top. It's a stage, sure, Charlie."

"Give me your hand," Charlie exclaimed, in a deep earnest voice. "Thank Heaven! we are out of the most dangerous hole we could have got into this side of either ocean."

"I don't suppose there has really been much danger since we got them tied up, has there?" Oscar asked, in astonishment at Charlie's earnestness. And he noticed, for the first time, how pale and haggard Charlie's face looked in the sunlight.

His friend smiled as he replied: "Since I rapped on the sod house door there has not been one minute when the chances were not better that the next one would find us dead than alive, yet here we are, with three of the biggest desperadoes in the country tied neck and heels, and the Deadwood stage coming up. Oscar Peterson, you are a trump, through and through. There isn't a ranger on the plains to-day who can hold a candle to you. And next to you, God bless your little Indian!"

"Don't you talk that way, Charlie," Oscar exclaimed excitedly, while tears filled his eyes. "I know who it was who did it all, with the help of the Indian's pony and guns. If I am ever one half as brave as you are I shall be satisfied. And when I think how much I owe to you "—

"Bosh!" Charlie muttered, turning quickly away and going over to the prisoners.

"Wake up, boys," he shouted; "you've had five hours to rest, and the cars are coming. Look alive, now. We haven't grub enough to offer you another meal, but here's hot coffee. Down with it, quickly, and be on your feet."

"What's the row?" the squatter asked sullenly, drinking the coffee, while Charlie untied their feet and prepared to tie their hands, and Oscar mounted Sancho and sat on guard.

"There's no row unless you make it, and we should

put a stop to that precious quick, I tell you. Uncle Sam's letter-box is coming, and we want to make a good-looking squad. See?"

"The stage!" An obvious shudder ran through the trio. Captain Bill glanced quickly about him, as though in search of some weapon. Oscar's rifle flew to his shoulder; Charlie stepped back and caught his pistol from his belt.

"Dead or alive, now," he exclaimed. "You fellows stand up; and do it quick! Now put your hands behind your backs and hold them still. One motion while I am tying them, and what's left of you will go to Deadwood on the tailboard of the stage."

The rope around their necks proved an excellent precaution against a sudden break, and Charlie finished his work without another move. When it was done Captain Bill muttered: "Look a-here! ef we hadn't a-let you off yesterday we'd 'a' been O K terday. Now money's what yer arter. You've got back yer kit. Take us ter Deadwood, an' yer in three thousand five hundred. Jest cut these ropes an' gin us back our mules an' shootin'-irons, an' we'll send ye, by the next stage, five thousand dollars in clean gold. Now that's fair."

Oscar started up the mules and pack horse, and formed them in line as Charlie replied: "So far as you're concerned, Captain Bill, I reckon you mean it to be fair; but lookin' at the matter from my side

I'm 'gin your biz, on principle. I may want ter go
through that gulch ag'in. And thar's others has es
good a right. Now I'll tell yer jest es 'tis. I'd ruther
turn you fellers over ter Uncle Sam, an' pay him five
thousand dollars out o' my own pocket, ter keep yer
out o' mischief, than ter let yer go ag'in in swap fur
the hull of Dakota."

"Fools we were not ter try our chances when we
had our hands free," the outlaw muttered.

As the stage approached the driver looked suspiciously at the little group, and drew up fifty yards away,
calling to know who they were and what they wanted,
while two men, who sat behind him to guard the mails,
made an ostentatious display of their rifles.

"Harry Porter! by the powers!" Charlie shouted,
catching off his hat and swinging it lustily.

The driver looked sharp from under his broad brim
for an instant, then, quickly tossing the reins to the
man who sat beside him, whose duty it was to handle
the long whip, he left the high seat at a single bound,
and made for Charlie as fast as his legs could carry
him.

Oscar did not dare to take his eyes for an instant
from the prisoners, but he overheard enough to know
that they were college classmates who had parted in
dress suits after the graduation reception, under the
shadow of the Cambridge elms, to meet in this way on
the Deadwood trail.

"I reckon you didn't get held up last night, in spite of your being so late," Charlie said.

"No, I didn't," his friend replied; "I hung up t'other side, and waited for daylight. It's getting too thick for me in there after dark. I haven't made a trip for three weeks without a scrimmage or a clean hold up. Look at that hat o' mine. There's three bullet holes come in it back there, at various times.

MEETING ON THE DEADWOOD TRAIL.

I said to myself, 'it's three times and out; and I'm not going to have my hat ruined completely,' so I hung up for daylight, though it'll make me late in."

"Well, you're right, Harry; it is three times and out," Charlie remarked. "There's your men. We treed them and brought them out of the gulch last night. If you will transport them to the Deadwood authorities, with our compliments, it will be the best thing you can do for that hat, now I tell you."

Harry stepped over and inspected the prisoners, stopping short before Captain Bill, taking off his hat, bowing very low, and saying: "How do you do, sir? I never was more delighted in my life. I should know you anywhere, mask or no mask. Look at that hole through the crown of my sombrero? It was a big double-barrel cannon of yours that put that there. It came precious near calling for my checks. Yes, sir; I'll see you safe to Deadwood, as cheerfully as ever I carried a bail o' goods in all my days. Haul up this way, Jerry," he called to the man who held the reins. "'*Tempus fugits*,' as my friend here has often remarked while he was loading paper guns with Latin powder and Greek shot. Just hustle in on the back seat there, now. That'll do." Then turning to the two men on the mail seat he said: "All the danger is inside, now. You can put up your rifles and get out your navies, and go in out of the wet."

The officers took the three men in hand. Oscar and Charlie refused Harry's urging that they go on with him, but Charlie got out the double-barreled roer and, consulting Oscar, presented it to his friend as a memento in which he had a personal interest. Then, promising to see him in Deadwood, they watched the stage drive away.

"Well, if that's not a mountain off, there never was one," Charlie said, with a sigh of relief. "Now let's have some grub, and then if you will watch out for three hours, while I sleep, I'll be ready for anything that comes along."

Fortunately nothing did come along, and two hours before sunset they started again.

"We'll make an easy stage this time," Charlie said, "and bunk early, so the horses will be ready for a daylight start, and look reasonably fresh. We want to put on all the style we can for Deadwood."

Ranches appeared occasionally, and many a little cluster of mining huts, as they neared Deadwood. The hills rose about them in ragged and irregular mound and cones, full of gorges and ravines, often covered with a low growth of scraggy pines, with gaunt dead trunks rising grim and black, testifying to some forest fire in years gone by.

"I don't wonder they have had trouble with Indians here," Oscar remarked. "If I were an Indian I would ask no better place to make myself at home."

"Well, they have just done it," Charlie replied. "There isn't a foot of ground about us that hasn't felt an Indian on the war path. Look at those graves down in the bottom of this gulch! 'Killed by the Indians.' That's the record you would find on the wooden tombstones there, if it is not obliterated. Times are a good deal changed since the first rush to these parts, and the furious objection which the Indian made at the start. Travelers used to bunch up in gangs of fifty or a hundred, if they could, and make a perfect caravan with their long line of teams. At night they would strike for the highest lump of land they could find, and back their carts, one after another, so as to make a circle round the top. They would cook and eat in there, and when the horses and mules or oxen had fed they would pull them into the corral,

"ONLY WAITING FOR A SHOW."

too, and all sleep together. It was the only way they could get through alive, for from one end to the other they were watched by the red skins, who were only waiting for a show to pounce upon them. When I was coming up the last time, we hit upon a party of eight that had been attacked and every scalp lifted. Some of the bodies were horribly mutilated. The wagons had been ransacked, and all the animals carried off. We could only do what hundreds had done before us under similar circumstances; dig a hole, put the bodies in it and cover them up, take a board from one of the wagons and plant it at the head, with all the names of the party that we could discover burned upon it with a hot iron, and at the bottom, 'Killed by Indians.' Then we went on our way again, cursing the red man."

In time the straggling camps and cabins assumed more prominence. The path was better beaten, and occasionally they met people walking or riding upon it. Gradually, too, as they came back again into civilization, it was evident that the entire atmosphere was different from what they had experienced before. The people they met, and everything pertaining to them, was different. There was nothing in any way to suggest the trading-post of Pembina. There was nothing to suggest the slightest resemblance to the farming town of Casselton. There was no odor of the shipping interests of Bismarck. Everything, everywhere, was mining, pure and simple. It was as if they had come out upon another world with another race of people. There had been miners in the streets of the other cities, but they seemed like strangers there. Oscar felt like just as much a stranger and as much out of place in entering Deadwood.

Here and there the mines appeared along the hill-

THEY ENTERED DEADWOOD.

sides and up the valleys and gulches — discolored patches where the earth had been thrown out, most of them sodden and heavy, indicative that the anxious searchers had dug and failed and gone away; while many were only just begun, and men were working with pick and shovel and wheelbarrow, or lounging about the most disconsolate of little shanties.

Even their language — the words they used and the way they used them — was unlike anything Oscar had ever heard, and he began to realize the truth of what Charlie had told him; that each of the great occupations of the frontier, with its isolated circle of devotees, had its own lingo; a lingo which came with it, and was as much a part of it as the pick, the rope, the bull-whip or the mode of dress.

It was difficult to tell just when they really entered Deadwood. It was growing dark, but to Oscar's wide-open eyes and nervously excited condition it seemed the strangest combination in which one could possibly find himself. There was nothing that was like the mines which he had seen in England, or the well-regulated mines on the estate at home. There was no order, system or harmony in anything; but a great, free race to guard against Indians, highwaymen and starvation, and make a fortune, if possible, regardless of any one else, and the quicker the better; from above the ground or underground; in gulch or cliff; by washing, crushing or smelting, and to exist, the while, in hole or dugout, log cabin, sod house, adobe hut, board shanty or tasteful residence — all of which were within sight at a single glance.

Now the houses stood so high above the street that to reach them one must literally climb, while within a stone's throw they would be so far below the street that only a ship's plank seemed required to walk into the second story windows, if they had any, or out upon the roof.

As they rode slowly down the narrow valley which forms one arm of the Y-shaped city, Oscar said with a shudder:

"I wouldn't change places with one of these fellows here if in the end I got a pile of dust as big as that hill."

Charlie turned slowly about in his saddle and asked, "Is there any one in the world with whom you would change places, Oscar?"

"Dear me! Thousands," Oscar exclaimed. "Why, I can hardly keep myself from envying almost everybody."

"You may envy people some particular advantages they have which if you had you could utilize," Charlie replied thoughtfully; "but you just go ahead, now, and fix on one solitary mortal with whom you would be willing to change places, body and soul — all circumstances, ambitions and conditions included, I mean."

"Maybe that's a little different," Oscar said, and rode on in silence for a moment. Then he exclaimed: "Why, upon my word, Charlie, I never thought of it that way. I don't believe that I should really care to change places that way with any one that I know. It sounds queer and conceited to say so, and surely I am not over-well satisfied with some circumstances in my own life."

"No one ever is," Charlie interrupted. "At least if he is, he is to be pitied. And on the other hand we know precious little about the skeletons in other people's closets. We only know the most hopeful and promising side, and yet, unless you strike an out and out fool, I don't believe you'll find the man who would be willing to swap, clean over, sight unseen, taking only what he thinks the condition of any other man that lives."

"What made those fellows stare at us that way as they passed?" Oscar asked abruptly.

"Did they? I didn't notice them. I was talking metaphysics, and I didn't even look at them," Charlie replied, with a careless laugh.

"They certainly did," Oscar repeated, decidedly. "They were looking at us very sharp, every one of them. As they came up abreast they slowed down a little, and then they looked back again after they were on ahead. They were certainly talking about us."

"And now we're talking about them, to pay them

back," Charlie observed, laughing. "I reckon 'twas only because we're strangers here. One would think that in a place like this, where everybody's a stranger, they'd get so used to such a sight as to turn away from it in disgust. But there's no place on earth like these mining towns for curiosity concerning new people. A New England village is nowhere. Thirteen years ago, while I was trying my luck here at losing everything, even to grub-stakes, there was a tenderfoot came sliding down the street at a lively pace, on a likely piece of horse flesh, taking an airing, and thinking himself a full-fledged frontier feller, when an old settler stepped out into the street and held him up, at the muzzle of a big navy. It was so sudden that he slid clean off his saddle. He was white as a sheet; but the miner quietly put up his shooter, looked him over, nodded pleasantly, and remarked, 'I say, stranger, when yer showin' yerself off in these parts, do it slow, so's folks kin git a good look at ye.' Then he walked away."

"I'd have been tempted to show him the end of my gun, about that time," Oscar remarked, with a laugh.

"He didn't mean any harm," Charlie explained. "It was a pretty rough way, but he evidently sized his man in advance, and only meant it for a joke. There's a good deal of harm done in taking these fellows' jokes too serious."

"But isn't there a lot of shooting done in earnest, too?" Oscar asked.

"There was at one time; but there's not so much of that now, I reckon," Charlie replied, quickly. "Many's the time that it was called a poor day for excitement in Deadwood if there wasn't a first-class shooting row somewhere, with one body, at least, to carry down the street. But to sample things on the strength of that is as wrong as it is popular. A frontier town, and a mining town at that, will always draw to it the meanest skunks that crawl, and they are the creatures who always fill up such holes as that."

He pointed to a liquor saloon they were passing, where, out of the open door, came the shouts and yells of a free fight of some sort.

"Birds of a feather flock together. If a fellow is one of them and gets in there, the risk is his own. When they get drunk, they are as much meaner in proportion as other people are when they get drunk. Those are the fellows who do the real shooting, as a rule. They're not very often able to hit the man they aim at, but they usually hit somebody in the saloon, and the chances are that it will prove a blessing to the place in the end, whoever it is; especially if the fellow who shoots loses his life for it, too."

"They tackle strangers, too, sometimes," Oscar remarked, referring, mentally, to the peculiar actions of the men who had just passed them.

"Anybody in a saloon must run his chances," Charlie replied; "and the greener he is, the greater the chances, of course, of attracting a bully's attention. Better not go to saloons at all. That's my opinion."

"But outside of the saloons?" Oscar insisted.

"Why, of course there are chances," Charlie admitted. "That's why you wear a six-shooter, and carry a rifle. As long as there are Indians on the plain, and fools in frontier towns, we shall have to be armed. It's an ounce of prevention, and is worth a pound of lead inside of the guns. If a fellow minds his own business, and neither swells, gets drunk, or loses his temper, so long as he looks as if he were well armed I would be willing to wager anything that he could live in Leadville with as little real use for powder as if he were in the city of Boston. If any one comes round a place like this and puts on airs, though, he's very likely to receive some suggestions on the great American dogma of equality. There was a sprig from somewhere came out here to invest a fortune in the mines, and struck Leadville in a pair of patent leather boots, a plug hat and a duster. The driver stopped his stage a good quarter of a mile from the hotel, so's he'd have to walk and give the fellers a sight. Well, he took his grip and began mincing along in the dust, and straightaway the fellers began to fall in behind him, close rank and single file, mincing along just the same, till there were about fifty men, like the tail of a comet, pulling in behind. His face was as white as a snowdrift, and he was the scaredest man you ever saw. Then some one struck up singing 'Does your mother know you're out?' and he made a break and ran into a restaurant; while the fellows gathered round the door and gave him a free concert."

"I say, Charlie," Oscar interrupted, "what did that fellow mean who rode up, just now, and clear round us, and there he goes back again, as fast as his horse can run?"

"Did he? I didn't notice," Charlie responded, carelessly. "Hope he saw all he wanted to. He's going off as though he was satisfied."

"What's the matter with you, Charlie?" Oscar muttered. "You don't seem to notice anything. Back there on the plain you knew if a grasshopper jumped, a mile away."

"That was back on the plain. This is the public thoroughfare of immortal Deadwood," Charlie returned, laughing.

"Well, I'm a heap more afraid here than I was there," Oscar said.

"And I was a heap more afraid there than I am here," Charlie added, "which makes all the difference between us, and the way we keep track of what is going on."

At that moment three men rode up to them. It was quite dark now, but they could see by the lights ahead that they were approaching the body of the Y, the center of the city, where Harry Porter, the college stage driver, had promised to secure rooms for them, and meet them on their arrival. The three men turned and rode back beside them. Presently one of them asked:

"Is them your mules, stranger?"

"Reckon they're as much mine as they are yours, 'tenerate," Charlie replied indifferently, swinging one leg over the side-pocket of his saddle.

"You jest hold yer hosses, now," returned the man. "I ain't a-jumpin' no claims ternight, nor drawin' no comparisons. I'm jest a-axin' ye, civil likes, be them your mules?"

"Can't ye see that they're anchored ter my saddle?"

"I'll 'low yer towin' on 'um," said the man; "but be ye towin' 'um on yer own account, or fur summon else? That's what I'm axin'."

Charlie laughed as he replied: "You fellers seems ter be powerful anxious 'bout them long-eared critters hangin' onter me. P'r'aps you'd better jest try lightin' on one of 'um, fur the sake on't, ef yer wanter find out quicker'n scat how much personal interest I take in him. Chin music's been plenty, and target shootin' scarce'n hens' teeth for a piece back, and we're kinder hankerin' fur variety. See?"

"You jest keep yer shootin' irons fur them as isn't stuffed so full o' lead a'ready that a bullet couldn't git into 'um edgewise," the man replied, and the three laughed and rode away toward the center again.

"Them's 'um. We're O K," they heard one of the men remark, as they started off at a rapid pace.

"I told you there was something wrong. What in the world does it mean?" Oscar muttered.

"Switched if I know," Charlie replied, swinging his foot. "They seem to take a lively interest in these mules. I presume they were stolen from some one, and like as not it was some one in Deadwood. Maybe their owner has spotted 'um."

"They don't take us for horse thieves, do they?" Oscar exclaimed indignantly.

"Shouldn't wonder," Charlie replied, with a short laugh, as though it was a good joke. "Wouldn't you, if your horse had been stolen, and you saw some one coming down the street, towing him by a lead line?"

"It would depend somewhat upon whether he looked like a horse thief or not," Oscar replied.

"Well, don't you flatter yourself that, after what we have been through, we are any great improvement on good, respectable horse thieves, so far as personal appearance is concerned," Charlie interrupted. "And all cats are black when the lights are out, you know."

Charlie finished his sentence with a low whistle, and suddenly swung himself back to an erect position on his saddle, and the two looked down the street.

Ahead of them there was an open space like a square. It was easy to see that a crowd of people was gathered there, and looking eagerly toward them; while flickering lights from various sources dancing over them made the scene more exciting and mysterious. To add to the peculiarity of the position, a voice from in front of the crowd could be distinctly heard, remarking: "Them's 'um, boys. Now mum's the word."

"If they've got a liberty pole or a lamp post handy, and a good rope, all they need is a couple of horse thieves, to have a first-class funeral there to-night," Charlie muttered.

"Do you think that we'd better go on?" Oscar asked.

"This is about the only road I see running that way," Charlie remarked. "You just hook on to this tow line, and let me ride a step or two ahead."

"Not if you're going to do any fighting, I won't," Oscar replied decidedly. "If that's it, we'll just drop the mules altogether, for I'm going with you, and if they hang one they can hang us both."

"There's many an honest man been hanged for a horse thief before this," Charlie answered. "But don't be alarmed. There'll be no hanging here to-night. They're laying for us, and no mistake; but all the fighting I shall do is with my tongue. If that don't fix it we'll let them put us up at the Government House till morning, if they insist on it; but I reckon they won't. Hold on to the mules, for if they think we stole them it would go against us bad to drop them; and whatever comes, don't touch your shooters if you value your life."

Oscar was satisfied, and took the lead lines, falling a little behind. As they approached the square the men fell back, leaving a passage between them. Without a moment's hesitation Charlie rode directly forward and Oscar followed close behind. It was the strangest sensation he had ever experienced. That line of grim and silent upturned faces looked hideous in the cross-lights and shadows, watching him as though he was the greatest curiosity in the world. Were the men only waiting for a signal from some one to drag him from his saddle, throw a rope about his neck and hang him for a horse thief? In the flaring lights of the square their seamed and eager faces looked it. If they would only say something, do something. It seemed as if it would be a relief to have them make the dash at him. Then he would fight, in spite of Charlie's admonition.

With every muscle strained, and his eyes fixed on Charlie, he rode on a few steps farther, when, just as they were in the very center of the crowd, the men closed in upon them from behind and formed a solid wall in front, while one big fellow caught the bridle of Charlie's horse.

Oscar cringed. He hugged his feet under Sancho and almost caught his pistol from his belt. It would have been a very doubtful struggle to have fought his way through that crowd of earnest men; but he felt that it would be easier to try it, at least, than to sit there waiting for them to treat him as they pleased. Charlie's example was all that restrained him. He saw Charlie deliberately stuff his hands into his pockets, lean back in his saddle, and remark:

"Well, stranger, do you make a livin' holdin' hosses 'out bein' axed? Ef that's the custom in these parts I'll gin ye a quarter an' yer kin let go; 'cause my critter'll stand, 'out a hitchin' post, whenever I git good an' ready ter stop, the which ain't jest this minit."

"Look a-here, Mister," the big man replied, without the least intention of dropping the bridle, "we hain't come out here to give or take no back talk. The fust thing we folks wants ter know is whar you two fellers come frum and whar yer goin'?"

As Oscar sat there, trembling and listening, he asked himself for the thousandth time what he should have done if he had taken that trip alone. He would really have trembled much less, and would doubtless have done precisely as Charlie did — made the best of everything; for while it is very true that they also serve who only stand and wait, any one who has tried it and can speak from experience, is sure to say that by far the most difficult task of all is that same standing and waiting. Oscar did not think of that, however. He simply appreciated the fact that he was frightened.

Instantly Charlie answered, " We come from Manitoba, gentlemen, and when you'll show me that where we're goin' is any of your biz, I'll let you know."

" Thet hain't sayin' nuthin' 'bout how ye cum by them mules, is it now, Mister ? " asked the big man at the bridle, with a suggestive grin ; and a voice from the crowd called : " Ded ye fetch 'um all the way frum Manitoby ? "

" You didn't axe me whar the mules come frum," Charlie responded, " or like enough I mought 'a' told yer "—

" Waal, go on an' tell us now," interrupted the big fellow, and the crowd gathered closer as Charlie quickly continued :

" Like enough I mought 'a' told yer that that come putty nigh bein' our own biz, jest now."

There was a wild yell from the crowd. Oscar started in his saddle ; yet no one seemed inclined to lay hands on him.

When the yelling ceased the spokesman continued : " That there's jest the gist on't, stranger. Them mules has been assayed as stolen property."

" I presume they are," was Charlie's cool response. " Hosses an' mules in the West is a good deal like umbrellas in the East."

" Waal, do you happen to know, too, stranger, the way we folks smelt up a vein o' hoss thieves, in these diggin's, when we strike it rich ? " the spokesman asked, and the words were no more than out of his mouth when Charlie replied:

"Ef you want points on handlin' hoss thieves, I'm yer man; but ef it's exercise in the art that ye're arter, and ye're prospectin' my way for a subject, I can tell yer at the start that ye've got the wrong pig by the ear. Now, then, pard, ye've come putty close on to hintin' at charges that no man makes ag'in me and lives. Ef you've got any honest doubts that you'd liked cleared away, I'll clear 'um. But you come one hair nearer to sayin' that I'm a hoss thief, and I'll put a ray o' sunlight inter you before you kin git yer mouth shut. Open up yer sluices, now; wash out the dirt and gin us the dust clean and straight. Say what ye have ter say, and say it quick."

"Waal, now, I'll tell yer, stranger, it's jest this way," said the man. "Thar ain't no call fur shootin' irons ternight, not but that I've been shot at in my day an' been able ter shoot back. Leastwise I've got firearms handy, an' I know how ter use 'um. But the hull on't is, we know them mules ter be stolen goods, an' we've see the fellers that straddled 'um. Now we don't make no pussonal charges till we're staked out an' know that we've got a sure thing. Nevertheless, we don't perpose ter let two sech fellers as you an' that youngster go no further through this town 'out payin' yer some attention. We've chipped in an' laid out as putty a spread as the town affords on short notice, which ain't no great, it's true, but we've come out ter axe ye ter honor us by grubbin' up with us. 'Tain't every day we comes acrost two fellers that kin hold up three o' the worst road agents in the country, an' we'd everlastin' like ter git a better look at yer. Will yer come?"

"That's more like biz," Charlie remarked, while Oscar hardly knew whether to laugh or cry in the sudden reaction. "Ef ye'll axe me ag'in, now, whar we're goin', I'll tell ye quick enough that we're goin' ter grub."

Some one shouted, "Three cheers for the hoss thieves!" and they were given lustily. Then a voice cried, "Three cheers for the youngster!" and the heart of Deadwood rang again.

In the momentary hush that followed a clear voice in the rear called, "Now, then, three more for them mules!" and in the roar of laughter which followed they started for the largest hall in Deadwood.

The dinner was one which might never find a counterpart. Abundant gold dust had done its best. Of all places in the world where highwaymen are hated and personal bravery admired, such a location as Deadwood in its earlier history has no equal. The three highwaymen had rendered the route from Bismarck almost deserted. Every effort had been made in vain to capture them. They had only become more daring and aggressive. Now, after soldiers, volunteers and all had failed, two travelers, one of them a boy, brought in — not proof that some one of the outlaws had been shot, but all three alive and well. No wonder they wanted to honor them.

The two leading hotels had been taxed to their utmost. They drained every market. Fruit was an expensive luxury that ordinarily found a poor sale, but from raisins to apples there could not have been found a dime's worth for sale when their purchase was completed. A trapper appeared with a bear, and instantly sold him, whole, for more than he expected to receive by peddling bear's stakes from house to house, all day. The bake shops turned out their best, no matter what it was, and the whole promiscuous upper ten of Deadwood society was on hand.

The company was an assortment as peculiar as the feast. There were men there who had honored the most artistic dining saloons of the refined East. There were men who were no strangers to banquets in the great cities of the Old World. There were men from homes where refinement was so pure and unaffected that an uncouth word or act would have been simply impossible. They were entertaining a Harvard graduate, too, and an Oxford student. But who would have thought it?

They were all in the Black Hills now, and the Black Hills as they were when all who were at the Black Hills were one. They were rough, hearty, boisterous, earnest men; quite capable of hating life's hypocrisies and honoring its nobilities, in spite of the coats of mental, physical and social tan that covered them.

There were men there who were manipulating millions, and men who were working on grub-stakes, but they, too, were all one; for it is one of the eccentricities of nature, that at the very places where gathering of gold and silver is the one ambition and energy of life, the possession of it has the least power to give an unworthy man influence and authority, and win for him the servile homage of his fellow men.

The dinner was a grand success, closing with the presentation of the purse of three thousand five hundred dollars. It was late when it was over, but as Harry Porter was to leave early in the morning, they sat in his room with him afterward.

The stage driver is a most important personage in a frontier town. He knows every one, and in his official capacity has to do with almost every one.

"Speaking of Manitoba Lake," Harry said, "I brought a fellow down some weeks ago, who said he had just been up there, investing; and he talked great about it. I told him I thought it would have been better for the States if he had stopped there; for he wasn't much liked in these parts. He's a first-class humbug, and humbugs don't go down here, you know. He was a first-class coward, too. Humbugs always are, I guess. We were held up, that night. Those fellows got the best of me by fastening a black rope across the road and throwing my leaders. Before I could get them on their feet again the fellows had the drop on us from behind the trees, where we couldn't get at them, and while we were at the horses they went through the stage. You ought to have seen that fellow shell out his watch and trinkets and dust. And how he did shake! He'll not show up here again, though. He had a claim that was panning out something great, and he tried to jump a poor fellow's claim lying next and freeze him out. The folks got on to him, though, and the committee waited on him and gave him forty-eight hours to give it back and git. They say he sold out at a pretty good figure. Those skunks generally do suck in the fat, somehow; but he's gone, and we're well rid of him. If he ever turns up in Manitoba, look out. A small man, short one little finger? Yes. That's him. So you've seen him before? Well, that's funny. I tell you, this is a mighty small world when you come right down to it. What? You want to strike him again? Well, that's funnier yet. You must think more of him than most folks; but I guess you'll be pretty apt to find him in the neighborhood of Leadville, unless he gets the good-by from there, too. His lawyer, here, told me yesterday that he had heard from him down there, and that he was taking a big pile of dust out of the ground from some claims he was working there. By the way,

Charlie, what have you been doing up in Manitoba, any way?"

"Oh! I've been camping out on the Half-circle-dash range, punching cows for a living." He was about to put another question when Harry interrupted:

"Half-circle-dash! Hold up a bit. Half-circle-dash! You don't say! I never thought of it from that time to this. It never occurred to me that you might be those fellows. I was looking for cowboys, and, in fact, when I met you I was so excited, finding who you were and seeing those agents along with you, that I never thought of it at all." He was fumbling away in his stage box. "I've got a letter for you somewhere here. It's the funniest thing out, I declare! You see, I was just coming up to the gulch, a little after daylight, instead of two o'clock in the morning as usual, when I ran on to a little Indian boy, sitting by the road, hugging the head of a white pony. The pony was dead as a door nail, and the boy was crying like water through a sluice sieve. I was kind of sorry for him, and held up till we made up a little purse between us, and passed it over. Come to find out, he could speak English like a book. He said the squaw from the sod house by the well got mad and killed his horse so he could not go on; but he had a letter for two Half-circle-dash fellows who were somewhere between there and Deadwood. Here it is. Only a piece of brown paper."

When they were alone, a little later, they opened the paper and read what the Indian had scratched with a bullet:

"Heap pale face tepee soon. Indian no more need. Great Spirit keep open eye. Indian go back now."

"Poor little fellow," Charlie said earnestly, as he laid down the paper. "So the squatter's squaw got

"THE BOY WAS CRYING."

wind of what had happened and killed his pony for the part he played. But the brave little chap wouldn't acknowledge it in the letter."

"I'd like to scalp her," Oscar muttered.

"Easy," Charlie interrupted. "That's the way I felt about all the Indians; but this little fellow has pulled my eyes open. His traits and characteristics are pure Indian, only he has directed them in a way that we can appreciate, and the result is we admire him. That squaw was doing precisely the same thing for the old squatter, and I begin to think that if I studied them more charitably, instead of hating them at sight, I should find a heap more nobility and story-book romance about them. The fact is, they never stop to think. They never have any half-way. If they believe they have cause to be friendly they do everything that comes to hand to show it, in a way so generous and self-sacrificing that one would be a brute not to admire them; while if they feel that they have cause for revenge they just reverse the whole. And the trouble is, we've got to admit, ninety-nine Indians out of every hundred, wherever you find them, have excellent cause for vengeance. I wish they were a little cleaner and a little less lazy and hoggish when they have nothing to do, if I have got to turn about and befriend them; but if they were they would not be Indians. That's all there is to it."

"Do you suppose that that boy will have to walk all the way back to Manitoba?" Oscar asked anxiously.

"O, no! He'll steal a horse directly, and be all right again," Charlie replied carelessly.

"Steal!" Oscar exclaimed indignantly.

"Certainly," said Charlie, laughing. "It's the nature of the beast. You are just as bad as I am. You think because an Indian has been kind to you that he never could steal a horse from any one, and I think because he steals horses that he can't have any nobility in him. Let's shake ourselves up, together, and we shall come at a better estimate of the Lo family. And now what are you going to do with your three thousand five hundred dollars?"

"Mine," Oscar exclaimed. "If ever a dollar belonged to any one, that money belongs to you."

"Look here!" Charlie interrupted quickly, "I've told you once that I was not dead struck on cash. I've got enough now to keep me, if I was to be blind or anything, and I wouldn't go saddle my horse to double it. On the other hand, this trip is yours, and any funerals along the way are your funerals. You can pay me back the expenses of the trip if you want to, to make yourself feel easy. More than that I will not touch, and that settles it."

Oscar saw that Charlie was thoroughly in earnest and replied:

"All right, Charlie. It's not worth fighting over, any way. It's good for nothing but to spend, and all that either of us could do with it would be to decide how to spend it to the best advantage. I've thought of one way; see if you agree with me? You take five hundred, for past expenses and future contingencies, and we'll devote the three thousand to giving that Indian boy an education and a chance to make the most of his good qualities."

"Good," said Charlie. "The next thing is to get hold of him."

"I've been thinking of that," Oscar replied. "He must have been the one who brought Sancho to me at the ranch house, and from the letter the keeper wrote I think he knew who it was. The pony came from the farm. I noticed the brand under his mane while I was riding, but I forgot to speak about it afterward. He never could have got those arms of father's except the keeper had given them to him. I think that keeper is a pretty square fellow, and if we write to him about it, and send him five hundred dollars to begin upon, it'll be all right, won't it?"

Charlie thought for a moment, and replied: "It's trusting a stranger, of course, but I liked his letter. It sounded like a straight man. At any rate, it is the only way to do at present. Now for the next step. I suppose we strike for Leadville?" Oscar nodded. "I don't know what you propose to do when you hit your man there, but I don't believe you will ever accomplish anything with him except by accident. He's a scamp, through and through. You must keep that in mind, and remember that a scamp is not influenced and affected according to the mental and moral laws that work in an honest mind. A wounded crane will fight, and a wounded deer will run as surely as oil will float and a stone sink in water; but you never can tell what a coward and a fraud will do when you drive him into a corner. You'll find that he's covered up his tracks too carefully to be caught by a straight hunt. He fired that shot as the price of a big deal for himself. Don't imagine that you are either going to shame him, confound him, or prove anything by straight, open work. You'll find that he isn't made that way. Lie low and wait for some accident to put him in your power, or I'm afraid you'll find he is more than a match for you."

"I'll remember what you say, Charlie," Oscar said, "and I know you are right, for you always are; but it is what I have come to accomplish, and with your help I am going to accomplish it."

Charlie gave his hand in a way that left no doubt as to the quality of aid he was to receive from that quarter.

CHAPTER XVI.

THE INDIAN QUESTION.

WITH at least a limited amount of absolute knowledge ahead of them, Oscar and Charlie were now in the greatest haste to reach their destination; but there was the difficulty, in shortening the journey by taking advantage of the railroad, that they had never seen the man they were after, while he had at least seen Oscar, and if he had heard of his departure from Manitoba he might be on the watch for him. If he watched anything it would be the railways and stage lines, and to have him forewarned would mean the greatest possible obstruction in their way. They decided to strike the trail again, and follow the most direct route through Wyoming to Leadville.

Deadwood had little that was of further interest to them, and the notoriety which they had gained was not at all to their tastes; so that as soon as the horses were in condition they started again down the famous Deadwood Gulch. There was no doubt as to the origin of its name. The hills were ragged and rocky about them, full of caverns and gorges which might easily have sheltered every Indian west of the Mississippi without betraying the presence of a single red skin, while here and there, like solitary sentinels, or in grim clusters, rose the gaunt dead trunks of trees.

Miners' shanties, singly or in little groups, were everywhere, and they frequently passed more extensive settlements sometimes dignified by the name of town, sometimes called cities, chiefly composed of liquor saloons and grocery stores. Some were only half-built and deserted, some already falling to ruin. For a time, too, there was company enough if they had desired it, and comparatively little fear of Indians, though the disturbances in the northern reservations had already reached the agencies to the west of them, and many reports were brought from Wyoming of the rough treatment which the settlers were receiving from the Sioux there.

For several days there was only the constantly changing magnificence of the mountains to make one hour differ from another. There was no excitement to keep them constantly on their guard, and no shooting, the game had been so effectually driven away by hungry miners. The depressing atmosphere of mines and mining, however, gradually disappeared as they reached the wilder tablelands of Wyoming.

"Mining may look well enough on paper," Oscar

THE LAST OF DEADWOOD GULCH.

said one day, "and it's fine to read about the bonanza kings, but I tell you there's too much sadness in the reality to suit me. I wouldn't spend my life digging in the Black Hills if I could own the whole of them to pay. There are too many deserted holes, too many ruined shanties, too many half-starved, ragged, wretched creatures about, and too many graves everywhere. I wish that the stories of failure could be told as often and graphically as the stories of success. I think some fellows would give up the idea of jumping into fortunes without working for them, then, and would come out on to the farms and ranches, instead of to the mines."

"Hold on, Oscar," Charlie interrupted, with a smile. "You are talking like a philosopher now, and philosopher is only another name for a poor man who has made a failure himself in the race for riches. It is not at all impossible that you will come out of this scrape a big rich mine owner yourself, coining money without lifting your finger, and you may wish, then, that you hadn't talked too strong on the other side."

"I said that I would not work at mining for the whole of the Black Hills, and it's a fact," Oscar insisted. "If I am poor as poverty I shall not come here to earn a living, I promise you. If I ever do own a big mine, as you say, I hope that I shall have the good sense to make the income accomplish something for the good of the world. At any rate, you'll never find me standing over it. Ranching and ranging are good enough for me, and I'd rather be a ranchman and ranger than the biggest mine owner in the country; so if I come out of this trip as poor as I began, which is all that I expect or wish, I'm just going to strike for some place under you, on the best ranch we can find, and do the best I can."

By degrees they lost sight of the signs of civilization again, and crossed the Indian trails leading to the various reservations, now and then passing small bands of Indians, who paid them no attention, however, beyond a guttural grunt or muttered "How?"

Again they began the precautions necessary in the doubtful Indian country, and again their eyes were open for every sign or footprint, and their ears for every sentiment which Panza might express.

"I didn't realize it then, but the fact that I felt sure that the little Indian was round made me feel a heap easier about red men, in coming through Dakota," Charlie said, and added, "I wish he were about here now."

Before sunset they built their fire in a sheltered gorge, using only dry sticks, to prevent smoke, and after supper moved on again for half a mile or more. The second night they selected a camp in a curious ravine, which seemed to have sunk down from a level of the tableland, through some action from below. There was a narrow entrance, a defile between the rocky ledges leading to it, and the bottom, containing not more than three or four acres, was thickly covered with grass and wild flowers. Except for that one defile it was completely walled in, and a little stream, trickling over the rocks, wound along the bottom and finally disappeared.

"What a glorious place this is," Oscar exclaimed. "We have only to turn the horses loose and go to sleep."

"It is the best thing that could be built," Charlie replied, "so long as no one knows that we are here. But it would be a tough place for us if a bunch of Indians should get wind of it, for there'd be no getting out, and no getting at them. I reckon we'd better keep the watch same as last night."

Whenever they were obliged to watch Charlie slept the first half of the night, giving Oscar the last half; for then he was in a better state to go to sleep quickly, and could sleep till the last moment in the morning.

The night was clear. There was a cold wind blowing over the tableland, but it could not reach their sheltered valley. Oscar was tired after the long day, and the still air made him sleepy. He was obliged to walk, most of the time, to keep awake, frequently passing the narrow entrance, and at every turn giving a sharp look along the ledges.

It was approaching twelve o'clock, and Oscar was very glad of it, when Panza, who had been lying near Sancho, stood up, looked about her in an uncertain way, and came over to where Oscar had seated himself for a moment. She was evidently disturbed. Her tail was between her legs, and she came crouching along in a most unusual way; for there were very few things which ever frightened her.

"What is it?" Oscar asked, patting her head; but she simply looked about her and crouched close to him. "I'll bet a cent there's a snake in the grass over there," he added, and was rising to go over and investigate when one of the horses stood up, and he noticed that the others were both awake. Suddenly Charlie sat upright, looked toward the horses, and then up the gorge. "What's the row, Charlie?" Oscar asked, coming toward him. "Here you and Panza and the horses were all sound asleep a moment ago, and yet you all seem to know that there's something wrong, while I have been wide awake and on guard, and I can't find out what it is to save me."

Charlie was slowly rising to his feet, in a way to indicate at least that there was nothing of any immediate importance. He stretched and yawned, and answered, "That's because we were in a position to receive the first reports. Just lie down and put your ear to the ground, and see what you think of it."

Oscar obeyed, listened for an instant, then springing to his feet he gasped, "What is it? For mercy's sake, Charlie, what is it?"

"What does it sound like?" Charlie asked.

"Is it an earthquake?" Oscar whispered.

"I never met one of those things," Charlie replied; "but I reckon they would shake the ground, and this is pretty steady."

"It sounds like ocean waves," Oscar added, listening again. "And it's growing louder. Yes; you can hear it standing up. It can't be thunder?" and he looked toward the sky.

"O, no!" said Charlie, with vexing deliberation. "Thunder usually comes from overhead. You'll have to guess again."

"Well, I know it's nothing serious," Oscar observed, "you take it so easy. It can't be Indians. But it's a horrible rumble now. Could a lot of big prairie schooners on the run make a noise like that?"

"I don't know," Charlie replied, walking over toward the horses; for they were all on their feet now, and growing uneasy. "It's not very often that you strike a lot of big prairie schooners on the run, and especially not at this time of night."

"It isn't Indians, is it?" Oscar asked, as they caught the horses and brought them together.

"Not by a large majority," Charlie replied, laughing. "Indians never tiptoed like that in my experience."

"It's a cloud burst, a flood," Oscar said, as the rumble grew louder, and the horses harder to manage; and he cast one quick, anxious glance up the narrow entrance to the ravine.

"It's coming from the wrong way for that. It's going toward the Rockies; don't you see?"

"I don't see anything, but I hear a good deal," Oscar replied, glad of a chance to pay Charlie back in a small way. "Now I'll bet I know what it is," he exclaimed. "It's one of those intermittent boiling springs, or the now-and-again geysers of Wyoming."

This time Charlie laughed outright. "Upon my word, Oscar," he replied, "you beat a Yankee for guessing. I shouldn't have supposed there could have been so many things to make a noise." By this time it had become a steady thunder, and the very ground seemed to tremble. "Ten years ago that would have meant a herd of buffalo ahead of a bunch of Indians; but now I reckon it's only a big drove of cattle on a stampede. Some ranch is changing its quarters, and the cows have started off for themselves. There, I can manage the horses now. Just you climb up that bluff, and I reckon you'll see a sight worth taking in. Only have a care that you don't get in front of them, and if they are headed for this hole in the ground give a yell, so I can get the horses out quicker than lightning; for they will not stop for fire or water. They'd fill this hole full, and then run over on the top if there were enough of them left, after making the bridge."

Oscar climbed the bluff, and the moment he reached the upper plain the noise sounded so much louder that for an instant he stood almost petrified, sure that the herd could not be fifty feet away.

In reality it was nearly half a mile away, but in the great wave of sound that swept over him there was the fierce tramping of twelve thousand feet, the bellowing of three thousand throats, the clashing of horns, the yelling of cowboys, and the howls of wild animals that were in the path, to escape or be run down.

The moment he could gather himself together Oscar looked away over the plain, and as Charlie had said, saw a sight that was worth taking in. A great dark shadow, like the shadow of a dense cloud sweeping over the landscape, came rolling onward. Oscar watched it carefully, for a moment, to be sure that the direction would not bring it too near the ravine, then he cast one quick, searching glance about him in every quarter — a habit which early becomes the second nature of every expert ranger — and sure that there was nothing else about him he turned again to admire the grand sight of three thousand cattle, packed in one solid mass, dashing madly forward, bellowing and groaning as they goaded each other on.

A great stampede is a sight full of anxiety to the ranchman, full of apprehension and danger to the cowboy, full of majesty and grandeur to one who can look at it without anxiety or apprehension.

The herd swept past within a quarter of a mile and thundered on, down into the distant valley. Oscar watched till the dense shadow blended with others in the distance, and the thunder began to die away; then he went back to Charlie, conscious of the strangest condition, which no one can explain or appreciate who has not realized, at some moment of life, the utter and puny helplessness of man before the blind force of brute muscle, centered as it is in a great stampede.

"Where do you suppose they came from?" he asked, as the little camp settled down to quiet again.

"It was just as likely from twenty miles away as from one," Charlie replied. "It's just about the time for the early round-up in this part of the country, and probably some big ranch is working its way West. It takes precious little to start a herd when they're bunched close and are uneasy, as they would be in this cold wind. I've seen them start at sight of a man getting off his horse. They are so used to seeing the two together that I suppose they consider the combination as one being, and to see him deliberately take himself apart was too much for them. A thunderstorm will very often start them, and sometimes they will start at nothing at all. Then if they once get running on blind nerve there is nothing under heaven can stop them till they are tired out. I've seen a herd go straight over a bluff into the Missouri River, swim across, as many as lived out the jump, and those that were not drowned in crossing, start and run again when they reached the other side."

"Tell me some more about cattle raising, Charlie," Oscar said, as he rolled himself up in his blanket. "That stampede has strung me all up, till I sha'n't get to sleep to-night, unless you can talk me to sleep."

Charlie sat down, and leaning back against his saddle began, in a slow monotone that was calculated to

"STEERING OVER THE TRACKLESS PLAIN."

make Oscar sleepy, if anything could. "The last thing I did with cattle, before striking the Half-circle-dash, was to move a ranch up this way. Not so far as this, for this was all Indians then. Nearly the whole of it belonged to the Sioux, the Crows, the Arapahoes and the Shoshones, and they were all-fired ugly if any one came too near their boundaries. With the first show of spring three of us started out with two pack mules, and a pretty tough time we had of it hunting for a good place for the range. As soon as we found a place we hurried back, to start the herd, so that it could have as much time on the new range as possible, to brace up from the tramp, before the next winter. There was upward of four thousand head, and three big four-mule schooners lugging grub and bedding. It was tough work steering them over the trackless plain, creeping along, so that they should not be over driven, looking out to strike water, enough of it, when we stopped for the night, and not too much of it when we had to cross a river. And all the while the cattle were nervous and fidgety, hunting for some excuse to run, and every step of the way we were open to sudden calls from ugly Indians. Altogether it was a big relief when we reached the range we had selected, and the cattle could spread themselves, while we ran up a ranch-house of cotton-wood logs — I say, Oscar, look up the gorge."

For a moment Oscar did not move. He could not see what looking up the gorge could have to do with the ranching experience which Charlie was relating. He was provoked, too; for Charlie knew very well that he was doing his best to go to sleep. If he should rouse enough to look up the gorge he would simply have to begin the struggle all over again. What did he care what there was up the gorge? He had seen enough for one night, and he proposed to go to sleep. He did not move.

"Oscar!"

There was something rather sharp and peremptory about that. Possibly it was something that required being looked at. He disapproved of the whole matter, however, and gave a grunt that was intended to convey a volume of his personal sentiments on the subject to Charlie. Then he cautiously opened one eye, part way, so that he should see as little as possible till he had investigated, and pushed back the blanket that was over his face.

The next instant he was sitting upright, rubbing his eyes vigorously; and even then he had not looked up the gorge. He had simply discovered that it was broad daylight, that breakfast was ready, and that he had been sound asleep for nearly six hours.

"Look up the gorge, Oscar," Charlie said again.

This time he did look up the gorge, and instantly started to his feet. Right against the bright eastern sky he discovered the narrow pass literally blocked with dark forms, above which horned heads were tossing, in eagerness to get at the tempting grass and water in the ravine. Alone in the very front stood a sturdy bull, the sunlight flashing along his back and polished horns. They were a fragment of the herd that had either become separated from the rest or had been too far in the rear to keep up their enthusiasm, and the present delay, against which they were protesting, was caused by the fact that the bull in the lead found himself unexpectedly brought face to face with Panza. Neither of them seemed satisfied as to the wisest course to follow under the circumstances, and while they were thinking it over Charlie said to Oscar: "Let's bring them down and round them up at that end of the ravine. They'll not be in our way, and we shall be obliging some fellow immensely."

They called Panza off, and, mounting, Oscar followed Charlie's orders, taking his first lesson as a cowboy. The cattle were a little restive, especially a bunch of stragglers which they brought in from the surrounding plain; but Charlie understood his business too thoroughly to have any trouble; the ravine made an excellent corral, and in a short time they were safely located, and Oscar and Charlie were eating their breakfast.

"This is the last of our meat," Charlie remarked. "Unless those cowboys get along in a hurry and hand us over the hind quarter of one of their steers, for salvage, we've got to shoot something or go hungry."

"What are you going to do with the cows?" Oscar asked.

"Leave 'um where they are," Charlie said. "We'll put a stick with a handkerchief on it on top of the knoll to mark the spot. They won't care to move away to-day, any way, and we shall surely meet some of the boys hunting for them, before noon."

"What's the matter with my taking Sancho and the shot-gun and making a little dash to see if I can see any of them or knock over anything for dinner?" Oscar asked.

"There's none, if you don't go out of call and if you're back in fifteen minutes. I'll be ready to start in that time," Charlie replied.

Oscar was off in an instant.

"Look out that you don't run into a bunch of Indians," Charlie called after him, but Oscar was too far away to hear. He marked their hiding place by sighting a dead tree and a mountain peak, in one direction, and two bowlders in a line in another; but it was too fine a morning to think of any further precautions. It was gloriously clear and cool, and it was the first time for days that he and Sancho had been free from the monotonous pace of a pilgrimage. Sancho started at a furious run. There was not a cowboy in sight; Oscar made sure of that, and then devoted his attention strictly to the ground about him, with his shot-gun ready to drop the first living thing that started up within reach.

The scene was one of the most magnificent that he had ever witnessed. The high tableland about him was glowing in its early summer and early morning glory. Broken and irregular hills and buttes, backed by the giant peaks of the Rocky Mountains, rose upon three sides, like the walls of a giant amphitheater. Only for an instant Oscar lifted his eyes to look at them, but he lost a prairie chicken in the act; for one rose directly in front of him, but before he was ready it had crossed the brow of a mound upon his right, and dropped down into a ravine beyond. Chagrined, he turned Sancho quickly in that direction. He caught sight of it again just as it was dropping into a little cluster of bushes half-way down the knoll, and had made a good dash toward it, watching for it to rise again, when he discovered, to his horror, a party of Indians, in full view, who had overpowered and robbed a white man sitting in their midst. They were indulging in a series of suggestive flourishes with their knives, about his head, while the poor fellow was pulling off his boots for them.

The Indians evidently saw Oscar at the same moment. His first thought, with a cold shiver, was to turn and run for his life. They had only the horse and rifle which they had stolen, between them. He remembered that he had wholly ignored Charlie's injunction to keep within call, and that he had nothing but a shot-gun. Before he had time to act upon it, however, he had changed his mind. It was not his nature to run from anything. He did not propose to leave a helpless fellow-being awaiting a horrible death.

Without a moment's thought he hugged his feet under Sancho and sent him bounding toward the group. He threw his gun to his shoulder, and at the top of his lungs shouted: "Hi, you red skins! I've got you now. Come on, boys! Come on!"

HE WAS PULLING OFF HIS BOOTS.

He saw the Indians hesitate and look at each other. He knew that if they stood their ground for another moment he would be in their midst, and they could dispose of him instantly. He saw the Indian standing by the captured horse catch the white man's rifle in his hand and lay his other hand upon the horse's neck. It meant that he would mount and fight. If he did there could be but one result. Quick as thought he leveled his gun between the broad bare shoulders, and thanking fortune, even then, that it was only loaded with comparatively harmless shot, and had little chance to kill, he pulled the trigger and shut his eyes.

There was one wild yell from the Indians, and as Oscar opened his eyes he saw the prisoner springing to his feet, catching his rifle in one hand before it had time to fall, and the bridle of his horse in the other, before the frightened animal could move, while the Indians were already several feet away, starting down the ravine like frightened deer.

"Don't stop to shoot," Oscar muttered, as he rode up. "Get into your outfit and on to your horse quicker than lightning, for I'm all alone, and if they have friends and horses near they'll be back in no time."

"You all alone?" the man gasped, looking up at him in blank astonishment.

"Yes, yes; can't you see without stopping to ask? They will see, too, if they look back. Give me your pistol. I've nothing but this shot-gun," Oscar muttered.

The man handed him his pistol without a word, and made good time in getting his belongings together. A professional fireman could not have done better. As one article after another flew into place, and Oscar reloaded his shot-gun he heard the man say to himself:

"Alone, and with nuthin' but a pea shooter. Well, I'll be busted!"

The moment he was ready they started up the hill as fast as their horses could carry them, and a little later dashed down the narrow path into the ravine, where Charlie sat upon his horse ready to start, ignorant that anything had happened.

The man proved to be one of the cowboys out looking up the lost cattle, and as Charlie listened to his story of the rescue his face grew sterner than Oscar had ever seen it, and he muttered:

"I'm glad it has turned out as it has; but now that I know what risks you'll run, Oscar, it's the last time you get out of my sight, in an Indian country, so long as I have one eye that will open."

"You're just right," said the cowboy. "'Twas the bravest thing I ever saw done, but it was foolish, no mistake. No man livin' would 'a' took such chances with only a pea shooter."

"Well, they're gone now, so let's talk of something else," Oscar interrupted.

"Wish I knew how fur and for how long they're gone," muttered the cowboy. "I must 'a' squatted right down in a nest on 'um. All night I was followin' a herd on a dead run, and soon's we had 'um rounded up part of us started back to pick up the others. We turned two lots, with three men each, but there was some fifty or sixty more. I see you've got 'um in here, for the which I'm all-fired grateful. Four of us kept on and kinder spread out. About an hour after sunup I was tarnal tired and hungry, and comin' to a good spot I pulled off the saddle while I ate a piece o' raw ham and a hunk o' bread I'd grabbed when we started. I'm sure I didn't see any Indians, and I'm sure I didn't hear any; but before I had three good bites they were all around me, within arm's length, and it's the strangest luck that they didn't brain me, first go off. I didn't show fight worth a cent, and when I found they were going to let me get my togs off first, I tell you I was slow about it, hopin' the fellers would come up."

"Well, I'm glad I got there, even if it was foolish," Oscar said.

"Hold on, youngster," the cowboy interrupted. "I kinder appreciate what you did for me, and don't you forget it. I only said 'twas foolish runnin' such a risk. I'd no more 'a' done what you did than I'd laid down in front o' that herd, last night. You're ready to start, ain't you? If you don't mind I'll go on with you fur mutual protection in case those fellows turn up again. We'll meet the boys somewhere, unless they're scalped — the which I guess not — and after seein' you safe away we can come back for the cows and stop here to-night."

They climbed the narrow path, but they were none too soon. As they reached the upper level Charlie muttered:

"There they are, now! They're coming for us in good shape! Send Panza back into the ravine with the pack horse, quick. We'll have to meet them on the nub. It's not a bad place, for they can't get at us from behind, and when they wheel they will be too far away to fire."

He quickly assigned the positions, in a half-circle, taking the center himself, with the bluff behind them. The cowboy's horse was down in an instant, and he was flat upon the ground, with the saddle for a rifle rest. Charlie dropped next. It was Oscar's first experience. He had tried the experiment once before, in the Indian camp, by Neepawa, but he had almost forgotten how it was done, and Sancho was so slow in obeying that he was hardly down when, with a wild yell, the Indians were upon them.

There were nine in all, all mounted, but only armed with pistols. Yelling and shooting they dashed furiously on, directly for the center of the little group, as though no power could stop them. Sancho began to struggle, and Oscar was obliged to lean upon his neck to keep him down. He could not blame the horse for

"HE WON'T DO IT AGAIN."

being frightened. His own hands were like ice. He knew that the Indians meant death without mercy. He knew that their only hope was in using their rifles; but he had not strength to lift the hammer. He could only crouch there, behind Sancho, vacantly staring at the approaching Indians.

When they were within fifty feet they suddenly wheeled to the right, dropped down behind their horses, till all that could be seen of them was a leg and arm, and clinging to the bare backs and leaning forward fired their pistols from under the horses' necks. The chief was not even armed with a pistol, but he used an Indian bow with a fury which at least inspired the rest and sent cold shivers down Oscar's back.

As they dashed past Oscar recognized the fellow whose back he had lashed with shot, and at the same instant the Indian recognized him. He was evidently on the watch for him, for he gave a fierce yelp, like a wounded wolf, brought his horse within thirty feet and fired; then whirled away. Oscar saw the dirt jump where the ball struck the ground close to him, and still he could not move.

Charlie's rifle was the first to sound, and Oscar saw an Indian fall, throwing his horse at the same time, and heard Charlie mutter:

"That fellow put a bullet through my hat, but he won't do it again."

The next instant the cowboy fired, and the chief

gave a fierce yell and fell headlong, while the cowboy remarked as he reloaded his Winchester:

"There's one less for Uncle Sam to feed, and he's a good one to have out of the way just now."

The moment the Indians had passed, they rode away and wheeled to come back in the opposite direction.

"Are you hurt, Oscar?" Charlie asked, glancing over his shoulder, the moment they were past, as he threw a fresh cartridge into his rifle.

"No, no! I'm all right," Oscar replied, shaking himself from his lethargy.

"Well, look sharp," muttered the cowboy. "They're holding their irons in their right hands, this trip, and they'll hit nearer. You stop where you are," he added, firing at a rather long range; but the foremost Indian fell, giving him time to reload before they were again upon them.

With a wild whoop they came again. Oscar ground his teeth and cocked his rifle while he watched them, determined that this time he would not flinch. Several times before he had aimed his rifle or pistol at an enemy, but with the exception of the use he had made of his shot-gun that morning, he had never pulled the trigger or really intended to fire upon a human being. He knew that it was a struggle for life and death between them now, and that their number was none too large if each one did his best. He bent to his rifle, determined to do his share.

They came within a hundred and fifty feet, this time, before they fired a shot.

"They mean biz; look out for them!" Charlie muttered.

Oscar singled out the one who had fired at him before.

They came within a hundred feet and opened fire. Oscar heard the sharp zip of a bullet passing over him, but his eyes were fixed upon the man he was watching, waiting to see his head appear.

Their yells were horrible, and the contortions of their savage faces, appearing under their horses' necks, were hideous. It has been the experience of too many to be counted simply the timidity of a few that there is nothing which can so completely unnerve a man and paralyze him to the heart, as the ghastly, distorted features of a frantic, desperate Indian.

It was no wonder that Oscar's heart failed him at first. It was much more remarkable that he lay there now, ready to meet them as they returned.

Suddenly, just as his fingers tightened upon the trigger, and he felt sure that another instant would bring in view the mark he waited for, the Indians gave a peculiar cry, and, like a flash, every horse had turned, and they were riding swiftly away.

As Oscar dropped his rifle, and looked after them in astonishment, he noticed that they were carrying away with them the bodies of those who had been shot.

He remembered what Charlie had told him of the way it was done, but it was all accomplished so quickly, while he was so intently following one horse with his rifle, that he had seen nothing of it.

The cowboy was on his feet in an instant.

"Easy," Charlie muttered. "Maybe they've only taken those fellows out of the way, and will be back again in a minute, madder than before."

"I guess by the way they went that they saw some one coming," the cowboy replied, "and it's high time our gang turned up."

"I hope so," Charlie said, rising cautiously. "I've got over caring to shoot Indians, but I haven't got to where I care to have them shoot me if I can help it. Are you all right, Oscar?"

"O, yes!" Oscar replied, springing to his feet, when he noticed that his shirt was wet with blood, and looking, found that a bullet had scratched his side.

"It's nothing but a touch. It'll be healed in a few days;" Charlie said, anxiously examining the spot. "But it was a close call. Thank God that a miss is as good as a mile."

"Why, I didn't know that I was hit at all, Charlie," Oscar exclaimed; "I wish now that I had fired. I could not get my strength. They took my breath away."

"That's natural," Charlie replied, as he cared for the wound. "It's precious few people who are good for much with Indians till they've been under fire

a good while longer than you have. And to stand out
a rush like that first one is all that anybody's nerves
could do. There! I reckon that will patch up all
right, and that some day you will be proud of that
scar. Halloo! What's struck our friend?"

The cowboy pulled off his hat and shouted, and a

THE COWBOYS' SERENADE.

moment later the three of whom he had spoken, came
dashing up.

Between experiences and congratulations it would
have been easy to laugh and listen, all day; for more
entertaining company could not easily be found than a
party of cowboys after a successful escapade.

Oscar and Charlie were in too much haste, however, to yield. They only waited long enough for another breakfast of broiled steaks, prairie pancakes and coffee, and with all they could carry of fresh beef, fastened to the pack, they started again, accompanied by the four as a guard of honor.

Oscar thought he had never enjoyed a half-day's ride so much in his life, and he began to understand the sunny side of the cowboy's nature, and the real character which Charlie had praised so highly.

They were full of stories and bubbling with wit, so that the strain of the morning wore away, and he entirely forgot that he was a wounded veteran, shot in a battle with the Indians.

The cowboys refused to turn back till the middle of the afternoon. Then they said good-by, and were a few feet away when one of them shouted:

"Here's to the youngster, and his little pea shooter!"

They all wheeled their horses about, and while Oscar and Charlie sat and watched and laughed, they sang the chorus of "Marching Through Georgia," emphasizing the cheers with shots from their pistols, while their horses, in an intensely amusing but ungainly bronco fashion, attempted to dance an accompaniment.

With the last note the horses wheeled again, and dashed away.

CHAPTER XVII.

THE LAST OF THE TRAIL.

"WELL, we have crossed Wyoming in safety, at any rate," Charlie said, when they entered Colorado. "If all goes well we shall stop to-night at a full-fledged cow-town. It will be the first time you have struck such a place, Oscar, and I'm anxious to see how you like it. You'll find it another eccentricity of the frontier, and another sample of what we were talking about as we entered Deadwood."

He was quite right. The people, their language, their dress, their manners, the buildings, the stores, all had a distinct individuality. It was no trading post, no farming town, no shipping point, no commercial center, no mining settlement. It was a cow-town, through and through. There was only one feature which had run through all alike; that curse of America's frontier life, the liquor saloon, was everywhere. Whether to attract the Indian trader, the farmer, the clerk, the miner or the cowboy, and make a friend of him, the glaring sign was the same, and omnipresent.

The town was rough and only half-finished, like the rest; but it was not depressing, as they had been. The streets were deep with dust, and the wooden sidewalks irregular and half-dilapidated, but it did not seem to matter so much as before. There were several ranchmen about worth their millions, and cowboys earning their forty dollars a month. There were Irish, Germans and English, all thoroughly Americanized. There were hunters in their buckskin shirts and caps, with shaggy beards and uncut hair, but with quick and resolute eyes, taking in everything. There were mule skinners in slouch hats and high-topped boots covered with dirt; stage drivers, whose bronzed faces were seamed with deep lines, suggestive of the troubled trails they followed. Here and there an Indian stalked silently and solemnly, wrapped in his long blanket; but over all there was an air of light-hearted freedom from care and anxiety. The people sauntered leisurely along with an independent, though somewhat ungainly swing, from not being much used to relying on their legs, or lounged in front of the boarding-houses.

Between the high sidewalks were heavy prairie schooners, with their great canopied tops, loading with supplies for the various ranches within a hundred miles. There were the pack mules of squatters and the smaller ranches, waiting to receive their burdens.

A REAL COW-TOWN.

A lumbering stage coach was ready to start for somewhere early the next morning, and tough and awkward but invaluable broncos darted about with the inevitable cowboys on their backs.

It was an ideal cattle town; that was all; but there was something in the atmosphere which Oscar found as attractive as the others had been repulsive. He wondered why, and even spoke of it to Charlie, but received only his favorite reply:

"I reckon it's the nature of the beast. It's so with everything. You take a violin into a room where a piano is being played, and when certain notes are struck it will vibrate. It always will for those notes, whether they come in a harmony or discord, and it never will for the rest. Square pegs will not fit close in round holes, and round pegs won't in square holes. You're not tuned for trading or mining, and there's nothing in them that vibrates in you. But when the big piano of life strikes a note on ranching, no matter how roughly, your violin vibrates. See?"

"I shouldn't wonder," Oscar observed, "and I hope you are right; for ever since I was old enough to know anything, it has been my ambition to be a ranchman and ranger, and I mean to carry it out some way, before I die. Let's turn in. I want to put in a good square night of it in a real bed, to see how it seems."

There was no further danger from Indians before them. There was nothing but cattle ranches, sheep farms and wild, branching spurs of the great mountains, between them and Leadville. They made long days and short nights, trusting to Panza to do the watching when they were not fortunate enough to strike a squatter's shanty or a ranch-house at the right time; keeping as good a place as possible, knowing that the horses had only to hold out a little longer, when they would have abundant time to rest.

The days were not monotonous, though they were of a milder type of excitement and of more steady pushing than before.

The fording of almost innumerable streams proved the most difficult work of this part of the journey, and once they were seriously delayed and came very near losing their pack horse.

Late in the afternoon they reached the bank of a river, or at least the dry bed where a river had been, under more favorable circumstances. At first Charlie was very decided that they had better cross and camp upon the other side, but everything was so much better where they were, that at last they decided to remain there, and, unsaddling, turned their horses out to feed, digging holes, for water, in the sand-bed of the river.

In the middle of the night Oscar was suddenly roused by a hideous yell. He woke with a start which sent a sharp pain to his finger tips, and perspiration to his forehead. For a moment he could not tell whether it was something real or a frightful dream that had roused him. He only knew that he was trembling from head to foot, and laying his hand on his rifle, he looked cautiously about him.

The night was dark. He could distinguish only the outlines of the horses, and of Panza close beside him. She was not asleep, and she was licking her chops in a fashion to indicate that something was not just to her liking; but she did not seem much disturbed. Charlie was lying on the ground at a little distance, apparently asleep.

Oscar made up his mind that it must have been a dream — though a very real and very bad one — and hoping that he might never dream out such a fiendish yell again, he turned over and was just dropping asleep once more, when, from all about him, from every side at once, there rang out the most frightful screech that could possibly be imagined.

It sounded as though all the Indians in the West had surrounded them, and as though each one was in the very act of scalping a pale face.

With a start which seemed to lift him completely from the ground, Oscar caught his rifle again and started to crawl to Charlie, wondering how he could possibly have slept through it; afraid to rise or speak lest he should attract attention, and shuddering as the fearful thought flashed through his mind that possibly Charlie might have been killed where he lay. He could almost touch him, when Charlie gave an impatient toss under his blanket, and, evidently speaking to himself, muttered:

"Plague take those coyotes! I can't sleep."

Oscar lay down again even more cautiously and quietly than he got up. He had been afraid of attracting the Indians and showing them where he was; but he was more afraid of attracting Charlie's attention and showing him what a fool he had been. He would have received very charitable attention, however, if he had attracted it; for every plainsman knows that there are no two things in nature which so closely resemble each other, in disposition, general habits and accomplishments, as coyotes and Indians; and many a man of long experience has shuddered for his scalp at the first yelp of a pack of coyotes in an Indian country. Oscar had occasionally seen them and often found traces of them. He had sometimes heard a solitary bark; but he had never heard their concerted howl before, and would have been very willing never to hear it again. They were not over sensitive concerning his wishes, however, and it was a long time before he could get to sleep. It seemed as though he had hardly succeeded, when he was roused by another incomprehensible noise. It was so soft and musical this time, that it was rather pleasant to listen to. Oscar was so sleepy that, though he knew there was something out of order, he had hard work to rouse himself sufficiently to wonder what it was. He thought there must be a pond somewhere that Panza had found, and that she was taking a bath in it. It sounded so. Then he decided that other travelers had reached the spot, and were pouring water into something for their horses. He remembered how hard it was for the horses to get their heads down into the holes they dug the night before, and thought it a very good idea. In time it came over him that the sound was steadily increasing, and, making a great struggle, he roused himself, sat erect, and looked about him.

There was a splashing, gurgling sound, very distinct now, and very close at hand. He did not propose to make a fool of himself twice in one night, so he took his rifle, and, rising quietly, was moving toward the noise, when, in a sleepy voice, Charlie muttered:

"It's no use, Oscar. We're caught on this side. It's too late now, and we've got to make the best of it."

"All right," Oscar replied, but he was wide awake at last, and proposed to see for himself what was going on. A moment later he discovered a bubbling, boiling, angry river rushing between the banks that were parched and dry the night before. It was a hundred feet wide, and apparently deep enough for navigation.

"These intermittent rivers are all-fired uncertain things," Charlie remarked, as they sat upon the ground eating their breakfast. "They live on storms and cloud-bursts in the mountains. They appear under the clearest sky, and the worst of it is, the mischief they work in their bottoms. That was all sand we dug in last night, you know, and the chances are that it is quicksand this morning. If we go down the river — for goodness knows how far — we shall strike the stage route, I suppose, and probably find a bridge of some sort, or a paved bottom, if they're not washed away. If we wait for the water to run off, it may take an hour or it may take a week. If we go ahead and try to cross here, we may find a bottom as hard as rock, or we may find no bottom at all. What do you say?"

"I don't much fancy running the risk of losing Sancho," Oscar replied; "but I'm sure I don't fancy losing a day hunting for a bridge that perhaps isn't there."

"I don't think there's much risk for Sancho," Charlie said; "he's too quick on his feet. We'll split up the line according to the value of the horses, for the first is not likely to do more than soften up the stuff. It's not over three or four feet deep if they don't cut through. Now we're all ready. I reckon this pack is high enough not to get wet. You start first. Hold your feet up behind. It's safer than in front if you may want to use them quick. Just make straight for the other side. If it's soft and Sancho's feet stick and he slows down, just start him on. Keep him going if you can, and if you find he's stuck, get off quick and swim ashore. Don't let your own feet touch bottom, either, and we'll easily get him out before he is fast."

This was a new experience for Oscar, and he watched carefully each dainty step which Sancho took in feeling his way across the river. Twice he needed a little urging, but Oscar was not sure that it was on account of a soft bottom, till, with only a slight wetting, he climbed the opposite bank and looked back to see Charlie in the middle of the stream, his feet in the water, using his spurs, his horse lunging and floundering, and the pack horse literally lying back in the lead line.

Charlie soon found that it was impossible to pull both horses through, and, dropping the line, only by the utmost urging got his own horse up the bank.

For a moment the pack horse struggled to follow, then deliberately gave up, and looking toward them stood perfectly still, sinking deeper and deeper.

"A horse is the biggest fool that breathes when there's anything out of order round his feet," Charlie muttered, as he caught the end of a coil of rope he had taken from the pack and hung on his saddle. "He'll kick his legs off if there's anything behind him that he doesn't understand. He'll thrash himself to pieces if the only thing that will save him is keeping still, and there's that idiot out there could come through well enough, if he would only flax round, but he won't move a hair, unless we can make him, till he has sunk above his shoulders, then he will deliberately lie down and drown. Well, he might as well die of a broken neck as that way," he added, as he fastened a wooden pin in a knot he had made, two feet from the end of the noose, to keep it from slipping too far. "If his spinal column holds, we'll save his life, and if not we'll save him from drowning. Many's the cow I've pulled out of a marsh by this means; but a cow's different. She's got horns to catch on to, where you won't choke her, and a backbone that is the toughest that's made. Now, then! I presume I'll scare that ninny so that he'll jump and try to throw himself," he muttered, as he swung the rope round his head.

"I'll swim out and put it on," Oscar said; but Charlie replied:

"O, no! I'll get it there;" and the rope went flying through the air.

The horse did attempt to dodge, but he threw his head up, instead of to one side, and the noose fell directly over it. Before he had time to drop his head Charlie had drawn the rope till the knot met the pin.

"Pretty close fit?" he asked the horse, and added, "It'll loosen round your windpipe and tighten over your ears directly, if it don't slip off." Then twisting the end over his saddle he started his horse up the bank.

For a moment the pack horse seemed inclined to rebel, and Oscar thought his neck would surely break.

Then he began to struggle and advanced a foot or two; but the moment Charlie stopped pulling he stood still.

"Look at that, will you?" Charlie muttered. "He thinks it's a seaside resort, and he wants to stay all summer. Or else he's bound to get his neck stretched if he can. It always was too short. Well, here's another try."

By slow degrees they brought him out, but it was nearly noon before they were in a condition to start again. When they were under way once more Oscar said:

"That was my first experience with quicksand, and I'll not have another if I can help it. The next time I shall vote to go round."

The scenery about them grew constantly more magnificent. Wild ravines and beetling ledges were in grand confusion; rivers cutting their paths through rocky gorges; cliffs and mountain peaks; dark defiles and beautiful ravines where the grass was green and the wild flowers in their glory.

"We're pretty well out of the cattle country, now," Charlie said, "and that's what we shall indulge in for the next stage." He pointed to a drove of sheep they were approaching. "There's lots of them in Colorado. And there's money in sheep, too. More than there is in cows, I reckon; but I would rather spend my life in state prison, if it wasn't for the name of it, than to be a sheep herder."

"I can't see why," Oscar said, as he stood watching the sheep.

"Why, just look at it," Charlie exclaimed in disgust. "All the year round they live in that little box of a cabin, with those corrals and sheep sheds about them. Every night the sheep have to be shut up, and

"THAT'S WHAT WE SHALL INDULGE IN."

at daylight they begin to bleat to get out again, while the herder is rushing down his breakfast. They are let out through a narrow shoot and counted, to be sure they're all there, and the herder starts after them, on foot, with a coat on his arm, in case of storm, a canteen hung on his shoulder and a book in his pocket. All he has to do is to walk on till they are ready to stop, and then stop till they are ready to go on again, and follow them if he can when they are frightened by a coyote or a piece of paper, and run like mad till they fetch up against a cliff, if they happen to start on a level with the bottom, or run right over the edge and break their necks, if they are on the top. They are nothing but lumps of mutton stuck on legs; all wool, and no sense. That dog along with him does all the work, and does it a great deal better than the man could. He does that same, day after day, the year round. The only change that comes, even with winter, is that he dresses a little warmer, and don't sit around quite so much. If a prairie storm breaks on him in the winter, before he expects it, the woolly idiots will start and run before the wind. If they get tuckered before they kill themselves by running over a cliff or the like, they stop and begin to bunch up, climbing higher and higher on top of each other, and if the storm proves at all long or severe, the bottom ones are, of course, smothered, and the coyotes and wolves get the top ones, while the herder sometimes saves a few from the middle. In the meantime he cannot leave them, no matter how long the storm lasts, though he has nothing to do but stand and look on and freeze to death. Sheep do have an everlasting pull on life, though, especially against starvation. That terribly tough winter, ten years ago, they dug some sheep out alive that had been under eleven feet of snow for three weeks. That sounds wild, but I think it's true. They said that the creatures had worked their way about till they reached the bottom, and got at the grass there. Then every night they have to be driven back to the ranch again, corraled and counted once more to see that none have been lost through the day. In May comes the lambing, and every one puts to like a professional hospital nurse to keep the little fools alive for the first three months or so, before they are able to take care of themselves. In June comes the shearing, and fellows get six cents apiece for barbering the stupid things. Then the biggest part of them have to be dipped in a big trough, with water and a little tobacco in it, to cure the scab. O, yes! there's money in it; but compare that life with the life of a cow-puncher, and what do you think of it?"

"Not much," Oscar replied, fully enthused with the prejudices of his chosen profession against sheep.

Their next stopping place for the night was a picturesque little village in this isolated sheep-raising district. It was, as it must be, a sheep-town.

"I declare!" Oscar exclaimed. "I thought we'd seen every variety of settlement imaginable; but if here isn't another lay-out. How woolly and stupid and pretty and neat everything is here!"

There were only three stores in the entire village, and two of those were locked. There was not a liquor sign to be seen anywhere.

They entered the only store that was open, but even then they had to rouse the dealer, who was sound asleep, stretched out upon the counter.

After hearing what they wanted, he yawned and stretched, and replied that he was out of it, but that the store opposite had some. They told him that the door was locked. He yawned again and stretched, and finally said that he believed "Bill did say he was goin' out to his sheep ranch, this arternoon." Thereupon he got up, invited them to follow him, led the way to the house next Bill's store, asked for the key, went in, put up the required articles, put the pay in the till, locked the door, returned the key, and went back to finish his nap.

"Did you ever see anything like it?" Oscar exclaimed. "Upon my word, I am so sleepy myself that I can hardly keep my eyes open. Let's turn in, and make a big daylight start."

The whole world could hardly produce a counterpart of the magnificent scenery which grew grander every hour about them, as they wound in and out among the deep defiles, climbed the steep declivities or crept along the sides of precipitous ledges, nearer and nearer to Leadville.

All in vain Oscar tried to arrange with himself some plan of action. He only knew that every step of advance made him so much the more anxious to be there, and at last, travel-worn, dusty, tired and sunburned, they entered Leadville; Leadville with all its ups and downs, socially and physically; Leadville, without a street that is level, without a citizen whose life has been more smooth; with all its smoke and dirt from the great smelting furnaces; with all its swift vicissitudes, from grub stakes, gone, to millions made in an hour. Leadville, high up among the grand mountains, how many strange people have come to you, with how many strange fears behind them, and how many strange hopes ahead? And how have you treated them? How have they gone away from you? And, of them all, who ever came to you with stranger hopes and stranger fears than Oscar Peterson? What have you in store for him? How will he go away from you?

CHAPTER XVIII.

THE MAN INSIDE.

OSCAR grew more and more thoughtful as they approached their destination, and at supper he hardly spoke a word. Charlie easily appreciated his silence, and knew that it would be better to respect it than try to interrupt it; hence, when Oscar proposed a walk, after supper, Charlie made an excuse that he must attend to some arrangements about the horses, so that Oscar could be left entirely to himself. He was not in need of advice or protection, now. He was upon the eve of a battle that must be skillfully fought, and he needed solitude to lay out his campaign.

Charlie was especially anxious, too, that Oscar should not ask his advice, for he felt utterly unable to give it. Except through some accident, he could not see how their mission in Leadville could possibly be accomplished, and accidents never happen when one is on the watch for them.

"I don't suppose there is any use in wearing this

thing," Oscar remarked, taking off his belt and pistol. "It seems odd to begin to be half-civilized again."

He laid the belt on the table and went out alone. He had been thinking all day, all the month, in fact, and there was nothing new to think about, yet he was thoroughly wrapped in his thoughts, and wandered down the street with his hands in his pockets, his hat pulled down over his forehead, and his eyes on the ground. He was asking himself what he had come there for; and to his utter astonishment he found that with all his thinking he had not thought out an answer to that first question. Surely he had come to find the man who shot his father; but what then? He wanted to kill him; but that was out of the question. He had not proof enough of anything to bring an open charge against him, and he began to realize the force of Charlie's advice — to wait till some accident should place the man in his power.

He had not thought much about it at the time when it was given, for they were still a long way from Leadville, and the rest of the journey demanded their immediate attention. Now there was nothing more to do. They had reached Leadville. In the morning they could easily find the man, and the thought that from that moment it was simply "wait," was almost more than he could endure, in prospect, even.

In his worn and dust-grimed clothes he was not an object to attract attention. No one noticed him, and he paid very little attention to any one. It was not so much that he was deeply engaged in thought, as that he was trying to think; for he smiled when a little boot-black accosted him with, "Shine yer boots, gent?" and looking down at his dusty boots he wondered how they would look if they really were shined. He heard the newsboys calling the *Chronicle, Eclipse* and *Reveille*, and wondered what the great world had been doing while he was so far away from it, out on the plains. He caught snatches of conversations, and said to himself that if he were to be dropped, blindfolded, into a frontier town, he was sure that he could tell, in an instant, what sort of a place it was. "How deep are you?" "Struck it rich?" "Contact," "Carbonates," "Claims," "Surveyed in," "Pans out," "Runs high," "How does she assay?" seemed to form the greater part of the English language, as it was spoken in a mining town, whether by high or low, magnate or pauper. He heard ragged and illiterate fellows talking of millions as though they were dimes, on one side of him, while on the other side a delicate and refined, but pale and haggard boy, not much older than himself, in the very best of English was asking for enough to purchase a loaf of bread to keep him from starvation. He caught a remark made by one of two men standing alone at the corner of an alley: "I don't go pards with nobody, Bill, but our claims ain't neither one of 'um worth what it orter be, unless'n they're joined. Now I'll tell yer what I'll do; I'll give or take at one million and a half, down."

Oscar was close beside them as the other replied: "Another fellow took out that claim for me, and I sha'n't have the papers, clean, for a week, yet. But I've got a place up in Manitoba — nigh a hundred thousand acres; mines, stock farm, wheat, cattle range, and a village included — that's worth more than two and a half millions, if it is a cent. I'll swap that for your claim."

By that time Oscar had turned slowly, and entered the dark alley behind them. As he passed he very carefully noted the features of one of the men. It was not the man who owned the farm in Manitoba. He stood with his back toward him. It was a striking face which he saw, however, and he felt sure that he should know it if he saw it again. He lost a sentence or two which followed, but the moment he knew that he was hidden in the shadows he turned and walked back. This time as he approached, one of them was saying: "It's time the stage was off, this minute. Let the thing lie open till I get back."

With that he started down the street. Oscar was close behind him. He gave one quick glance at the man who was left behind. It was not the man from Manitoba, so he fixed his eyes upon the other and followed. There was no time to consider what to do He was simply determined not to lose sight of him.

A man was holding the stage door open, evidently waiting for him, as he hurried up. He entered without a word. The door closed with a bang, the whip sounded with an impatient crack, and the stage started.

Oscar reached the spot in time to catch a single glimpse of the interior. There were several people there; he could not tell how many, and a lantern, dimly burning, hung in the center of the stage.

"Where is that stage going?" Oscar asked the man who had stood by the door; but he was out of patience at the best; he had just turned to speak to a policeman, and withal Oscar was so little acquainted with the localities in the neighborhood of Leadville, that he could only make out from the short reply that, after several stops, the stage connected with an early morning express train, somewhere, and then returned to Leadville.

The stage was already almost out of sight. He turned quickly to the two men, exclaiming, "Will one of you please send to the Ranchman's Hotel and tell Half-circle-dash Charlie that I have taken this stage and will be back in the morning?" and without waiting for an answer he started on a run after the stage.

The reply was not very polite or promising, and if Oscar had heard it, it would only have added to the difficulties of his present situation, by making it very doubtful if Charlie's anxiety over his non-appearance was to be relieved. He would not have stopped, however, for he had done the best he could to notify Charlie, and he proposed to follow the man inside the stage at all hazards.

There may have been other and wiser ways to have accomplished the end, but he had no time to sit down and think it over, and a boy of sixteen may be pardoned, at such a moment, for following his first impulse at the expense of sober second thought.

The policeman and his companion expressed their opinions in a thoroughly Western and purely American fashion, as they watched the retreating figure, then they laughed, and dropped the matter entirely.

Three hours later, when the policeman was being relieved, the officer in charge asked him if he had seen anything of a young ranger without firearms, who had been missing since early in the evening, and whose absence was causing considerable excitement in the Ranchman's Hotel. He replied that he had not, but as he was walking home he recalled the incident, and went round to the hotel to see if there was any connection between the two.

In the meantime Oscar had a good run to overtake the stage, which gave him time to remember that he had no money with him to pay his fare, and that he could hardly accomplish what he was after by riding inside, even if he had. He did not stop to consider any other means to the same end, but decided to catch on behind and, if possible, find a seat on the baggage truck. He found the great leather boot drawn down, but there was only a single trunk beneath it and room enough to stow himself away. Before long it began to rain. The night was cold and the boot was, after all, a great convenience.

"If this trunk should stop before he does, it would be pretty bad for me," he said to himself, as he clung to the leather straps to prevent being jolted from the rack altogether; for the road was rough and the night as dark as it might be.

Only a few miles out the stage stopped at a mining settlement, and two men got out. With fear and trembling Oscar peeked from under the curtain; but the trunk was not disturbed, and he was sure, both from their voices and dress, that neither of them was the man he was following. A moment later they were rumbling and bumping on again, and soon it was evident, from the sounds, that they were dropping down into a gulch of some sort.

The rain rattled upon the leather curtain. The wind rushed and sighed among the branches of pine-trees. The brake groaned and grated as it was held almost continually against the wheels. The horses' hoofs splashed upon the wet road, and now and then the sharp crack of the whip was followed by a lurch of the coach, and Oscar had to cling desperately to the straps for a moment, till the horses slowed down again.

Suddenly there was a change. There was a shout from in front and a sharp crack of the whip; but the stage did not start up with a jerk. It simply jolted to one side and stood still. Something must have broken. Oscar cautiously lifted a corner of the curtain. The coach was close against a rocky ledge, on that side, and the ledge was bright as day. He was sure that no stage lantern gave a light like that, and as his eye ran along the dark shadow cast by the coach, against the rock, he could easily mark the outlines of the driver and whipman, and that their hands were up. It flashed upon him, then, that the stage had been held up, and that they were in the hands of highwaymen. He smiled as he thought of the ludicrous side of the situation, so far as he was concerned, and wondered what he had about him that he could give up, in case they should look under the boot.

In an instant, however, before a word had been spoken, there was a crash from a revolver, and a sharp groan from the man inside, followed by the remark from outside the stage, "Ef yer hedden't 'a' pulled yer shooter, Bill, ye'd not 'a' kotched it quite so quick, mebbe."

The whole situation was thus entirely changed. That man inside was something in which Oscar took a lively interest. The highwaymen were upon the right and toward the front. The rocky ledge was on the left. Quickly emerging from his hiding-place, at the most distant corner, Oscar stepped upon the wheel and cautiously looked over the top of the stage. Only two men were visible — two shadows, in the light which the ledge reflected back from a powerful dark lantern which one of them held full upon the stage. With the other hand he covered the two upon the box, with a heavy six-shooter. The other man was evidently the one who fired the shot, and, pistol in hand, he was now slowly approaching the coach.

Oscar felt for his pistol, forgetting that he had left it at the hotel. For an instant he hesitated. The sense of being unarmed weakened him. His head was in the light of the lantern, but the attention of the two men was so thoroughly absorbed that neither of them thought of looking at that back corner of the roof. He could easily climb down again, and doubtless remain hidden, or he could even show himself without much fear of harm. The only thing that he could not do without danger was to attempt to check those men. But it looked as though they intended to kill the man inside, and that one thing Oscar was determined to resist. How should he do it? Why had he left his pistol behind him?

These thoughts flashed across his mind, but his eyes were busy looking about him. Two iron shoes, used to hold the back wheels, upon the worst hills, lay on the roof of the coach, within his reach. While that lantern burned he was helpless. It was the lightning work of the brain in an emergency. He caught one of those iron shoes — the one without a chain — and with all his strength hurled it at the lantern.

If he missed it, his work would be over. And if he had calculated his chances of missing, he would never have fired that shoe. But he did not calculate anything. He fired the shoe, and the next instant the iron crashed into the lantern, smashing it to atoms and striking the man behind it a sharp blow. His pistol flashed, but without aim, and did no harm, while a volley of curses sounded in the darkness, mingling with the groans of the man inside.

Oscar threw himself upon the top of the stage, caught the other iron shoe in his hand, and lying at full length, holding the end of the shoe over the edge of the iron rail, in much the appearance and outline of a pistol, he shouted:

"Now, then, gentlemen, the first man to move gets a touch of this." He tapped the shoe against the rail.

All that they could see in the darkness was just as good as a large navy revolver, and what they heard could not have been better made by the barrel of a six-shooter. Only waiting a moment to note the effect, Oscar continued, "Drive on, Jerry; the road is clear."

To his own absolute astonishment, the whipman cracked his whip, the driver took his foot from the brake and caught up the reins, the horses started at a rapid pace, and the two shadows stood motionless till they were lost in the darkness.

What Oscar really did expect, he himself could not have told. Realizing his own position, it did not seem possible to him that men should be such fools. His words were only the inspiration of the intense emergency of the moment. He did not know how closely he had imitated the clear, fearless voice of authority with which Charlie gave his commands to the three highwaymen in the other gulch. It seemed so utterly absurd that two road agents could be reduced, and two armed stage men relieved of fear and set at liberty, by a sixteen-year-old boy, holding an iron stage shoe in his hand, that he lay there, in silence, trying to make himself believe that it was a dream.

He was quickly reminded of the reality, however, for before the stage was out of hearing, one of the fellows behind called:

"Yer needn't 'a' been so tarnal pertickeler. We ain't a-jumpin' no claims ternight. All we wanted was the man inside. Reckon he's got a dose o' int'rest, any way, and he'll git the principal afore he hears the end on us."

Then all was still but the splashing of the rain, and the wheels and the horses' feet, and the cracking of the whip and the groaning of the man inside.

"Where in thunder did you come aboard?" the man asked, without looking back.

"I climbed up here when you were standing by the rock," Oscar replied quickly; and to prevent the man from questioning him further he asked, "Where did those two men come from?"

"Reckon they're two we brought from Leadville, who got off at Happy Holler, and skipped across the gulch," the man muttered in a surly way; for it does not increase a stage driver's good nature to be held up.

"What's the matter with the man inside?" Oscar asked.

"Reckon he's got a hole in him," the whipman replied, and the two laughed.

"I mean, what did they want of him?" Oscar repeated rather sharply, for he did not relish their fun.

"Dunno," ejaculated the driver. "Mebbe he's been jumpin' some claim; got their diggin's surveyed in ag'in 'um, or suthin'. They acted like they'd been livin' on snaps fur one while, ter hold up a stage with only one man in it, and go shoot him the first lick."

"What's snaps?" Oscar said, simply to keep the man talking for a moment more, while he thought out what to do.

"Waal, I reckon you ain't frum these diggin's, nor nowhar in Collerady," the driver replied, and turned his attention to the horses. Oscar thought that was all the response he was to receive, and was not at all particular for more, but a moment later the man continued: "When a feller can't wash his livin' outer the ground, in these parts, he's got ter take his gun, hasn't he, ef he don't wanter starve, and go out an' snap at suthin'; and ef he don't bag no more'n these ones did ternight, he's jest got ter live on them snaps, hasn't he?"

Oscar was not in a mood to reply. He simply remarked:

"Haul up a second, please; I want to see if I can do anything for the man inside."

The driver was grouty, and evidently more anxious to get out of the gulch than stop to attend to his passenger. At first he did not seem inclined to slow down at all. Oscar was determined, however, and as he deliberately stepped between the two, the driver reluctantly put his foot on the brake.

"Whar's yer irons?" he asked, as Oscar passed in front of him. "Better not leave 'um up here, fur ye mought want 'um ag'in."

"I haven't got any," Oscar replied, as he felt for the first step down. "I didn't have anything but your old brake-shoe. The man inside has got a pistol, and I can borrow that if necessary."

The driver grabbed him by the shoulder, and stared at him for a moment by the light of the box lantern.

"You hain't got no irons?" he muttered. "Waal, I'm blowed! But you hain't, and that's no lie. Jim, jest you take a good look at this youngster, will ye? an' be ready to swear to't; fur when I tell the boys 'bout this night's biz, thar ain't a soul in Leadville will believe me, well es they know me." Then turning to Oscar, in a manner very different from before, he added: "Yes, sir; I'll hold up fur yer ter git inside, sir; an' excuse me fur not invitin' yer outer the reen afore. I didn't notict yer hadn't got yer gum-coat on. An' 'low me ter say, sir, whens'ever yer my way ag'in, jest you squat on any claim o' mine you come acrost. I'll allers count it an honor, an' it'll never cost yer a dime."

The moment the man let go of his shoulder, Oscar jumped, and as he entered and drew the coach door together behind him, the stage started again.

All was still and dark inside. Oscar lit a match, and found the swinging lantern. It had evidently been extinguished as a precaution, before the hold-up. It gave out a dim, flickering light, but enough to disclose the form of the wounded man, lying upon the back seat. He was breathing heavily, and occasionally groaning.

Oscar had had very little experience in gun-shot wounds, but he found the bullet-hole in the man's side, did what he could to stop the blood, arranged the seats so that he could lie more comfortably and could not fall, and then turned away with a shudder, and sat down with his back toward him. Neither of them had spoken a word.

There was one mark which he could easily have

found, which would have told him at once if this was the man he was seeking; but Oscar did not dare to look for it. He did not dare to know, alone in that dim, rumbling stage coach, that the helpless being lying on the seat behind him, was the man who shot his father.

His fingers were clutched till the nails cut into his palms. He ground his teeth till they ached. He knew that he was right. He knew that if he looked he should find a finger missing upon one hand. Every throb of his heart told him that he was close beside the man he wanted. He knew that the man was in his power, to do precisely as he would with him; that a better and safer opportunity could not have been prepared. He remembered Charlie's warning, that there would be no chance for him in an open struggle for justice. Had he not said to himself, early in the evening, that his only hope lay in some accident that should place the man in his power — and had not the accident occurred, even without his waiting for an hour? And was there not something almost providential in the strange combination of incidents which had led him on, step by step, to this most perfect situation he could have planned?

The man was conscious, fully conscious, enough to realize that it was revenge, and understand who it was that would accomplish it; yet if his dead body was taken from the stage at the next stopping-place, even the driver on the box would never dream but what it was the bullet that had killed him.

Every nerve and muscle in Oscar's body trembled and quivered. He longed to turn about and catch the man by the throat; to watch him struggle and strangle; to look into his eyes and see him die, while he whispered in his ear, "You could escape the law, you coward! but you could not escape from me."

Why was he brought there if not for that? Every savage passion of his nature seemed boiling and seething in him. He shuddered to realize what fearful thoughts he was capable of thinking, and to know that only one slender thread of doubt, which an instant could dissipate, was restraining him from putting those horrible thoughts into actions that would live with him just as long as his heart beat. He clung to that doubt, for strength to resist the temptation, as a drowning man might to a straw.

The man behind became more restless, moaning and talking to himself.

"I must get away from here," he muttered. "I must sell out and get away. Why didn't I kill the boy, too? Then I could have got a clean title to the mine without waiting. I could sell out and go tomorrow. I'll kill him. Yes, yes! I'll kill him yet."

Oscar covered his ears with his hands, and clutched his elbows between his knees.

"What?" the man behind him shrieked. "I did

not kill his father either? He has got well and come after me?"

Then he shrieked again, and began to struggle, and Oscar turned and held him on the seat, to prevent his falling or injuring himself, and talked to him to quiet him. The slender thread had broken, but he found, to his astonishment, that after all he had a will that was stronger without its help. He had not laid a finger on the man, except to care for him, when the stage stopped at the shanty tavern of another mining settlement, and the driver opened the door.

The innkeeper was much more accustomed than Oscar to the treatment of gun-shot wounds. The man was delirious now, but he was soon in bed, in spite of his struggles, and after a hot drink, which the innkeeper prepared, he sank into a heavy, restless sleep.

Oscar learned that the same stage would pass in two hours, on its return to Leadville, and while he watched at the bedside he wrote to Charlie, briefly recounting the circumstances, and asking him to come at once with —

There his hand rebelled. Every force of nature in him urged him to drop the pen. Was this doing the duty for which he had come all the way from Manitoba? Was this taking advantage of the opportunities which Providence had placed within his reach?

He hesitated for a moment. He looked steadily into the sleeper's face. He saw the hand, with a missing finger, twitching and clutching, as it lay, uneasy, on the spread.

"If I know what my duty is, I can do it," he muttered, and a moment later he turned to the paper, and in a firm hand finished the sentence — "with a doctor."

He did not realize it then, perhaps he never will, but it is true, nevertheless, that if his entire life should be as crowded with acts of bravery as his short trip from Manitoba to Leadville, when they are all summed up in one, they will not equal the real courage required for that one act, by the bedside of the wounded man.

Oscar was astonished to find how easy it was for him after that to bathe the wound with arnica and witch-hazel, steeped over the tavern fire; to administer the golden-rod tea and the sleeping-mixture, whenever the man began to moan, and to do all that he would for any sufferer, for the man he found inside the coach.

It was as if he had been laboriously climbing a steep hill, where every step was harder than the one before, to find that the last, almost despairing struggle had suddenly brought him to the summit, and that from that instant the path was leading down the hill again, making each step easier than the last. He even found himself anxiously counting the time, eagerly listening for the sound of horses' feet, that should announce the arrival of Charlie and the doctor.

CHAPTER XIX.

"I AM AFRAID TO DIE."

BEFORE ten o'clock Charlie came with the doctor. He was a rough and hardened frontiersman, like all the rest, dabbling as much in mines as in medicine; but as skillful and experienced in bullet wounds as a surgeon in an army hospital.

They found Oscar looking worn and haggard after the excitement of the night, the long watch and the fierce battle with himself, but hard at work.

While the doctor was probing the wound and making his examination, Oscar and Charlie stood at the little window, looking down the wild mining gulch.

"How in the world could you do this for that fiend?" Charlie asked abruptly.

"I don't know," Oscar said, shaking his head. "Somehow I can't seem to help it. I don't believe he'll escape, but I think that after all I would rather have him go, than think always that I did it when he couldn't protect himself."

"Maybe you're right, Oscar," Charlie replied. "At any rate, if that's the way you feel, I'd certainly act it out. But if it were my case, I would lift that man's scalp and wear it for a charm, like an Indian."

"Is this fellow anything in particular to either of you?" the doctor asked, coming to the window.

"We never set eyes on him before," Charlie answered quickly.

"I never saw him till last night," Oscar replied more slowly.

"Well, he's pretty well fixed for dust, I'm told, but there's no use sending to Leadville to hunt up friends, for he hasn't got any there," the doctor continued. "I don't know whether he's got folks somewhere else or not; but whatever he wants to do with his dust, he's got to do it pretty sudden. He'll start off without it before sunup to-morrow. There's nothing I can do for him. The youngster's done all there's any use in. 'Twon't stretch him out more'n a few hours, but if you think it's worth your while to keep on with what you're doing, it'll ease him along a little. He's coming to himself, I see, and it's likely he'll be tolerably clear from now on till he dies. I must be goin' now, for I've got to get back. Is there anything I can do for you in Leadville?"

"Look a-here, doctor," Charlie said in a low tone. "It's true that neither of us ever saw that man till this trip, but we know a pile about him that's not to his praise. In fact, that's what brought us here from Manitoba. We just got in last night, and the first thing the youngster saw him taking that stage, and was afraid he was going to skip, and followed to see which trail he took. That's how he happened to be on hand. Now if he's going to die, and he's the coward I think he is, the chances are that he'll have a powerful weight o' something besides dust to unload; and it strikes me that it'll be for the best good of all concerned to have the unloading done in proper shape. If you don't mind sending down the best lawyer in Leadville, quick as he can get here, I think it'll be a wise thing. Here's a hundred-dollar bill for our part, in case it proves a fool's errand."

"It strikes me that's a pretty clean idea, that'll pan out well," the doctor replied, putting the bill in his pocket. "I'll have the right man here as soon as horses can cover the ground; but he won't die before night," and with that he went out.

Very slowly the wounded man came back to consciousness, and even Charlie found himself working as hard as Oscar; but with him, as he took every opportunity to explain to Oscar, it was only a savage determination that the man should not die till after the lawyer came.

"You saved my life last night, and I shall pay you well for it," the man muttered, as Oscar bent over him, bathing the wound. "I feel better now, only a little weak. I shall be all right in the morning. You don't think there's any danger of my dying, do you?" And an hour later, after drinking something which the innkeeper had prepared for him, he whispered: "I feel better. O, yes! I certainly feel better. I am not going to die."

Oscar and Charlie decided that it would be better to tell the lawyer all they knew before he saw the wounded man, that he might understand better what they expected.

The man was sleeping, and they stood together at the window as some one drove up from Leadville. It was doubtless the lawyer, and Charlie quickly left the room to meet him; while Oscar, still standing by the window, also recognized in him the man he saw at the corner of the alley the night before, offering a million and a half for the mining claim. Doctors or lawyers, boot-blacks or newsboys, living in Leadville, were, almost of necessity, interested in mining. It was so much in the atmosphere that they could not help it.

Charlie had only been gone a moment when the man awoke. It was evident that his strength was failing. He pointed to a glass of water standing on the table, and drank it ravenously; then looking up, he whispered:

"I have seen you before. Do you live in Leadville?"

Oscar shook his head.

"In Deadwood?" the man asked.

Again Oscar shook his head.

"I have surely seen you somewhere," the man said feebly, closing his eyes as if trying to think.

Sunburned, weather-beaten, developed and hardened by trials, dangers, exposure and sharp experiences with the stern realities of life, it was a very different face from the schoolboy's he had seen, and yet it was the same. No wonder the dying man remembered it, and yet could not remember.

He opened his eyes again and whispered:

"Don't you remember me? Where is it I have seen you?"

More in pity than with any thought of revenge, Oscar replied:

"You may have seen me, but I never saw you until last night."

"Where have I seen you? Your face haunts me," the man said, with a shudder. "Tell me — tell me where have I seen you?"

Oscar thrust his hands deep into his pockets, lest they should move before he could stop them, as he replied:

"You saw me in a yacht, on the shores of Manitoba Lake."

"Who are you — who are you?" the wounded man gasped, starting on the bed.

"I AM OSCAR PETERSON."

"I am Oscar Peterson: Ranchman and Ranger," Oscar said; for that little sign had become so firmly imbedded in every thought, as a vital part of himself, that in the intense excitement of the moment the words fell from his lips unconsciously, as though he was repeating only his name.

For a moment there was the silence of death in the little room. The wounded man shut his eyes, and a great shudder shook the very bed upon which he was lying. Oscar was afraid he was dying, and was upon the point of going for Charlie, when he opened his eyes again, and tried to call for help. But his voice was so weak that it could not have been heard even beyond the thin board partitions of the miner's shanty tavern.

Oscar stepped back a little, and in a low voice replied:

"You need not be afraid of me. I have had chances enough to kill you, and I wanted to a great deal more than I do now. You killed my father! You sneaking coward! You killed him because he trusted you, and gave you a chance to make yourself rich by it. But I have not hurt you. No! and I am not going to now. I have done all I can to save your life. I have tried, but it's no use. The doctor says that no power can keep you alive until sunrise to-morrow."

"I die? I will not die! I can't die," the man shrieked, pushing himself up till he leaned upon his elbow, with his back against the wall, and shook his fist at Oscar. "You take that back. It is a lie! It is you who are trying to kill me, but I will not die to-night. You wouldn't kill a helpless man, would you?"

Then a sudden change came over him, and opening

his clinched hand, he stretched it toward Oscar, and his voice trembled and almost failed as he pleaded:

"No, no, no! There must be something more that you can do. Oh! try again. Try just once more to save me, for I do not want to die. No, no! I cannot die."

At that moment Charlie entered with the lawyer.

"Halloo, Bill!" the latter said, in a cold, careless way, seating himself by the table, with paper, pen and ink. "Doc Hutch was round this noon; said you'd got yer come-upances at last, and couldn't live the night out, and I'd best git round ter see if yer wanted to put anything on paper 'bout by-gones, 'fore yer went across ter whar they say thar ain't no keepin' things secret, Bill. Then anything ye've got ter say about the stuff yer leavin' behind yer, I'm here to write it down. Don't forget, Bill, that this is the last shovelful ye'll h'ist out o' diggin's on this side, an' if ye want yer dirt to pan out anything, when it's washed and assayed over there, you've got ter have some of the real stuff in it, even if it goes in with the very last shovelful. Go on, now, Bill; I'm ready. You do the talkin' an' I'll write it down. Then you can sign it, and they'll know, over there, what it amounts to. Go on!"

The dying man was thoroughly sobered by this rough, plain statement. He was silent for a time, still leaning against the wall; then, speaking slowly, in a low, weak voice, and pointing a trembling hand toward Oscar, he said:

"He is the one who owns that claim next to yours. It belonged to his father, and I shot him. I shot him to get that mine. I made out the papers, and signed his name myself. Write it down, and I'll sign it."

The lawyer wrote, and the dying man watched him in silence till the last word was transcribed in legal form. Then he made a struggle, as though he felt life ebbing and would drag it back till this, at least, was accomplished, and steadying himself continued:

"There's more to write. That farm I told you of — the one I offered you in Manitoba — that was his father's. I had an old deed of it, which he used to borrow money when he bought the mine. I made a new one. I copied all the names. Then I made a bill of sale and signed it. They are recorded in Winnipeg. Every name on them but the Winnipeg lawyer's is a forgery. I fooled him. Yes, I did it; and it's all fraud — all fraud. Write it down and I'll sign it. Write it down."

Again there was a moment's pause, while the pen flew over the paper; but this time the man was in greater haste.

"Write faster!" he gasped; "and write that my own claims — you know them — and everything else I hand over to him. Write that I'm sorry; write it down, and I'll sign it. I haven't any relatives, and

Mr. Peterson was about the only friend I ever had. I killed him. Write it down. Now, quick! Let me sign it."

The moment the lawyer passed him the pen, he clutched it, and leaned over the table.

"What?" he muttered. "You want my real name, too — the old name?"

A sob shook the dying man as he wrote the old name, and even when it was finished, and the pen had fallen from his hand, he leaned heavily upon the edge of the bed, still staring at it.

"I haven't seen that name," he said, "since the last time my mother wrote to me before she died; more'n twenty years ago."

He fell back on the pillow, and lifting his right hand took the legal oath.

Charlie signed the paper as one witness, and he, too, hesitated for a moment, and tried hard to hide two glistening tears as he wrote " the old name " under the one by which he was known on the plains. His occupation he indicated by the simple word " Cowboy."

When it came to Oscar to sign the paper, he had but one name to write; and as for his occupation, it was easily indicated. He copied the old sign; and he, too, realized a strange sensation, but it came from the future to him, not from the past, as he saw the first real and legal imprint of the dream of his life:

"Oscar Peterson: Ranchman and Ranger."

The wounded man lay with his eyes shut, breathing heavily. The lawyer signed and sealed the paper, and handed it to Oscar with his card, saying:

"If you will call at my office in Leadville, I will see that this is put through all right, and set you on the track of your property. I should like to see you before you take any steps in the matter."

Then turning to the bed he took the hand that had lost a finger, lying perfectly still, now, on the cover, and in a gentler tone than he had spoken, said:

"Good-by, Bill! I guess you've done a straight thing for once, any way, before handing in your checks. The folks this side'll give ye credit for it, 'tenerate, and I reckon ye'll find it's better than havin' nuthin' at all to stand on, at the Judgment Day."

Oscar and Charlie were left alone again with the poor dying wretch, and they did their very best to relieve his last moments. There was no longer any thought of vengeance or revenge. Such feelings were all gone. It was not that he had returned the property; surely not that he had left more. It is doubtful if a thought of money entered the minds of either of them as they worked. In Oscar's mind, at least, only one thought kept on and on, always repeating that sentence — 'Write that I'm sorry;' and he had nothing but pity for the poor frightened coward who was struggling and trembling upon the shelving brink of an open grave. But even if bitter feelings had remained; even if he had felt, still, as he did while sitting in the stage, he would have been satisfied — more than satisfied — that he had waited. He would have counted his revenge more perfect than if his hands had followed their inclination, and, in reality, only put a villain more quickly and easily out of agony.

That night they watched a scene more graphic than all the preaching and teaching in the world; while a soul, steeped in twenty years of crime, clung to the tottering walls of the wretched cabin it had polluted. "Don't let me die. I can't die," the poor fellow groaned. "Oh! try something more! Only save me till morning! Only one hour more!" And when his strength was gone — all gone; when his hands were cold and his lips were white, and his glassy eyes fixed on the rude rafters, his last, gasping, shuddering words as life went out, were:

"I am afraid to die."

CHAPTER XX.

THE PAST AND THE FUTURE.

THE sun shone over Happy Hollow and down the gulch beyond, when two mourners —they were real mourners — followed the innkeeper's mule cart, bearing a plain pine box that covered all that was left to earth of the man who was afraid to die.

There were a dozen or more graves upon the hillside, about the one which had been dug that morning. They were all alike; with wooden head-pieces, and nothing more.

Whatever respect they could show to senseless clay was freely extended to the dead, and when that was accomplished, they paid the innkeeper and returned to Leadville.

The lawyer had studied carefully upon the case, as there were many complications in the way of an immediate settlement.

"It will be different," he said, "with the Manitoba estate. This acknowledgment of forgery will be sufficient. By the appointment of a guardian you will be able to take possession there at once. This tangle here will take more time and patience. I have this proposition to make to you, which is in a line with an offer I made to Bill, the night he was shot. The original claim of yours is worth, to me, one million and a half. You might make it pay you bigger if you work it just right, but the chances are it wouldn't do half so well by you. The other claims he spoke of are doubtful. They may pan out as good as this one, but their chances are better for nothing than they are for much, and I don't want to risk too much on chances. I will place two million dollars in Government bonds, in trust for you, the interest to be yours as it falls due, the bonds to be delivered when you are twenty-one years old, in exchange for a clean surrender of all these claims in Leadville. There is no rush about it. Think it over and sleep on it. Go out and take a look at the claims with some one who knows what diggings are, and come in to-morrow morning and let me know."

Oscar did not look at the mines. He had no ambition to remain in Leadville, under any circumstances. He simply went to Charlie and reported the lawyer's proposition.

"Take it quick," Charlie exclaimed.

"That would be one way," Oscar replied, "but there's another way that I would much rather do. I would like to turn these claims over to you. You understand mining, and can run them, and I have all that I could possibly use or care for, in getting back the estate. Won't you please take them, Charlie?"

Charlie slowly leaned back in his chair, slowly lifted his feet to the table, slowly stuffed his hands into his pockets, never once taking his eyes from Oscar. When he was safely balanced, he said:

"Do you mean take the claims and own them and run them for myself?"

"Of course I do; and please do, Charlie. I don't want them or the money."

Charlie stared in silence for a moment, then he replied:

"I must say, Oscar Peterson, you are about as reckless and about as brave and about as generous as any man I ever struck, in real life or a story book. If I hadn't forgotten my Cicero I'd make you an oration; but whether it was in Greek or Latin, in good straight English or only in imagination, my dear friend, it would wind up just the same. It would be as full of admiration and appreciation and of thanks as it was of words, Oscar, but it would have to wind up with 'excuse me, please.' For the fact is I don't want it. I shouldn't know what to do with it if I had it, and besides, I have every prospect of striking another job, within a day or two, that is much more to my taste, though there may not so much dust wash out of it."

"Another job! Where?" Oscar asked, and his face fell.

"Well, it's a friend of mine," Charlie replied, slowly. "He owns a big ranch and range. He's a good fellow, and has struck it rich, lately. I flatter myself he'll be good enough to give me the care of that ranch if I ask him, and I'd rather have it than forty mines."

"Where is it, Charlie?" Oscar asked, and his lip quivered in spite of him.

"Why, it's up alongside of Manitoba Lake," Charlie said. "Do you think I can get a job?"

Oscar did not reply, for he had very nearly upset Charlie's chair, in the vigor with which he grabbed his hand. A moment later Charlie continued: "I knew how it would all turn out. Didn't I tell you so at the ranch-house, when you wanted me to pack up all my outfit and have it sent South? And now if you will excuse me from stopping in Leadville, I'm in a furious hurry to get back to the ranch, for if those cattle are handled right, in the fall round up, there'll be a pile of good money to show for it."

So they went back to Manitoba together. This time they went all the way by rail, with two of the horses and Panza alone in a large padded car, chartered for their sole use. They stopped at Winnipeg to adjust the title to the estate, which was easily accomplished, and when that matter was settled, and the lawyer who did the work had been paid, Charlie was turning to leave, still anxious to be on the way; but Oscar caught him by the arm, exclaiming:

"Hold on one minute, Charlie. There's one more thing to do. I haven't spoken of it, because I knew you would try to crawl out, in some way, but it can't be done. I never should have seen an acre of that estate again if it hadn't been for you, and you have confessed that you want to stay there. Now, you are going into partnership with me, and we are going to start in with the whole estate, as stock in trade, share and share alike. There's no getting out of it. The papers are all made out, like the mine matter, as well as they can be till I am twenty-one, and you have got to sign them, and sign them quickly, without a word. I tell you straight, I will not go back to Manitoba Lake, until you do."

"That's biz. Load up a pen and I'll blaze away," Charlie replied, in that happy abandon with which he surrendered, either to the highwaymen or to Oscar, when he found they had "the drop" on him, as gracefully and cheerfully as though it were something he had been anticipating and arranging for all the time.

The last day they made again on horseback, and it was as full of happiness and hope as the first day had been full of sadness and anxiety. Oscar had succeeded in forcing back the tears as he looked for the last time upon the disappearing butte; but he did not even try to restrain them as he saw the familiar outline rise slowly out of the clear horizon in front of them, and marked the sharp lines of the little speck of black upon its summit, which meant that he was almost home.

During the day they planned out their future. Charlie was to take the ranch and range under his special care. Oscar was to have the stock farm and wheat fields, and if they found that the keeper who had been in charge during their absence, was the man they thought him, and would accept the position, he was to have the mines under his direction, upon a salary or commission.

There was but one cloud which darkened the joy of their return, and even that had its silver lining.

Their very first inquiries were concerning their mysterious Indian. Oscar could scarcely believe his senses when the keeper assured them that it was none other than Wenononee, the little Indian girl, who had followed them; but when they heard the story of the way she stole Sancho from the stable, and then came back and told the keeper, saying that they would starve and freeze and die before they would let the young master suffer such a sacrifice to save them, and how she had touched his heart and made him ashamed of the part he had played, till he was only too glad to help her carry out the rest of her plan, Charlie turned to Oscar, saying:

"Didn't I have the right of it when I stuck to it that you'd been doing something for an Indian?"

The cloud came when they learned the rest: that Wenononee had walked all the way back, safely returning the rifle, the belt, and the pistol, but that exposure and hardship had so thoroughly broken her down that she was rapidly following her mother, who died while she was away.

Oscar felt as though he could willingly have given his life to save hers, and, though that was impossible, money and kindness were lavished upon her till her last months of life were made so peaceful and happy that she said:

"Me heap too glad for Indian girl. When Great Spirit speak and Weno go, she cannot know the difference. This Heaven. That Heaven. If here, if there, all Heaven."

That was the silver lining.

Oscar and Charlie were standing, one day, by Weno's arm-chair, just outside the cabin door. They had been looking backward, while Weno recounted a part of her journey, and told them how they had missed a warning she had put up; that they should not stop at the squatter's sod house.

"I tell you what it is, Charlie," Oscar said, "I learned more about farming and ranching and ranging, about mining and hunting and hólding my own, on that trip, than I might in a lifetime, without it; but the best and biggest lesson of all is what I've learned about people. No matter what color of skin or kind of clothes makes one differ from another, how the heart does show through; and what a world of difference it makes with the evening, whether the sun is setting in clouds or in a clear sky. I wish that everybody in this world who thinks enough of gold to wrong another to obtain it, could see the sun go down in such a storm as we saw it in the gulch by Happy Hollow, and then come here and sit for an hour in the beautiful light of Wenononee's sunset."

www.ingramcontent.com/pod-product-compliance
Lightning Source LLC
Chambersburg PA
CBHW030428300426
44112CB00009B/904